PHIZ

By the same author

Fasten Your Seat Belts! History and Heroism in the Pan Am Cabin

PHIZ

The Man Who Drew Dickens

Valerie Browne Lester

Chatto & Windus
LONDON

Published by Chatto & Windus 2004

2 4 6 8 10 9 7 5 3 1

First published in Great Britain in 2004 by
Chatto & Windus
Random House, 20 Vauxhall Bridge Road,
London SW1V 2SA

Random House Australia (Pty) Limited
20 Alfred Street, Milsons Point, Sydney,
New South Wales 2061, Australia

Random House New Zealand Limited
18 Poland Road, Glenfield,
Auckland 10, New Zealand

Random House (Pty) Limited
Endulini, 5A Jubilee Road, Parktown 2193, South Africa

The Random House Group Limited Reg. No. 954009
www.randomhouse.co.uk

A CIP catalogue record for this book
is available from the British Library

ISBN 0-7011-7742-X

Papers used by Random House are natural,
recyclable products made from wood grown in sustainable forests;
the manufacturing processes conform to the environmental
regulations of the country of origin

Typeset by Palimpsest Book Production Limited,
Polmont, Stirlingshire
Printed and bound in Great Britain by
Biddles Ltd, King's Lynn

In memory of my parents
Phiz and Petra Browne
and in celebration of the new generation
Kiri, Linus Hablot, Emma, and Kate

Contents

List of Illustrations

22 Title page, *The Knight of Gwynne*. Engraving from 1839 portrait by Samuel Lover.

Plate Section 2

23 Phiz, 'The Country Manager', c. 1839. Oil. (Private collection.)
24 Phiz, small oil painting, possibly illustrating *The Vicar of Wakefield*, c. 1845.
25 Harrison Ainsworth, c. 1830.
26 Title page, Harrison Ainsworth, *Mervyn Clitheroe*, 1858.
27 'The Conjurors Interrupted', *Mervyn Clitheroe*, 1858.
28 Sketch for 'The Mausoleum at Chesney Wold', *Bleak House*, 1852–3. Black crayon. (Rare Book Department, The Free Library of Philadelphia.)
29 'The Ferry', Charles Dickens, *Little Dorrit*, 1857.
30 'Damocles', *Little Dorrit*.
31 Edgar Athelstane and Alice Domenica Browne, c. 1867.
32 Charles Michael Browne, c. 1880.
33 'Ayah', Charles Michael Browne, c. 1880. (Margaret MacKenzie.)
34 Emma and Eliza Browne, c. 1865.
35 Walter Browne, c. 1865.
36 Gordon Browne, c. 1920.
37 Robert Young, c. 1885.
38 Fred Barnard, c 1890.
39 Luke Fildes, c. 1910.
40 Emily Dickinson manuscript page, c. 1859. Wood engraving and pencil. (By permission of the Houghton Library, Harvard University MS Am 118.5 (B175) © The President and fellows of Harvard College.)
41 Susannah, with her grandchildren by Charles Michael and Josephine, c. 1890.
42 Phiz, self-portrait resembling Prospero, c. 1887. Oil. (Philip Pirages.)
43 Phiz having his head 'taken off', c. 1874.
44 Phiz's grave in Brighton.

Illustrations in the text

All illustrations are by Phiz, unless otherwise stated. The author's name is given on first mention of a book title, and the date indicates the first appearance of the illustration in print, sometimes before a book appeared in volume form.

MICHEL BRUNEAU (1703–1748) M. HELENE DESCHARMES (1705–1747)

become

MICHAEL AND ELEANOR BROWNE

2 children including

SIMON (1729–1797) M. ANN LODER (1735–1833)

11 children including

ANN (1760–1843)

M. THOMAS MOXON

6 children

JOHN HENRY (1767–1843)

M. CHARLOTTE PENLEAZE

13 children

WILLIAM LODER (1771–1855)

M. KATHERINE HUNTER

14/15 children

*KATHERINE ANN (1793–1862) CHARLOTTE AMELIA (1795–1803) EDWARD (1796–1808) WILLIAM FREDERICK (1797–1818) EMMA LOUISA (1798–1882) HENRY ALBERT (1799–1883) LUCINDA SARAH (1801–1850) CHARLES ALFRED (1802–1866), GORDON DAVIS (1805–1844) EDGAR (1806–1833) SEPTIMUS (1807–1821) OCTAVIUS (1809–1876) ADELAIDE MATILDA (1812–1830) HABLOT KNIGHT ('PHIZ') (adopted, 1815–1882) DECIMUS ('1816–1869)

★KATHERINE ANN + NICOLAS HABLOT

HABLOT KNIGHT ('PHIZ') M. SUSANNAH REYNOLDS
12 children

★EDGAR ATHLESTANE (1842–1917) CHARLES MICHAEL (1843–1900) WALTER ROBERT GEOFFREY (1845–1912)
KATE (1846, lived 2 days) FREDERICK (1847, lived 1 day) EMMA GRANT (1848–?)
ELIZA MARY (1850–?) THOMAS HABLOT (1854–1932) MABEL ANNA (1856–?)
GORDON FREDERICK (1858–1932) BEATRICE ALICE (1860–?) ARTHUR JOHN (1862–1864)

★EDGAR ATHELSTANE M. ALICE DOMENICA BROWNE
6 children including

HABLOT JOHN MOXON (1869–1953) M. MILLICENT RABAN HIGGINS

HABLOT ROBERT EDGAR ('PHIZ') (1905–1984) M. PETRA ELSIE TAINSH

VALERIE JEAN (1939–) M. JAMES TRELOAR LESTER
2 children, 4 grandchildren

Prologue

'Look here, old fellow: will you come to my rooms to assist me with a plate I have to etch?'[1] shouted Hablot Browne to Robert Young, hammering on his friend's door. The twenty-year-old Browne had just received a commission to illustrate *The Pickwick Papers*, and had already drawn his first two images on the etching plate. Determined not to wreck the steel in his hurry to meet Charles Dickens's crushing deadline, he sought Young's skill with the tricky biting-in process. Only too aware of the fate of the book's two previous illustrators, Browne had resolved to present the author with a technically perfect etching. He was confident that Young, already a wizard with acid on steel at the age of nineteen, would do justice to the plate.

Young grabbed his walking stick, and they hurried to the studio they had rented in the attic of 3 Furnival's Inn, Browne slowing his pace to keep time with Young's limping gait. Both were good-looking, of medium height, and well built, except for Young's wasted leg. Browne sprang up the stairs ahead of Young, and lit candles and lamps to provide as much light as possible for the demanding task. They set to work, dipping the

'First Appearance of Mr Samuel Weller', *The Pickwick Papers*, 1836

I

steel plate in the acid–bath time and again, adding details here and there, and burnishing away mistakes. They laboured all night to perfect the plate, and at dawn were finally satisfied. The publishers, Chapman and Hall, were satisfied too and, most importantly, so was Charles Dickens.

Browne entered the world of *Pickwick* in its fourth monthly part, at the key moment where Mr Pickwick meets Sam Weller, and the scene he illustrated became the most famous happy encounter in literature as well as a reminder of his own happy meeting with Dickens. He paid particular attention to Weller, Dickens's newest creation: 'It was in the yard of one of these inns – of no less celebrated a one than the White Hart – that a man was busily employed in brushing the dirt off a pair of boots. . . . He was habited in a coarse-striped waistcoat, with black calico sleeves, and blue glass buttons; drab breeches and leggings. A bright red handker-chief was wound in a very loose and unstudied style round his neck, and an old white hat was carelessly thrown on one side of his head.' Browne caught Sam's jauntiness, and Sam, in words and images, ran away with the public's imagination.

Edgar Browne, the artist's oldest son, remembered how sharply Sam Weller caught the public's fancy: 'Some years ago, one pouring wet day, I took refuge in a little curiosity shop near Leicester Square. The propri-etor, partly to pass the time, and partly to magnify himself a little, told me that he was a kind of literary character, having stitched the first numbers of *Pickwick*, which he considered a failure, till the fourth number; then the sales went up with such a bound that he had to employ hands to carry out his contract. "It was Sam Weller that did it," he said; then after a pause, "and the illustrations."'[2]

I

Huguenots, Patriarchs, and the Talent for the Tiny

It seemed like a miracle. Just when Charles Dickens and his publishers thought *The Pickwick Papers* doomed for lack of an illustrator, a curly-haired young man appeared out of nowhere, etching needle in hand, willing, gifted, and trained. Their luck held; for the next twenty-three years, Hablot Knight Browne (1815–1882), better known to the world as 'Phiz', worked and developed his art alongside Charles Dickens. But the artist makes the barest ripple in the oceans of material about the author. Biographers relegate him to the shadows, and describe him as almost pathologically self-effacing, but although Browne certainly kept his private life private, he was far from being a cipher. There is far more to him and his background than the point of a stylus.

Some say that drawing is a skill that can be learned, while others insist the gift is inborn. More than that, it can be argued that certain individuals

Simon Browne, Moth and dragonfly

inherit a gift within a gift; that is, an innate talent for a specific kind of art. In the case of Hablot Browne, 'immortal "Phiz"',[1] the specific skill he was blessed with – the talent for the tiny – enabled him to work on a scale peculiarly suited to early nineteenth-century book illustration. This talent was characteristic of his family, as evident when one examines the professions in previous eras.

The Brownes were, and still are, passionately proud of their Huguenot ancestry. They are descended from families who fled from Mons (Hainaut) and Langres (Champagne) as a result of religious persecution sometime between the St Bartholomew's Day Massacre of 1572 and the Revocation of the Edict of Nantes in 1685. They settled in London, becoming members of the thriving colony of French silk merchants and weavers in Spitalfields. Precious little is known about their background in Europe, and even Charles Gordon Browne and Algernon Sidney Bicknell, authors of the 1903 hand-written *Notes to Assist the Future Authors of the History of the Huguenot Family of Browne*,[2] have nothing to say on the topic. Phiz's uncle, John Henry Browne, just two generations beyond his Huguenot ancestors confesses: 'All the information I can give you of my fore-fathers lies in a very small compass. *Simon* the son of *Michael & Eleanor Browne* was born 25 Sept. 1729 & I recollect my Father [Simon] telling me that he was born in Spitalfields & was the son of a maker of the wires used in weaving velvets. It appears that he had a turn for mechanics, for my Father used to show me some of the parts of a watch which he said his Father had made, but which was then without a case, & the parts of it were kept in a small box.'[3] This turn for the mechanics of watchmaking is an early allusion to the Browne family's gift for working on a minute scale.

Various family researchers have scrabbled hard and long at the Huguenot Library in London trying to find the elusive ancestor who became Michael Browne and promptly forgot his French name. 'The name Brunet or Brunel was never spoken of,' continues John Henry Browne. 'My father used to say [the name] was probably Le Brun; & accordingly I put the name of Le Brun in some of my French schoolbooks.'[4] Calling themselves Le Brun was wishful thinking on the part of Simon and John Henry, who probably wanted to ally themselves with Charles Le Brun (1619–1690), the famous artist at the court of Louis XIV. Phiz's cousin, Charles St Denys Moxon, brushes aside this notion, saying, 'Le Brun was a Parisian in high favour at court – no Huguenot, or if he were, not a man at all likely to sacrifice his interests for the sake of his religious views.'[5]

Another notion the Brownes entertained was that the artists in the family (which included almost everyone) inherited their skill from a connection with the internationally fashionable portrait painter, Elizabeth Vigée Le Brun (1755–1842). This had no foundation in fact as she was Le Brun by marriage, not by birth.

Time and again, the efforts of family researchers to trace a Brunet, Brunel, or Le Brun proved fruitless. Recently, however, it occurred to me that since the Brownes had cousins called Descharmes,[6] the mysterious French ancestor might well have married a Descharmes (*cherchez la femme!*), and that indeed turned out to be the case. On Christmas Day in 1722 at the Huguenot chapel of St Jean, Spitalfields, Hélène Elisabeth Descharmes married Michel Bruneau.[7] BRUNEAU! They never mentioned the name again, and became Michael and Eleanor Brown (sic), desiring to assimilate as quickly as possible, like so many other Huguenots who could not afford to be suspected as spies for France.

Michael and Eleanor lived on Brick Lane, just a stone's throw from the site where magnificent Christ Church, Spitalfields, was under construction. Designed by Nicholas Hawksmoor, it was completed in 1729, the year of their son Simon's birth. (Little Simon was named after his uncle/godfather, Simon Descharmes, a noted clockmaker.) The gleaming new building played an important part in Michael and Eleanor's lives, and they were buried there when they died within three months of each other, Eleanor in October 1747, Michael in January 1748.[8]

A memorial ring of intertwined bands of gold and black enamel, minutely engraved with the words 'Eleanor Browne ob. 26. Oct. 1747 aet. 42. Michael Browne ob. 11 Jan. 1747/48 aet. 44'[9] descended through the family. It clearly demonstrated Simon's talent for calligraphy and the ingenuity with which he could fabricate intricate objects. It is on this ring that Browne appears spelt with an 'E' for the first time.

Simon Browne (1729–1797), Phiz's grandfather, a dazzlingly gifted calligrapher and artist, can be regarded as the patriarch and progenitor of the modern Browne family. He was diminutive and courtly, a French scholar who could relate a fund of anecdotes about the Huguenots and their various trials and tribulations while remaining obstinately ignorant of his French patronymic. After the deaths of his parents, he left London – for love.[10] The object of his affection, Ann Loder, was the daughter of a Bermondsey wool stapler who, finding more call for his trade in Norwich, packed up his family and set forth, with Simon in pursuit. On 6 October 1754, at the age of twenty-five, Simon married twenty-year-old Ann, at St Stephen's, Norwich.[11]

Once established in Norwich, Simon Browne became a writing teacher, and established a boys' school at St Stephen's. He and Ann lived nearby at 3 Assembly House Yard, in an attractive house with a walled garden, now called 'The Chantry'. Simon's business card announced: 'English, Writing, Arithmetic, Merchant's Accompts, etc. taught and Young Gentlemen boarded by S. Browne in Saint Stephen's, Norwich. The languages, dancing, music & drawing by able Masters.' He also maintained a good business as a letterer and designer, and his work included the design of banknotes for Gurney's Bank. He was a dedicated Freemason, and for three years wrote and decorated the minutes for the oldest Masons' lodge in Norwich, the Maid's Head.[12]

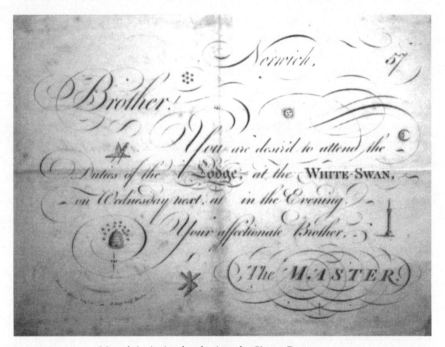

Mason's invitation handwritten by Simon Browne, 1757

Simon's talent went beyond transforming handwriting into written art. Some of his purely decorative efforts are masterworks, and his reputation spread as far as London where he became known as 'the Norwich pen man'.[13] C.G. Browne also comments on the elegance of Simon's work, noting that his designs and drawings were so extraordinarily minute and the workmanship so fine 'that it is almost impossible to detect, even with a powerful magnifying glass, that they are executed by hand in pen & ink and as there were no steel pens in those days, it is marvellous that a quill could have served his purpose. In the most complicated flourishes, curves & patterns ornamented with very minute insects or animals, there is no trace of his pen ever having slipped or failed him.'[14] His masterpiece was a painting of a harp whose strings form a poem which begins at the wider end with the words 'Some magic is embraced within thy simple form.'

A quick glance at, say, the frontispiece for *Martin Chuzzlewit* reveals that Simon's knack for detail and delight in flourishes continued to whirl from the etching needle of his grandson, Phiz – the same confident accuracy, the same deftness of touch.

In contrast to her genteel, courtly husband, Ann Loder Browne, Phiz's grandmother, was obstinate and irascible. She bore eleven children in twenty-one years, seven of whom survived into adulthood. She managed to find time to run her own boarding school for young ladies near St Stephen's churchyard, staffed by her daughters, Wilhelmina, Elizabeth, Ann, Charlotte, and Lucinda. After her run of girls, Ann produced three boys, John Henry, William Loder, and George. George died when he was six weeks old, leaving William Loder the baby of the family, basking in the attention of his mother and five sisters, and, as indicated by later events, becoming indulged and mischievous.

Simon Browne died on 1 May 1797, but Ann lived on for another thirty-eight years,[15] in a house in Tombland, a street just outside the Norwich cathedral close. She was cared for to the end by an aged man-servant whom she referred to as 'my fac-to-tum, my old John'.[16] In 1830, her grandson Charles St Denys Moxon was taken as a young boy to see her. She was ninety-six and totally blind, but he clearly remembered her saying, 'Bring him here, that I may see him.' She felt all over his face and pronounced, 'I know what he is like now.' She would have done the same with Phiz, showing him how to *feel* an image by absorbing information through his fingertips. The act of stroking horses, dogs, and cats is reflected in the ease and pleasure with which he sketched them; in human terms, the charm of his images of young women reflects his particular delight in the curve of a neck and shoulders.

Phiz's uncle, John Henry Browne, was another powerful influence. Like his father Simon, John Henry had exquisite handwriting, and drawing and painting were his passions. His work resembled that of the Norwich School, and was eagerly sought by collectors in Norfolk. He was a parish priest and a headmaster, first at his father's school in Norwich, and then for forty-three years in nearby Hingham at the Endowed Grammar School, where he hired Monsieur Francis Noverre, a celebrated French dancing-master, to teach dancing to the boys, and 'Old Crome' to teach drawing and painting. John Crome (1768–1821) was the founder of the Norwich School, the Norfolk landscape was his subject matter, and his paintings combined strict adherence to nature with a flowing, romantic atmosphere. 'Old Crome' spent his holidays with the Brownes, and the headmaster accompanied him on sketching expeditions and shared his love of the Dutch masters. John Henry's influence shows up in the spacious, roman-tic, watercolour landscapes that Phiz enjoyed painting throughout his life.

John Henry proposed to Katherine Hunter of Cambridge in March 1792, but she refused him. Three years later, he married Charlotte Ann Penleaze, and their happy marriage produced thirteen children. He was a handsome man, but an eccentric dresser. 'To the end of his life he dressed as a cleric of the old school, his suit of black reaching only to below the knees, with gaiters for walking, or black silk stockings and shoes, whilst his ordinary hat was the "shovel" since then exclusively adopted by bishops and archdeacons.'[17] People stopped in the street to stare at him as he alighted like a bee here and there, drawing sketches or painting water-colours. The image of his uncle lodged in Phiz's memory, to reappear as the prototype of certain 'clerics of the old school' in his illustrations.

Phiz's aunt and uncle were regarded as universal peacemakers. Their establishment at School House formed the pattern of a Christian home and haven of rest, and seemed to exemplify the ideal Victorian family. Little Phiz could not but notice the vivid contrast between John Henry's family and his own.

Phiz's immediate family provides clues to the sometimes ghoulish, pathetic, and tragic subject matter that recurs in his work. His official father, William Loder Browne, was feckless and often absent; his official mother, Katherine, was ambitious and opinionated. They were unhappy with each other, and moved their enormous number of children from place to place, never allowing them to feel a sense of permanence or constancy. Journeys, debt, betrayal, partings, and a steady succession of deaths were commonplace in Phiz's early life. On the other hand, he honed his keen wit among his ebullient brothers and sisters, a talent later turned to good use.

William Loder Browne was born in Norwich in 1771, and educated by his father, Simon Browne. He showed early talent as an artist as well as exceptional facility as a linguist. On 7 July 1792, in London, he married eighteen-year-old Katherine Hunter, daughter of Colonel Thomas Hunter and his wife, Sarah – the same Katherine Hunter to whom his brother, John Henry, had proposed in March of the same year, just four months previously.[18] William was twenty-one the day before the wedding, but Katherine was a minor and needed her parents' permission. The wording of the marriage register,[19] for which her parents are witnesses, suggests that William stole his brother's girl and made off with her, her parents got wind of it, and Colonel Hunter applied his shotgun to William's head. It is easy to suspect a pregnancy which failed to go full term. After the birth on 3 November 1793 of William and Katherine's first child, Kate, Katherine proceeded to produce a baby a year for seven years before her rate of production slowed a little.

What was it that made Katherine so desirable to the two brothers? She was 'a handsome young lady, very good-looking, most particular in her notions, and having, it is said, a great idea of her own importance'.[20] Her good looks, her energy, some family money, and her links to society probably had much to do with her attraction. As the daughter of a colonel, she believed in maintaining significant connections, and these bore fruit when she later needed help with her children's education and careers.

After their marriage, William and Katherine lived in London, first at 306 High Holborn, opposite the George and Blue Boar tavern. John Henry Browne visited them in Holborn for the christening of their second daughter, and told one of his sisters that Katherine 'is in the straw with another of the petticoat gentry, named also by yr Brother [i.e. baptised by him], Charlotte Amelia. The worst part of that story is that her Mother from Cambridge, after having been with her about 3 weeks, was taken ill on Saturday sennt. & died there on the Monday following, which unhappy Circumstance has thrown her whole Family both in Town & Country, as may well be supposed into much Consternation & Trouble.'[21] Indeed.

John Henry sheds light on William's nature in another letter, following the death of their father. It is instructive if you read between the lines:

I wrote to you my dear William last Monday with a heavy heart. In spite of the conviction we feel that the last sigh of such a Father as our's wafts his soul to the regions of peace & happiness, we cannot but perceive, nor perceive without a tear, that we have suffered an irreparable loss. Even the recollection of his virtues serves in many a moment only to deepen regret for what cannot be recalled. The void occasioned by Death cannot be filled up by argument. It must be generally closed by Time & Employment. If this power over Grief were not more effectual than our boasted Reason the sorrows of Life would end only in the Grave. The last offices of respect to his Body will be performed tomorrow morning. It will be interred in the same spot as our Grandmother & Uncle. We wish to hear from you. The situation & feelings of Mrs Moxon & my Aunt[22] render us anxious for a letter. Mr F. Noverre conveys this from me & will return on Thursday but I hope you will not wait for that opportunity. Your Mother desires her love to you & to all the family. She continues better than we had expected.

I remain my dear William

Yours very sincerely & affectionately

J.H. Browne[23]

John Henry is clearly disturbed by William's failure to respond to his original letter. He hopes, but senses it unlikely, that William will arrive in time for their father's funeral. It would be interesting to know whether Monsieur Noverre (the celebrated dancing master at Hingham), executing a *grand jeté en l'air*, was successful in delivering the letter and whether William stirred himself enough to arrive at the graveside in time. John Henry's remark that the void occasioned by Death must be closed by Time and Employment is a serious jab at his brother. Indeed, it is a complete mystery how William supported his family during the first fourteen years of his marriage. However, he was certainly not above using his charm to prey on the kindness of friends and relatives, including John Henry himself.

As their family continued to grow, William and Katherine moved several times in quick succession: from High Holborn to the Old Kent Road, a country road in those days, and then to Box Hill in Surrey. In 1802, they settled in Kennington and began attending St Mary's, Lambeth, where their eighth, ninth, and tenth children were baptised. Eventually, necessity (and perhaps another sharp prod from Colonel Hunter) forced William into steady employment. In 1807 he and his wife's brother started working in partnership as merchants and warehousemen under the name of 'Browne & Hunter'.

By 1812, William and Katherine had eleven living children, out of a total of thirteen; Charlotte Amelia, their second child, and Edward, their third, had died at eight and twelve years old respectively. Two more children were still to come, one of whom was Hablot Knight Browne, 'Phiz'.

2

The French Captain's Woman

Waterloo! Waterloo! Waterloo! morne plaine!
Victor Hugo, *Les Châtiments*

Katherine Browne found it increasingly difficult to make ends meet, in spite of William's employment with her brother; but by asserting her strong will and her independence she found a solution to the family's financial problems. During the short-lived peace between Napoleon's abdication in March 1814 and the Battle of Waterloo in June 1815 she migrated with most of her children across the Channel to France, where the cost of living was lower and the weather often milder. She chose St Omer, a small town in the Pas de Calais. The fact that William did not accompany her is freighted with significance: Phiz was conceived while the family was abroad.

France must have seemed like paradise after the appallingly cold English winter of 1813–14, a winter spent struggling to keep her children warm

V. Lester, 'Grenadier à cheval'

and healthy. (London had celebrated the great chill by holding a Frost Fair on the frozen Thames.) But Katherine had other reasons for moving: her marriage was beginning to show severe cracks, and at some time either in 1808–9 or 1811, her eldest daughter, Kate, had met and formed a liaison with Captain Nicolas Hablot, a prisoner of war, captured during Napoleon's Peninsular campaign, who was on parole in England.[1] A *grenadier à cheval* in Napoleon's Imperial Guard, and a member of the Old Guard (seasoned officers who had served their emperor with unusual loyalty and heroism), he was no ordinary soldier. Coming from a military family herself, Mrs Browne would have been impressed by this member of the military elite and eager to further her daughter's prospects by moving to France.

In a story reminiscent of John Fowles's *The French Lieutenant's Woman*, Kate became the French Captain's Woman, and as a result of recent research, it is now evident to all but the most blinkered that Nicolas Hablot and Kate Browne were Phiz's natural parents. The story that William and Katherine were Phiz's parents was resolutely maintained in the nineteenth century; in that era when families were large and women continued to bear children as long as they remained fertile, it often happened that a mother passed off her daughter's illegitimate child as her own. This appears to have been the case with Kate, Captain Hablot, and his little namesake.

Who was the mysterious Nicolas Hablot, the man always referred to as Kate's fiancé? The French Army records at Vincennes throw light on his military history, personality, and physique, and go a long way towards explaining why Phiz differed so markedly from his brothers and sisters, even as he still inherited the Browne family's artistic talent through Kate.

Nicolas Hablot was born in Dugny-sur-Meuse, a small farming village near Verdun, on 4 November 1781, the youngest of six children. At the age of seventeen, he enlisted in the 15th Regiment of the Cavalry, and later became a horse grenadier. In a special report in his service record,[2] he is described as having distinguished morals, good principles, little fortune, superb physique, and no wife or children. He served in l'Armée du Rhin, l'Armée d'Italie, and La Grande Armée; he fought in Spain in the Peninsular War in 1808, in Germany in 1809, and again in Spain in 1810 and 1811. At some point during these years, after being seized in Spain or Portugal and brought to England as a prisoner of war, Nicolas Hablot met the Browne family.

Although captured conscripts were mainly detained on notorious hulks, officers were treated decently. A number of towns across England were designated parole areas where officers were billeted and, having pledged their word of honour not to try to escape, they were allowed to walk about freely, provided they stayed within a one-mile radius of their billets. The men, often perceived as heroic and dashing, inevitably became a source of much attraction for young English women, and many formed alliances. Kate Browne would have been in her late teens during the time of Nicolas Hablot's parole, and doubtless immediately intrigued by his gallant reputation and his height. Admission to the Imperial Guard was restricted to men between 1.78 and 1.84 metres (5 feet 10 inches and 6 feet and half an inch), who were of robust constitution, and who had performed heroically, been wounded, or had given proof of bravery, patriotism, discipline, and exemplary conduct in several campaigns. They were also required to be able to read and write. Nicolas Hablot, in turn, would have been delighted by the ease with which he could converse in his native language with the attractive, dainty, bookish, francophile Miss Browne. (Simon Browne's descendants all had a gift for languages and French was much spoken in the family.[3])

At some time in 1811 or 1812, Nicolas Hablot returned to France, probably traded for a British officer of equivalent rank whom the French had captured. He then served in Napoleon's disastrous Russian campaign of 1812 and, unlike most of his fellow cavalry officers, survived the retreat from Moscow and rallied again to serve his Emperor in Saxony and at Montmirail, where on 18 February 1814 his index finger was slashed off by a blow from a sabre.

Why Mrs Browne lit on St Omer as her destination in France is a mystery, but it is possible that Hablot was convalescing there after Montmirail, nursing his wounded hand. Or – to speculate a little – if he wrote to Mrs Browne expressing honourable intentions towards Kate and heaping praise on the charms of St Omer, he could have been the catalyst that propelled the escape from London. Whatever her reasons, Katherine Browne arrived there at some point during 1814. The children were aged from twenty down to one: Kate, Emma Louisa, Lucinda Sarah, Gordon Davis, Edgar, Septimus, Octavius, and Adelaide Matilda. The three oldest boys were elsewhere: Charles Alfred was already in France, studying at Mr Tomkins's school in Boulogne; William Frederick was a boarder at Christ's Hospital, the London boys' school; and Henry Albert remained in England to continue his classical education.

The family travelled by coach to Dover, where they found the captain of a suitable vessel, haggled over the fare, and waited until the weather and tide declared the time of departure. Their first trip abroad must have been an exciting event for the Browne children after being cooped up in London for so long. At last they left the white cliffs of Dover behind them and glimpsed the long-forbidden territory across the water. How thrilling it must have been to board the vessel and to watch its great sails filling. Perhaps Captain Hablot met them at the port and supplied them with a diligence – or two, or three – to transport them the twenty-two miles from Calais to St Omer. On his magnificent black horse, wearing the uniform of the *Grenadiers à Cheval*, he would have astonished the children. Over his powdered hair, he sported a huge 'beehive' – a black bearskin headdress with brass chinscales and a scarlet plume. He wore a blue coat with scarlet trim, a white waistcoat, white hide breeches, and white leather gloves. His knee-high black riding boots were adorned with gleaming spurs. (Kate's little brother, Octavius, became fascinated with these boots and spurs, and remembered playing with them as a little boy.[4])

France provided an idyllic change for Mrs Browne. St Omer was a charming little town with an excellent *lycée*, and schools of music and art were an added attraction. It also boasted a medieval cathedral full of works of art including an immense thirteenth-century statue of Christ with the Virgin and St John, a twelfth-century wooden Virgin Mary – the focus of pilgrimages – and a thirteenth-century memorial to St Omer himself, a seventh-century bishop. Katherine Browne and her children could shop in the bustling marketplace, parade in the public gardens, and drive down wide streets lined with attractive sixteenth- and seventeenth-century houses, passing the statue of Jacqueline Robin who in 1711, when the town was besieged by the Duke of Marlborough and Prince Eugène, risked her life to smuggle provisions to the starving citizens inside the fortifications.

For the first time in twenty-three years Katherine was free from the bondage of child-bearing. As the seasons changed, 1814 became 1815, and as the children became fluent in the language of their adopted country and healthier because of clean air, she started to enjoy herself. Her older children helped take care of the younger ones, which left her time to indulge the youngest of all, Adelaide, the apple of her eye, without worrying that yet another child was on its way.

Her idyll was short-lived. On Sunday, 5 March 1815, word reached Paris that Napoleon had escaped from Elba, landed in Provence, and was crossing the Maritime Alps and making for the capital, amassing soldiers along the way. The gouty Bourbon king, Louis XVIII, was persuaded to leave Paris on 19 March, fulfilling Wellington's pronouncement that no sovereign can be sovereign without an army. The government also packed up and left the capital that night. Twenty-four hours later Napoleon entered Paris.

Napoleon, 'Boney', the banished bogeyman, the warrior, the thief, the demon of childhood nightmares, was back. The expatriate community bundled its possessions together and scurried to the coast to catch the first sailing vessels back to the safety of England. With the scare of war coming ever closer and with Kate's fiancé returning to the field of battle, Mrs Browne rounded up her family and joined the fleeing Britons. But before Kate left France for ever, she and Nicolas became engaged, and he presented her with a gold ring, inscribed with the words *'je t'aime'*.[5]

Napoleon's response to the Allied Powers' declaration that he was an outlaw was to declare war, a war which culminated in his defeat at the Battle of Waterloo on 18 June 1815. Nicolas Hablot, loyal and seasoned officer that he was, able once more to wield his sabre strongly although awkwardly, responded to the call to arms, leaped into the saddle, and vanished from Kate's life.

Military skill, timing, and luck on the part of the British and the Prussians finally got the better of the French at the Battle of Waterloo. Towards the end of the day's fighting, Napoleon, the man who had for so long dominated the European stage, lost his ultimate gamble. In a last, desperate measure, he sent the *crème de la crème*, his Imperial Guard, up the hill of St Jean to clear the English from the height they had held all day. Like a giant tidal wave, the Guard rolled up the hill and crested, stopped dead in their tracks by artillery, 'which hurled death from the English line. . . . Then at last the English troops rushed from the post from which no enemy had been able to dislodge them, and the Guard turned and fled.'[6]

'*La Garde cède! La Garde récule,*' came the terrible cry.

Nicolas Hablot was in the thick of things. The Old Guard formed squares but was forced back by the fleeing troops. Napoleon, after sheltering in one of the squares, left for Genappe, hoping to rally his men. As Scott Bowden writes:

> Behind him, the Old Guard continued to cover the retreat. . . . The fighting withdrawal of the Old Guard was a model of valour and cool determination. General Cambronne's reputed reply to a summons to surrender – 'The Guard dies but never surrenders' – may be a myth, but it reflects the spirit of these last desperate hours. Large numbers of the *élite* of the French army gave their lives to cover the flight of their compatriots.[7]

Back in London, Kate could have opened *The Times* on Thursday, 22 June 1815, to read Wellington's dispatch:

> The attack succeeded in every point; the enemy was forced from his position on the heights, and fled in the utmost confusion, leaving behind him, as far as I could judge, one hundred and fifty pieces of cannon . . . I continued the pursuit till long after dark, and then discontinued it only on account of the fatigue of our troops . . . and because I found myself on the same road with Marshal Blucher, who assured me of his intention to follow the enemy through the night; he has sent me word this morning that he had taken sixty pieces of cannon belonging to the Imperial Guard.[8]

On the next page came the official bulletin from Downing Street:

> The 18th of June, we trust, will satisfy the most incredulous. Two hundred and ten pieces of cannon! When, where, or how is this loss to be repaired? Besides, what has become of his invincible guard?[9]

What, indeed?

The Browne family naturally assumed that Captain Hablot lost his life at Waterloo. Indeed, Phiz's oldest son, Edgar, states this on the first page of *Phiz and Dickens*[10] as uncontrovertible fact, a statement echoed by others. However, as she never received confirmation of his death, Kate may have lived in a state of anxiety for years, always hoping that Nicolas had miraculously survived. She never married, but wore his ring to her dying day.

3
Births and Names

Hablot, as a Christian name, seemed odd.[1]

Alec Guinness

[Captain Hablot] must have been sadly missed by the Browne family
or they would not have named their latest baby . . . after him. Or
could it be – and perhaps I shouldn't suggest this – the deceased
French soldier was the baby's father?[2]

Cedric Dickens

Soon after her return to England early in 1815, and in a short-lived bout
of reunion enthusiasm with her husband, Mrs Browne became pregnant
with the child who would be named Edward Augustus Decimus (but
called Decimus or 'Dec' by the family). Despite the fact that the exact
birth dates of all her other children are clearly recorded in the family
papers, the date of Decimus's birth is variously left blank, described as circa

Kate Browne, woodland scene, 1815

17

1815 or 1816, called 'unknown, probably 1815',[3] and marked by similarly evasive or plainly inaccurate statements. The true date was kept secret because of the birth of Hablot Knight Browne on 10 July 1815. This baby was immediately enveloped in a 'sentimental' atmosphere because of the presumed death of Captain Hablot at Waterloo. To add to Kate's loss and grief, it appears that the birth was difficult (which never seemed to have been the case with Katherine's deliveries) and the baby's life endangered, since an emergency call was made to the Reverend Henry White to come and baptise him immediately, giving him the name Hablot Knight Nonus Browne.

Five months later, on 21 December, the same clergyman officially christened the same infant at St Mary's, Lambeth, this time dropping Nonus from the collection of names. (On the baptismal certificate, White is referred to as 'preacher at the asylum', the nearby Bethlehem Hospital for Lunatics, otherwise known as Bedlam.) At the same time, he christened three-year-old Adelaide, who had missed out on baptism before the departure for France. Hablot Knight Browne's certificate declares that he is the son of William Loder and Katherine Browne. This, fortuitously, is no lie – William was the baby's adoptive father, and Kate's given name was Katherine. William is described as a merchant of Kennington Lane, and the baby's birthdate is given as 11 June 1815, a date at odds with Edgar Browne's claim that his father was born in July, and also at odds with Hablot's death certificate and the date given on the order of service for his funeral. It appears that Hablot's true birthdate, 10 July, was pushed back by a month to make room for Decimus's arrival at a respectable interval. The family archives are again significantly silent about a baptismal date for Decimus.

It is clear that family historians knew that little Hablot was not the child of his official parents, but one effort to tell the truth was squelched. The pages concerning Hablot Knight Browne in the copy of the family history have been excised and rewritten.

Why did the child receive the name Hablot – a surname – as his peculiar Christian name instead of the more accessible Nicolas, and in place of the family's frontrunning choice, Nonus? Probably because Kate wanted to make sure that she 'legitimised' her son by giving him his father's family name, even though Hablot would be an awkward label for an English boy to sport. In a mongrelised version of French and English, the Brownes aspirated the 'H' but dropped the 't' and pronounced it 'Hablo', a name they stuck to, even after he became known as 'Phiz' to the general public. As for the boy's middle name, Knight, given to him in honour of Admiral

Sir John Knight, the word translates into *chevalier* in French, and is another reminder of Captain Hablot, a *chevalier*, cavalry officer, in the Imperial Guard.

At some point during 1815, Kate drew a picture which offers a tantalising clue about the environment in which Phiz may have been conceived, even as it brings to mind *A Midsummer Night's Dream*. It is evidence of Kate's artistic inheritance and stylistic influence on her son's work.

Mrs Browne finally decided that the coast was clear for Decimus's baptism, and the ceremony took place at St Mary Aldermary, Holborn, on 26 January 1823. The date of birth is given as 12 January 1817. As the Brownes were already adept at fudging dates (and it is far easier to misrepresent a child's age when he is seven than a babe in arms), the true date of Decimus's birth would have been exactly one year earlier.

Kate Browne, 'Hecate', 1828

4

Abandoned!

The England that Mrs Browne and her children returned to in 1815 was a miserable place, seething with popular discontent, suffering a post-war economic crisis, traumatised by the maimed bodies returning from France, clinging to its eighteenth-century past, and beginning to feel the effects of the industrial revolution which had put so many out of work. King George III had declined into madness, and his eldest son, a fretful lump of blubber, was acting as regent. The country grieved for the loss of life at Waterloo.

All the same, Kennington Lane, where Hablot Knight Browne was born and lived his earliest years, was a pleasant street, far from the centre of London. Lined with small Queen Anne houses, it was not far from Vauxhall Gardens, then a favourite recreation place for Londoners. To the south, London soon gave way to the open countryside of Surrey and a welcome whiff of fresh air; but to the north-east lay stinking Lambeth Marsh, beyond which John Rennie's Waterloo Bridge was slowly making its way, arch by

'Repentance', c. 1828

arch, across the Thames (built between 1811 and 1817, it was described by Canova as the noblest bridge in the world). Due east, beyond the Elephant and Castle, the roads became country lanes; while on Kennington's western border, the Thames flowed between the Houses of Parliament and Lambeth Palace before making its noisome, freighted way towards the sea.

The state of the nation seemed to mirror the state of Katherine's crumbling and impoverished marriage. But her real troubles were just beginning. In 1818 she received the news of the death of one son, William Frederick, in Mauritius, and in 1821 she learned that Septimus had died at sea. To add to these woes, her husband fell out with his brother-in-law, and the partnership of 'Browne & Hunter' was dissolved. William was, once again, failing to provide for his enormous family. What could she do? What could he do?

In 1822,[2] when Phiz was seven, he vanished into thin air.

William Loder Browne, merchant of Kennington Lane, died to his past – and was resurrected as William L. Breton,[3] thus reclaiming his French roots, and becoming an artist, bachelor, and person to his own liking. He abandoned his native country, his wife and children, and sailed to the United States, settling in Philadelphia, where he lived the rest of his life, working as an artist and drawing teacher. (Alfred Moxon records in his notebook 100 years after the event, without citing evidence, that William ran away with some unspecified 'trust funds', adding that Katherine was to blame for running him into debt.)

William was fifty-one when he sailed, but probably lied about his age as well as his name. With his youthful bearing and spectacularly good health, he could pass for a much younger man. His American friend, Charles V. Hagner, admits that there was an air of mystery about him and adds that William told him he was a self-made artist whose first attempts at drawing were made during his journey to Philadelphia. This has to be another of William's deceptions; no son of Simon Browne could escape drawing lessons. He was clearly distancing himself from any artistic background through which his past might be traced. 'Although a man of intelligence and education,' Hagner continues, 'he was a thorough John Bull, a constitutional grumbler; in his view there was nothing right in this country – nothing wrong in his own.'[4]

On his arrival, William started painting Philadelphia's antiquarian buildings, and found himself a ready market. He even had an uncanny aptitude for recreating buildings that no longer existed, using verbal descriptions or existing sketches.[5] He worked mainly in watercolours, occasionally

William Breton, 'Railroad Depot at Philadelphia', c. 1830

produced wood engravings, and later became one of Philadelphia's first lithographers. The author John Fanning Watson so admired Breton's rather primitive style that he invited him to illustrate *Annals of Philadelphia and Pennsylvania, in the Olden-Time*, a detailed record of the earliest days of Philadelphia,[6] and their lengthy, happy collaboration presages that of Dickens and Phiz which began six years later.

Dickens's novels were available to William in Philadelphia, where they were extraordinarily popular, and when the author visited Philadelphia in March of 1842, 600 people stood in line to shake his hand at the United States Hotel. As an artist, William may have been particularly fascinated by the illustrations, having heard from his sister, Ann Moxon (with whom he did not sever ties), about the meteoric rise of the young illustrator known to the public as Phiz.

After living his reinvented life for thirty-three years, William L. Breton died in Philadelphia on 14 August 1855. One family historian records that: 'After travelling 40 miles – ten of which were on foot – taking a light supper and playing with a child, he sat down in his arm chair, and was found dead in it, as it were asleep, in the morning. Tho' 84 years of age, he suffered from no illness and his eyesight and hearing were very good.'[7]

William died intestate, but the inventory and valuation of his possessions is revealing. He owned 302 books and 132 magazines, twenty-two framed pictures, a box of pictures and papers, a camera, paint supplies and drawing paper, two armchairs, a table and four chairs, a wardrobe, a bureau, a bookcase, a silver watch, spectacles, cutlery, and $115 in cash. He was certainly not destitute; in fact, judging from the quantity of his possessions and the fact he had not made a will, it can be inferred that he was relatively prosperous, still enjoyed his profession, read a great deal, and had no intention of dying.

In his Preface to *Notes*, Charles Gordon Browne writes, 'There have no doubt, as in almost every family history been some shady characters & doubtful episodes, but on the whole the character of our forefathers has been that of men determined & energetic, & of a brain power well above the average, & for the most part truthful, honest, hardworking and respected.'[8] While blessed with the family brain power and energy, William L. Browne/ Breton is clearly the frontrunning shady character to which his grandson refers. Nonetheless, his talent and zeal continued to flow down the generations.

Phiz cannot have had an easy childhood, having witnessed the strains in William and Katherine's marriage. Abandoned by two fathers, he then suffered further abandonment as a result of death and emigration among his siblings. However, he had a sunny disposition and could entertain himself for hours on end. He drew and drew and drew; there was never enough paper. He drew on whatever he could find – in the margins of letters, on tracing paper, on both sides of scraps of paper. Even if Katherine Browne paid little attention to his efforts, preferring instead to focus her interest on the beautiful and gifted Adelaide, he received encouragement from his brothers and sisters, most of whom were artistically talented, and all of whom played important parts in the forming of his character. Unfortunately, no images of Phiz's siblings as children have come to light, but it is safe to assume that most of the family took after Simon Browne in physique and were small and slight; Gordon and Octavius are both described this way as young men, and photographs of Henry Albert, Charles, and Octavius in later years show them with light eyes and fair, curly hair.

After the return from France, the two eldest daughters, Kate and Emma, helped support the family, Kate by teaching French and Emma by giving lessons in music and general education. Kate was said to have been 'most conservative, hospitable, low-Church & easily offended, but at the same time quite willing to forgive and forget', while Emma was 'most amiable and essentially a lady in everything, having all the good qualities of the Brownes and none of their failings'[9] (which can be taken as meaning that she was witty, artistic, unpretentious, and paid her bills on time).

Henry Albert, whose interests were religion and classical languages, studied at Oxford and in the 1820s, after ordination, worked as a tutor to the sixth Viscount Galway. He later became rector at Toft in Lincolnshire, where he spent the rest of his life. The adjective 'amiable', used regularly in descriptions of other members of the family, and certainly the most cited, if not overworked, description of Phiz once he enters the world of Dickens, is not a word that portrays Henry Albert. In describing him, Charles Gordon Browne says,

> It is difficult to understand the character of Henry Albert Browne. After becoming Rector or before, he broke off all communication with his mother and family. Hablot said that his mother, whose means were at the time very small had asked him if he would receive him [Hablot] & teach him a little Latin etc. which he resented angrily; also that his sister Kate said he had told her & his mother that he could not associate with people who had allowed his sister Lucinda to marry an Unitarian. But whatever the grievance may have been, he never would have anything to do with his family all his life, & told his children he had no relations.[10]

Though this grumbling and cutting himself off from his family puts one in mind of William Loder Browne, Henry Albert certainly seems to have had nothing of the spirit of that adventurous artist in his make-up. A prude to end all prudes, he was sixteen at the time of Phiz's birth, an age at which sex is insistent and a sister's pregnancy doubly shaming and embarrassing.

By contrast, his sister Lucinda was by all accounts a delightful person and universal favourite. She spoke fluent French and played the piano and the harp (an ideal instrument to advertise lovely hands, elegant shoulders, and a charming neck). Like her father, she looked younger than her age, a trait she encouraged in another instance of date-fudging; she claimed a birthdate of 1804 when the actual date was 1801. Lucinda enjoyed society and had her own connections and ambitions. These social connections would later play a crucial part in Phiz's life, but until she married she, too, may have been forced to help out the family, by teaching music.

As a teenager the next child in line, Charles Alfred, was appointed a midshipman in the Royal Navy, with help from a family connection. Later, through the intervention of yet another connection, he obtained a Cadetship in the Honourable East India Company's Military College at Addiscombe where he attained high distinction upon graduation. His skill as a linguist was renowned; shortly after he joined the Madras Army in 1820, he passed examinations in four Asian languages and went on to write grammar books in Hindustani and Persian. Charles Alfred was liberal, courteous, hospitable, generous to a fault, and although he experienced a spiritual revelation, never forced his religious views on others. 'Besides being extra-ordinarily strong & active,' the family history declares, 'he had an amazing love of & capacity for work, often continuing his labours till 5 in the morning, & once for a whole fortnight he spent 22 hours daily either on horseback or at his desk . . . His love of children too was only equalled by their love of him.'[11]

Gordon Davis, the next brother, was one of the first settlers in New Zealand, where he went during the 1820s, while Edgar was a gifted artist and draughtsman, and the particular friend of his sister Lucinda. Phiz must have had an especially strong attachment to this brother because he named his eldest son after him. Very little is known about Edgar's life, but he may have worked as an artist before spending a year in Barcelona. In 1829 he sailed via the Baltic Sea to Latvia, and died of pleurisy in Riga on 5 January 1833, leaving behind a large collection of sketches in a book – sadly lost – which also contained sketches by other members of the family such as Hablot Knight Browne, Adelaide M. Browne, William Browne, F.S. Browne, C. St D. Moxon, J.E. Moxon, as well as by outsiders such as George Cruikshank, Conrad Masters, and Angus Hume. Perhaps this collection will come to light some day.

The next child, Septimus, was sent to school at Botesdale in Suffolk, receiving a commercial education. He left school early and became a midshipman in the Royal Navy but died of fever during his return from the West Indies when he was about fifteen. The *Notes*, however, insist that he drowned at sea. (It is entirely possible, even probable, that he had fever *and* drowned.) Octavius, the brother next in line, told this to one of his nephews:

Septimus was drowned in a hurricane in returning from the West Indies. Some time before this event was known at home, he (Octavius) had just gone to bed one night and put the candle out, when on turning round he saw Septimus standing between the bed & the wall; the moon was shining brightly through the window, which enabled him to see that the figure was dressed in uniform, & the face was pale & sad. Involuntarily he closed his eyes, & when he opened them again the form had disappeared. Jumping up he immediately went to his brother Edgar in another room, & told him what he had seen. He had been chatting with Edgar & when he wished him goodnight he was brushing his hair. Now when he came back, Octavius said, Edgar was still brushing his hair, which proved he said, that he had not had time to go to sleep. Shortly afterwards came the news of Septimus being dead, & the date & hour of his death agreed with those of the appearance he had witnessed.[12]

Charles Gordon Browne wonders 'whether Octavius allowed for the difference in longitude. He probably did, as he was an absolutely truthful man, & too sharp to have overlooked so simple a ground for scepticism.' Phiz would have been the impressionable age of six when Septimus died.

Octavius, like his older brother, Charles Alfred, was known for his generosity, and on many occasions helped other members of his family. He was born on 2 November 1809, and as a small boy was sent to Merchant Taylors' School, where he was starved and bullied to such an extent that he nearly died. He was quickly removed and sent to the gentler school at Botesdale in pastoral Suffolk which Septimus already attended and where Hablot would soon follow him. William Loder Browne's sister, Ann, and her husband, Thomas Moxon, took care of some of the school fees, and Octavius himself cleared the final debt. He left Botesdale at the age of sixteen and a half and went to work to support his family, earning £100 a year. The kindly Moxons must have been instrumental in securing this post for him because in those years an income of £100 was exceptionally high for one so young.

The two children with whom Hablot would have spent the most time were the artistically gifted Adelaide, born three years before him, and Edward Augustus Decimus – who arrived embarrassingly soon after him.

This, then, is the household in which Hablot Knight Browne lived. It is a home where people are constantly leaving, one way or another: in 1818, when Hablot was three, William Frederick died in Mauritius and Henry Albert left for Oxford. Charles Alfred joined the Madras Army when Hablot was five; Septimus died at sea when Hablot was six. By 1822, when Hablot was seven, Octavius was at school in Suffolk, and

William Loder Browne disappeared from England. The household attrition continued when Gordon Davis set off for Australia and New Zealand when Hablot was about ten. Adelaide, who shared Hablot's christening day and his artistic genius, died when he was fifteen. Edgar died in Riga when Hablot was eighteen and Decimus left for Australia when Hablot, who had just become Phiz, was in his twenties.

Is it any wonder that solemn Death, or sometimes hideously hilarious Death, wanders so frequently into Phiz's creations? Is it any wonder that Phiz became such a devoted family man when the time came for him to marry and have children?

5

The Young Printmaker

In Phiz's youth, London was crammed with people, soot-laden, disease-ridden, and stinking. A pall of smoke, sometimes ten miles wide, hung over the city. The rain dripped filth, open sewers carried away the contents of chamber pots, and streets were soggy with mud, rubbish, and horse manure. Cholera, scarlet fever, typhoid fever, smallpox, and diphtheria took tremendous tolls, as did the common cold. Nonetheless, London beamed brilliance. It was the same city Hogarth had inhabited, and where Dickens, Trollope, and Thackeray were living, a city where Phiz grew up to the sounds of street musicians and players and was constantly amused by visual delights.

The printshops were magnets for the populace in general, and provided free entertainment for young and old, rich and poor. The Browne family, with their artistic inheritance, paid particular attention to them. While the life of London scrawled images on the ground of Phiz's memory, the represented world of prints bit even deeper. Wherever the boy turned, his eye

'John Gilpin's Race', 1832

28

was attracted by images, not just in the shops but on the streets themselves where illustrations were often displayed on the inside of open umbrel-
las. Crowds gathered in front of booksellers' windows to see the latest
pictures, sometimes scandalous caricatures of famous people, sometimes
engravings of prize fights or of murderers and criminals at work. The illit-
erate imagined stories to fit the images; the wealthy acquired expensive
treasures as decorations and diversions in their own homes where looking
at a series of good-looking prints could be the high point of a gala event.

Phiz banked the images in his formidable mental storehouse. In this
way Bruegel's knotty characters, Holbein's 'Dance of Death', Hogarth's
'Rake's Progress' and 'Gin Lane' (without a doubt Hogarth was the most
influential of Phiz's artistic forerunners), Bewick's natural world, Blake's
angels, Gillray's caricatures, and Cruikshank's – well – everything, all entered
the boy's memory palace and inhabited it. Later on, Seymour's designs for
Mr Pickwick, Daumier's '*La Garde-Malade*', and Pugin's architectural
embellishments added further furnishing. Just as some musicians play exclusively by ear and never care to learn how to read music, so Phiz played
by eye and did not care to draw from the actual. He absorbed what he
saw and translated it, but perhaps what is more important, he used fancy.

William Thackeray, four years older than Phiz, also responded to the
printshops enthusiastically, and remembered them all:

> Knight's in Sweeting's Alley; Fairburn's, in a court off Ludgate Hill;
> Home's, in Fleet Street – bright, enchanted palaces. . . . How we
> used to stray miles out of the way on holidays, in order to ponder
> for an hour before that delightful window in Sweeting's Alley! In
> walks through Fleet Street, to vanish abruptly down Fairburn's passage,
> to his 'charming gratis' exhibition. There used to be a crowd round
> the window in those days, of grinning, good-natured mechanics, who
> spelt the songs, and spoke them out for the benefit of the company,
> and who received the points of humour with a general sympathis-
> ing roar.[1]

At some point, probably just after William Loder Browne vanished in
1822, the rest of the family moved to Euston Square, within easy walking
distance of the British Museum, then under construction on the site of
Montagu House. Phiz, whose childish doodles almost always included
horses, soon discovered the Elgin marbles and spent much of his time
admiring and sketching them. About a year later he was sent to the

Reverend William Haddock's Botesdale school on the Norfolk–Suffolk border, where Septimus and Octavius had preceded him. Phiz's uncle, John Henry Browne, headmaster at Hingham, had probably recommended this 'commercial' school for his three nephews because Mrs Browne's precarious financial state required that the boys be trained to earn a living. His own school would have been too expensive and too exclusive (he could ill afford to take on three boys as charity cases), but close enough for him to keep his eye on them.

At Botesdale, Mr Haddock recognised the new arrival's talent and believed a great future lay in store for the budding artist. He encouraged him to paint in watercolours, to draw in pen and ink or pencil, and to go on sketching expeditions in the countryside. Phiz's love of watercolour painting never left him, nor did his love of open skies. In contrast to his early years in a marital war zone in crowded London, his years at Botesdale were blissful. With Mr Haddock's encouragement, he thrived, and, after Phiz left, the headmaster stayed in touch and visited the young artist in London to celebrate the success he had so confidently foretold.

Phiz did not leave Botesdale by choice. He was removed by his brother-in-law, Elhanan Bicknell, who had married Phiz's twenty-eight-year-old sister, Lucinda Browne, in 1829, when Phiz was fourteen. Bicknell, like Mr Haddock, was fascinated by Phiz's talent, and resolved to encourage it, while at the same time ensuring that the young man could earn a living. He had quickly realised that Mrs Browne would always be dependent on the kindness of relatives, and was determined that Phiz would stand on his own financial feet.

Born in 1788, Elhanan was thirteen years older than Lucinda (although she insisted he was sixteen years older), a large, handsome, red-faced man, already twice a widower. In politics he was an advanced Liberal; in religion he was a Unitarian. It was his adherence to this religion with its emphasis on freedom from formal doctrine that so inflamed his censorious brother-in-law, Henry Albert Browne. As a young man, Bicknell endured a dismal training to become a farmer, until a couple of friends, aware of his remarkable financial talent, begged him to join them in a daring venture. This was the sperm whale oil business, and the two young men were absolutely right about its potential. With Elhanan at the financial helm, the business took off.

Always interested in art and artists, the prosperous Bicknell invested heavily in modern British paintings, especially the work of J.M.W. Turner. Edgar Browne rightly points out Bicknell's collecting canniness:

There is nothing remarkable in a rich man making a collection of pictures, but it was not so common in the early Victorian days, and this was done entirely at first hand, on his own judgment, and without the aid or intervention of dealers. He had a most extensive knowledge of the works of contemporary English painters, and he must have had a shrewd idea of their pecuniary value and prospects, as the collection sold for about three times its original cost, fetching something about eighty thousand pounds. The sale made a great stir. There were 122 oils, including ten important Turners, and 270 watercolours.[2]

Phiz enjoyed visiting the Bicknells, happy in the lively, artistic atmosphere of their well-run household at Herne Hill, and revelling in the powerful influence of the building itself. A particular house – a palace of memories and images – often exists in a growing child's mind, a house that more than any other exerts influence on an artistic imagination; the spacious Herne Hill mansion, its walls covered with contemporary paintings, played this role in Phiz's life. Bicknell had completely redesigned it, adding two large wings at either end so that he could display his collection throughout the entire ground floor. The centrepiece was the old low-ceilinged drawing room, its walls lined with mahogany and covered by white and gold rococo panels whose gold mouldings served as frames for watercolours. On the doors leading into the drawing room, Bicknell had set Turner's 'Rivers of France'. (A tinted engraving by Phiz, after Turner's 'On the Scheldt', shows up in the catalogue of Sotheby's 1887 auction of Phiz's artistic estate. It would be interesting to know at what point he executed it. Was it a juvenile rendering, executed as a gift for Elhanan Bicknell, or a mature work created to secure the memory of golden days at Herne Hill?)

If Elhanan Bicknell was Lucinda's great coup, the lovely, musically talented Lucinda was certainly Elhanan's. Edgar Browne claims that, in addition to her charm and good looks, 'My aunt was a notable woman, and managed her household affairs with a skill truly early Victorian. She had that art of organising which comes from natural capability, and which made the management of a big house and wealth no more difficult to her than a cottage home would have been, and she always seemed to have leisure for various pursuits.'[3]

The Bicknells' neighbour, John Ruskin, was four years younger than Phiz, and Edgar describes him as that 'vehement young man'. He was a regular visitor and greatly attached to Lucinda to whom he would read 'long screeds of a work in manuscript'.[4] He often turned the house on its ear in his search for drawing materials when he felt impelled to paint a beautiful flower just coming to perfection in the Bicknells' conservatory.

Phiz desired nothing more than to be a fine artist like those he met at Herne Hill, and was probably astounded by his uncle's sudden, draconian decision in 1831 to remove him from Botesdale and to apprentice him with Edward and William Finden, the leading engravers of the day. But Bicknell was a shrewd businessman and confident that a thorough training would turn the boy's talent to material gain.

The Findens ran their engraving business at 18–19 Southampton Place in Bloomsbury and produced fine prints of all kinds for book illustrations, for annuals, and for framing. The studio was a pleasant spot and the thirty apprentices and assistants worked congenially in its various rooms, several of them often engaged on a single line engraving. Here Phiz learned his technical skills, and made those lifelong friendships which influenced and sustained him throughout his long career. Most significant among his new friends were Henry Winkles and Robert Young. The former gave him his first commission as a book illustrator and the latter became not only his working partner but his closest friend, and remained Phiz's champion for the rest of his life.

Observe the consensus on how Phiz spent his time during his apprenticeship. David Croal Thomson, author of *The Life and Labours of Hablôt Knight Browne* (whose circumflex on Hablot is his own invention), comments:

No greater mistake could have been made than in apprenticing a youth with the aesthetic temperament of Hablôt Browne to a partly mechanical and always monotonous business like that of an engraver. It is easily believed, therefore, that with engraving after the manner of Finden, Hablôt Browne troubled himself very little. He was faithful enough to go regularly to his workshop, but after a time he only made believe he was drawing, and would sit at his engraver's desk, with its little drawer open, reading a favourite author. A writer with brilliant imagery was his delight, and Shakespeare's poems and Butler's 'Hudibras' were the books most frequently found in his hands. As he read, even under the eyes of his master, he would make rapid sketches of the scenes as they presented themselves to his mind.[5]

Frederic Kitton, author of *Phiz: A Memoir*, agrees that 'Line-engraving did not find much favour with the future "Phiz", the process being too tedious. Finden would probably occupy some weeks to produce a small plate, which by the quicker process of etching, could have been executed in as many hours.'[6] Arthur Allchin adds:

Hablot Browne . . . made little progress in line-engraving, and Finden was in the habit of sending [him] with plates to the printers to super-intend the taking of proofs. These absences from the studio seemed very congenial to Browne's taste, and he received many commenda-tions for the despatch and diligence he displayed, although had his masters been aware that their apprentice, leaving the printer to work his will, was spending his time, and filling his sketch-book, among the antiques at the British Museum, they would probably have had their proof-pulling overlooked by some steadier youth, and the sadly neglected plate on Browne's desk would have been the gainer by some few strokes from his burin.[7] [A burin is a sharp, grooved steel tool used in engraving.]

Edgar Browne admits that his father 'was not always solicitous for the finish of his plates but was accustomed to etch little original sketches on the margin, which would be printed off and afterwards obliterated, and served more for amusement than edification. Similar little sketches are frequently made seriously by engravers, and are termed remarques.'[8]

Even though he was surrounded by friends and making good progress with engraving in spite of himself, Phiz played hookey more and more frequently, disagreed with his teachers, neglected his work, and clearly demonstrated an artistic energy ill suited to the drudgery of line-engraving. He detested the slavishness and repetition of engraving, which entailed using a burin to copy the work of others onto a metal plate. He much preferred etching, a speedy technique where he could draw his own designs by running an etching needle through wax onto steel or copper plates, and acid would do the tedious job of biting-in for him. (Steel plates had been used exclusively for banknotes until 1823, when it was discovered that they worked just as well for illustrations.) His hand was sure, his needle unhesitating, and his lines were as deft, swift, and spontaneous as those of his manually nimble forebear, Simon Browne.

When Phiz was about eighteen, he asked Elhanan Bicknell to cancel his indentures, a request which was not well received. Bicknell, ever the businessman, recognised the commercial value of engravings and believed in investing in them. He was convinced that engraving, at which Phiz was extraordinarily gifted in spite of himself, was the road to a steady income. He insisted that Phiz continue his training. Phiz dug in his heels. Like water dripping on a stone, he importuned Bicknell to free him from his indentures. The brothers Finden also had to be persuaded to release the young man whose desk drawer was stuffed with sketches, whose remarques revealed his genius, and whose skill at etching had already been appreciated. In 1832, at the age of seventeen, Phiz had won the Society of Arts silver medal for the best illustration of a historical subject. The same society then awarded him another prize for his large etching (19½" x 12½") entitled *John Gilpin's Race*,[9] at the head of this chapter.

It was a worthy prizewinner, especially for one so young. Its size alone was impressive since etching becomes exponentially more difficult as it increases in size. The large image illustrates William Cowper's jolly poem 'The Diverting History of John Gilpin', and was possibly Phiz's competitive response to a minute 1828 wood engraving[10] of the same subject by the already great George Cruikshank (1792–1878). Phiz mimics many details of the older artist's picture and even signs 'H.K. Browne' on the same sort of toll-keeper's cottage at exactly the same spot on which Cruikshank has signed 'G. Cruik'. The artists both illustrate the following lines:

> Away went Gilpin, neck or nought;
> Away went hat and wig! –
> He little dreamt, when he set out,
> Of running such a rig.
>
> The wind did blow, the cloak did fly
> Like streamer long and gay,
> Till, loop and button failing both,
> At last it flew away.[11]

George Cruikshank was much in the public eye, having found fame as a political caricaturist in the 1810s and 1820s. Like Phiz, he relied on a brilliant native gift rather than serious academic training, and by 1815, the year of Phiz's birth and James Gillray's death, Cruikshank had already succeeded Gillray in the matter of satirical illustration. Phiz, in turn, was considerably influenced by Cruikshank, and hence by Gillray as well. And in 1837, the names of Phiz and Cruikshank would be inextricably bound together. In that year they worked concurrently, for Charles Dickens – Phiz on *Pickwick Papers* and Cruikshank on *Oliver Twist*. Such is the effect on the public memory of two of Cruikshank's illustrations, 'Oliver's asking for more' and 'Fagin in the Condemned Cell', that Cruikshank is thought by some to be Dickens's principal illustrator, ironic when one remembers that Cruikshank illustrated only one of Dickens's novels while Phiz illustrated ten.[12]

Phiz's love of horses is patently evident in 'John Gilpin', from the care he lavishes on them at the expense of the sketchy background. The meticulously drawn horses of the foreground hurtle across the scene from left to right towards the open toll gate, their back hoofs concealed in a cloud of dust. John Gilpin, in the lead, hatless, cloak billowing out behind him, is in trouble; he has lost hold of his reins and his feet have escaped the stirrups, leaving him clinging desperately to his horse's neck. The other riders, with two exceptions, race forward confidently, whip arms raised to sting their horses into speed. The two exceptions are engaged in the dangerous sport of slugging it out while galloping. Presciently, John Gilpin closely resembles Mr Pickwick, and by pushing that visual parallel a step further, one could even say that he is closely followed by a jaunty Sam Weller, kitted out in full jockey fig.

With the arrogance of youth, Phiz was determined to enter the art world on his own terms. In this attempt, he had the financial encouragement of Finden's superintendent, John Greville Fennell, who was already placing his watercolours with the dealer, Adolphus Ackerman. Fennell offered to pay off the next two years of the boy's indentures, and although Phiz's battle with Elhanan Bicknell was hard won – he must have sworn black and blue that he would never again ask for help – and although the Findens were reluctant to let him go, they all recognised that he could not abide line-engraving's tedious copying process and was yearning to draw and paint and etch his own images. Phiz was finally released from his apprenticeship, his indentures were cancelled, and he flung himself right into London's literary and artistic scene.

In partnership with Robert Young, he rented a small studio in the attic at 3 Furnival's Inn, Holborn, unaware that Charles Dickens, then a young parliamentary reporter, was living first at No. 13 and then at No. 15.[13] Furnival's was an Inn of Chancery attached to Lincoln's Inn, and formed a pleasing quadrangle, inhabited mostly by lawyers, except for the section which comprised Wood's Hotel, opposite the carriage entrance at High Holborn. Wood's was a respectable establishment, well known to country visitors who wanted the comforts and safety of home, including family prayers morning and night. The artists' studio was on the left of the entrance into Furnival's Inn; Dickens's chambers were on the right. 'I shall never be so happy again as in those Chambers three Storeys high – never if I roll in wealth and fame. I would hire them to keep empty, if I could afford it,'[14] cried Dickens after his move to Doughty Street. The peaceful atmosphere of Furnival's Inn was in marked contrast with the seedy locales nearby, including the notorious Field-lane and its gin palaces.

With a studio at Furnival's Inn and lodgings at 14 Bedford Place, Phiz was well set up. Bedford Place connected Russell Square with Bloomsbury Square, and was part of the well-managed Bedford Estates, an exclusively residential area, sweeter-smelling than its neighbours because of its underground sewer. The houses were uniform, each with a back garden or courtyard leading down to mews where horses were stabled. As a struggling artist, Phiz would have lived at the back of the house, unless his room were in the garret or basement. A room in the back would be small, but offered the opportunity for horse-gazing.

Whether at home or at work, Phiz was never far from his beloved British Museum. On 20 February 1834, he made his first use of its library, then called 'The King's Library', located in a wing on the east side (construction work on the Great Reading Room did not begin until 1847). His first name appears as 'Hablow' in the records, and a Mr Tyndale is his referee.

Once established in the studio eyrie, Phiz launched into drawing and painting in watercolour. His attempts at oil painting were less successful because he had little training and never enough time or patience to grasp full control of the medium. He and Young made a pact to produce at least three pictures a day each, and at first Phiz made good on his promise, managing to pay his share of the rent from sales of his drawings, a considerable achievement as the rent of even a small back room in Bedford Place was not cheap. After working all day, he attended evening sessions at the Life-School in St Martin's Lane, where he first met William Thackeray.[15] Phiz enjoyed the sessions, not because he knuckled under, but rather because he was absorbing what others did and how they did it, again stocking his visual memory. William Etty's nudes received his special admiration; Etty would often arrange the models in groups of three or four in classical poses, adorned with flowers and fruit, and surrounded by drapery, vases, and pedestals (burning incense the while to create an exotic atmosphere for those drawing his tableaux).[16] These poses made a lasting impression on Phiz; time and again he reverted to classical poses when no other subject came to mind.

Even husbanding resources and subsisting on the simplest of food, Phiz and Young eventually found it hard to pay their rents. In desperation, they decided to earn money by adding printmaking, book illustration, and even picture cleaning[17] to their sketching and drawing. Young became immediately and ever after in demand because of his skill with the final process of etching: the manipulation of acid and the touching up of the plates. Phiz soon acquired his first commission, from Henry Winkles, his other great friend from Finden's, already the successful publisher of 'pretty books'. Winkles needed his help with an ambitious project – a three-volume book

St. Paul's Cathedral, *Winkles' Cathedrals*, 1835

which he called *The Architectural and Picturesque Illustrations of the Cathedral Churches of England and Wales*, but which is usually referred to by its familiar title, *Winkles' Cathedrals*. Winkles would sketch a bare architectural outline, and leave it to Phiz to add light and life to the scene, and to draw the images onto the plates. (Coincidentally, back in Philadelphia, just a few years earlier, William L. Breton had completed a series of large lithographic images of that city's churches, designed to show the variety of Christian denominations which thrived there, including Friends, Episcopalians, Catholics, Unitarians, Presbyterians, and African Episcopalians.)

Winkles' Cathedrals became a beautiful, popular, large-scale book, and Phiz's contributions are astonishingly fine, considering he was at the time between nineteen and twenty years old. He prepared twenty-six images of the total of sixty-one in Volume I; in technique they reflect his technical training at Finden's, but in spirit they are much more lively than those of the other contributors because of his skill with chiaroscuro and the addition of charming little groups of people and elegant horses. He contributed fewer images to Volume II (nine of the fifty-nine), and none at all to Volume III – by then he was finding other more exciting ventures.

6

The Collaborators

They were as suited to each other and to the common creation of a unique thing as Gilbert and Sullivan. No other illustrator ever created the true Dickens atmosphere, in which clerks are clerks and yet at the same time elves.

G.K. Chesterton[1]

Enter Charles Dickens.

The actual moment when Hablot Knight Browne and Charles Dickens first met is a subject of vigorous debate, but it is generally believed the momentous encounter occurred when they joined forces on Dickens's first novel, *The Pickwick Papers*. There are, however, clues to earlier encounters.

They may have met as boys. A mysterious, handwritten play exists called *The Stratagems of Rozanza, A Venetian Comedietta*.[2] The author? One C.J.H. Dickens. The artist? H. Knight. The handwriting? Not Dickens's; for nearly

'Constables and Beggars', *Sunday Under Three Heads*, 1836

Two men and mirror, *The Stratagems of Rozanza*, 1828

a century it was said to resemble that of Dickens's mother, an idea now disproved.[3] The little book contains four illustrations in pen and ink, one pencil sketch, and one finished coloured picture of two tiny figures. The drawings are scratchy and immature; two are signed 'H Knight fecit 1828', two are signed merely 'H Knight 1828', and the other two are unsigned. The handwriting of the signatures varies, as is often the case with children's signatures, but one in particular is very similar to Phiz's. The drawings themselves seem less spirited than other Phiz juvenilia, but this could be the result of the formal nature of the subject matter.

In 1828, Phiz was thirteen and Dickens – already mad about the theatre – was sixteen years old. They were close neighbours: Phiz returned home to Euston Square during his school holidays; Dickens, working at the time as a law clerk, returned home to Fitzroy Square, a stone's throw away. It is not unreasonable to surmise that the boys struck up an acquaintance on the street, became friends, and launched themselves on their first cooperative venture. Not unreasonable, but unlikely.

F.G. Kitton believes that Phiz and Dickens were still unknown to each other even as they collaborated on *Sunday Under Three Heads* in early 1836.[4]

Yet even if they had not already worked together on *Rozanza*, it would have been almost impossible for them not to be acquainted by the mid-1830s. Both men operated within the same literary, artistic, and geographical confines. Both held reading tickets at the British Museum library. Both had quarters in Furnival's Inn, and laid eyes on each other regularly, coming and going. And Dickens, who constantly registered the visually extraordinary, had surely noticed Phiz's prize-winning etching of John Gilpin in printsellers' windows and the illustrations for *Winkles' Cathedrals*, which began appearing in monthly parts in 1835. He was too inquisitive a man not to inform himself about the artist. Phiz, too, would have been curious about the dashing (in both senses of the word) young man who lived across from his studio.

In the years after *Rozanza* and before *Pickwick*, Dickens learned shorthand and worked as a parliamentary reporter; Phiz shook the dust of Finden's from his feet, painted watercolours, cleaned pictures, and practised printmaking. In early 1836, on John Greville Fennell's recommendation, he was designing three wood engravings for Chapman and Hall's *Library of Fiction* (in which his fat man opposite p. 93 is a ringer for Tony Weller). For the same publisher, he also provided title page vignettes and three engravings for the aforementioned pamphlet, *Sunday Under Three Heads − As it is; as Sabbath Bills would make it; as it might be made*. The pseudonymous author, Timothy Sparks (Charles Dickens), his pen dripping with sarcasm, dedicated the satire to the Bishop of London. The work itself aimed at the extreme Sabbatarians and in particular Sir Andrew Agnew, whose Sabbath Observances Bill was decried by those who believed it had been designed with the express purpose of denying recreation to poor people on their one day of rest. To believe that Dickens and Phiz were still unacquainted at the time the pamphlet was written seems myopic.

Phiz's designs for *Sunday Under Three Heads* are tiny ($3\frac{1}{4}$" x $2\frac{3}{4}$"), full of vigour, and aptly carry out the author's intent, but the actual cutting, executed by others, is coarse − although, to be fair, it is extremely hard to do truly fine work on such a minute scale. One of the three engravings illustrates the words, 'See how the men all rush to join the crowd that are making their way down the street, and how loud the execrations of the mob become as they draw nearer.'[5] This tiny illustration, in which figures less than an inch tall are bursting with character, is already recognisably Phiz's work. The easy, confident sketching of the buildings in the background (festooned with figures hanging from the windows) is a reminder of his architectural renderings for Winkles; his strong, caricatured constables and beggars offer clues to how he will approach such types in the future; and, leaping forward to the end of his career with Dickens, the two female figures screaming in from the right will continue to scream in 'The Sea Rises', one of Phiz's last images for Dickens, in *A Tale of Two Cities*.

Phiz was ripe for Dickens, and they were destined for true partnership in June of 1836.

But first, to set the scene: the name Nimrod, that of the 'mighty hunter' in Genesis 10: 9, was popularised in the early 1830s by the writer Robert Surtees (1803–1864) and the illustrator Robert Seymour (1798–1836). They both enjoyed the comic contrast provided by the Bible's hunter and their own incompetent sportsmen. Between 1832 and 1834, Surtees contributed a series of papers by 'Nimrod' to the *New Sporting Magazine*, a periodical he edited. These papers described the sporting adventures of Jorrocks, a cockney grocer (who would later play a part in Phiz's history). Then, in 1835, Seymour presented the publishers Chapman and Hall with a collection of drawings illustrating the adventures of the 'Nimrod Club,' a group of cockney would-be sportsmen.

Robert Seymour needed an author to 'write up' each picture, that is, to provide text to support the narrative contained within the image. This was a common practice, and one in which author was subordinate to artist. The publishers cast about for such a writer with little success until the name of Dickens was put forward. Born in 1812, Dickens was fourteen years younger than Seymour, and had already gained a reputation for his journalism and his written sketches. He accepted the commission to write twenty-four pages of text for each four illustrations, to be published in monthly parts. From the start he was unable to contain his ambition.

Seymour, although illegitimate in the real sense, was a rightful heir to the tradition of Hogarth and Gillray. He was small, overworked, married with three children, and highly popular with the public. Before he invented the Nimrod Club, he had illustrated *Maxims and Hints for an Angler* (1833), which purported to be the minutes of the Houghton Fishing Club, with text by Richard Penn. This little volume contains a character who looks uncommonly like Mr Pickwick. Seymour next produced the highly successful *Cockney Sporting Sketches*, which includes a cockney Sam, 'wery' like Sam Weller. Feeling strongly that more business could be mined from this sporting vein, he put together a portfolio of drawings that illustrated the adventures of his Nimrod Club. His professional reputation was golden, and when Charles Dickens was hired to work with him, Seymour naturally assumed the young man would feel truly privileged. Dickens, however, had no intention of playing second fiddle to anyone. He quickly changed the title of the work to *The Pickwick Papers* and effectively drowned Seymour's images in a sea of brilliant prose.

The working relationship rapidly went from bad to worse. In the course of preparing the second monthly instalment of *Pickwick*, Dickens wanted time off for his honeymoon. He quickly provided a burst of text by wedging a macabre story, written earlier, within the larger narrative. Called 'The Stroller's Tale', it was a gruesome story of a pantomine actor's inexorable, drunken decline into delirium tremens and death, and was completely at odds with the artist's original concept. Watching his comic brainchild, his Nimrod Club, vanish proved maddening for Seymour, who was said to be 'sensitive' and 'very highly strung,'[6] euphemisms which could shade a painful inferiority complex and some mental imbalance. Matters came to a head when he failed to satisfy Dickens with his picture of the dying clown. In a letter asking for changes, the author summoned him to a meeting on Sunday, 17 April 1836. No one knows exactly what happened at that meeting, but early on the morning of 19 April, Seymour wrote a note to his wife, saying, 'Best and dearest of wives – for best of wives you have been to me – blame, I charge you, not any one, it is my own weakness and infirmity . . .'[7] Then he took up his fowling piece, went out into his garden, and blew out his brains.

Inevitably, Seymour's tragic act gave *Pickwick* some bad publicity and sales slumped. The need for a competent illustrator was vital to keep the venture afloat. 'Why was not William Heath appointed? Why not Onwhyn? Or Sibson?' ask Dexter and Ley, authors of *The Origin of Pickwick*. They answer their own question: '. . . for the same reason that Cruikshank was not. All Dickens wanted was a competent artist who, if not young and absolutely unknown . . . [would be] a man unlikely to thrust his own personality into the forefront, one who would work to instructions, and accept a position subordinate to the author. Such a man was not easy to find . . .'[8] The publishers turned to John Jackson, the foremost wood engraver of the day, for a recommendation. He suggested Robert Buss (1804–1875), an artist and established book illustrator, a steady, congenial man, a hard worker. But Buss had two fatal flaws. He was older than Dickens and he was inexperienced in the art of etching. Harried by author and publishers to supply two illustrations with all haste, he managed to complete the designs but, feeling uneasy about the etching, he stalled. He explains what happened: 'I was, in an evil hour, induced to *place my designs*

Robert Seymour, 'The Dying Clown', *The Pickwick Papers*

in the hands of an experienced engraver to be etched and "bitten-in" . . . [which meant that] *the free touch of an original work was entirely wanting.'*[9]

Buss's illustrations were deemed unacceptable by Dickens, and the artist was summarily dismissed. He never recovered from Dickens's slight, but remained gracious about Phiz's accomplishment, remarking, 'I have always admired his clever and spirited etchings, and cannot help thinking that those who have glorified Dickens might have bestowed some higher praise upon Phiz, for it is indisputable that much of Dickens's popularity is due to the admirable way in which Phiz illustrated his works.'[10] During the course of his life, Buss occasionally painted watercolours of Dickens characters, and in 1872, two years after Dickens's death, he celebrated both the author and his illustrators in a much reproduced but unfinished picture, 'Dickens's Dream'.

The news of Buss's dismissal hissed around the artistic community, whose members, says Edgar Browne, '. . . however they might hold themselves aloof, lived in a ring fence, and were continually in touch with one another. News spread mysteriously, as it is said to do amongst the Indians, [and] there was a constant intercommunication between authors, artists, engravers, printers, and the like.'[11] Artists, including Alfred Forrester ('Crowquill') and William Lee began lining up to take Buss's place.

Those who claim to have recommended Phiz to Dickens jockey for position. John Greville Fennell trumpets, 'It was I who, while superintending E. & W. Finden's establishment, sold his first drawing to Adolphus Ackermann, and induced him (H.K.B.) to reproduce Buss's two illustrations (viz. The Cricket Match and The Fat Boy Awake on this Occasion Only), which I sent down to Chapman & Hall.'[12] Joseph Grego asserts that the 'influential master of wood-engraving, Mr John Jackson, the zealous friend of both Seymour and Buss, was fated to influence Edward Chapman in selecting young Hablôt [sic] Knight Browne as the future and well-nigh life-long artistic coadjutor of Dickens.'[13] According to Grego, Chapman had visited Jackson's atelier where his eye fell on a print of 'John Gilpin's Ride', which immediately impelled him to recommend Phiz.

Robert Young, Phiz's working partner, claims that the artist himself made the first move (and who should know better than Young?).[14] Phiz had seen Buss's two illustrations and was convinced that he worked better on steel. He would have had no hesitation about putting himself forward. After all, he was 'a brave man, [and] faced danger with calmness';[15] as a teenager he had followed his own destiny after staring down the great Elhanan Bicknell. He had nothing to lose and much to gain by allying himself with a man whose star was rising and whose remarkable sense of humour matched his own keen wit.

Visualise the scene as the two ebullient young men discuss their plans at their first meeting:

It is June. The artist has dressed more carefully than usual by putting aside his customary grey in exchange for white ducks, and by yanking a comb through his unruly locks. The author marks the newcomer's medium height and sturdy frame – long of body, short of shank – handsome head with light brown curls, olive skin, sensitive mouth, and penetrating hazel eyes. He also perceives that Phiz is not a careful dresser; in spite of the impressive ducks, there is 'nothing flamboyant or suggestive of Bohemia about him'.[16] Younger than Dickens – Phiz is twenty, Dickens is twenty-four – he appears immediately attractive as a co-worker after the likes of Seymour, Buss, and George Cruikshank (who had illustrated *Sketches by Boz* early in 1836) – those older, temperamental, experienced illustrators the author has already contended with.

In turn, Phiz notes the trim young author's sartorial splendour: swallow-tail coat, crimson velvet waistcoat, frothing satin stock with double breast-pin, long wavy hair. Most of all he is struck by the gleaming, quick eyes and the vigorous intelligence.

Phiz was delighted to illustrate text – it was engraving other people's designs that drove him to distraction – and Dickens was relieved to meet a man who was both adept at etching and congenial. Why, the artist was so modest as to offer to sign the mysterious and self-effacing name 'N.E.M.O.' – 'No One' – to his work! Phiz was playing with a quasi-palindromic Latin acronym: *Nemo est meum (n)omen*. The prospect of working together on *Pickwick* pleased both of them, but Dickens admitted that he had one more applicant to interview.

When William Makepeace Thackeray showed up with his portfolio, he learned that he was too late.[17] Dickens had already made up his mind and had given Phiz the go-ahead for the first two designs. Thackeray was a gracious loser. Remembering Phiz from the life school in St Martin's Lane, he made his way to his rival's lodgings (then in Newman Street) with the intention of being the first to congratulate him. That accomplished, the future author of *Vanity Fair* and Dickens's anointed illustrator set off to celebrate at the local pub, where they consumed a hearty meal of sausages, and knocked back several bottles of stout.[18]

It was later that night, after Phiz had completed two designs and drawn them on the plate, that he rushed to Robert Young's lodgings and dragged him back to their studio to oversee the biting-in of 'The First Appearance of Mr Samuel Weller' (seen here in the Prologue) and its partner on the plate, 'The Break-down'. (Each octavo steel plate contained two images, a convenience for the printer in terms of cost and ease of printing.) Enlisting the aid of Young ensured that the biting-in was brilliantly executed, and Young recounts that while he and Phiz laboured through-out the night, they 'both indulged in flights of fancy as to the final outcome of the good fortune that was then dawning on the young artist'.[19]

Although the subject and image for 'The Break-down' appear before 'The First Appearance of Mr Samuel Weller' in the text and in bound editions of the book, Phiz actually drew Sam Weller first,[20] an image that reveals in microcosm why the collaboration between Dickens and Phiz was so success-ful. Sam's jauntiness, Perker's dapper stance, the firm solidity of Pickwick and Wardle, the inquisitive dog, the easy architectural competence, and, espe-cially, the idiosyncratic details such as the two boys cavorting on top of a gigantic hay wain, steam rising from a platter carried by a buxom maid, and

page 89

'The Break-down', *The Pickwick Papers*

a line of billowing laundry – all showed the public, straining to visualise *The Pickwick Papers*, that here, at last, was the right man.

Dickens had taken on far more commissions in 1836 than anyone in his right mind should, and Phiz and Young continued to work lickety-split. An early, undated letter from Phiz to Young shows the pressure they were under:

My dear 'Co', – Pray help me in an emergency; put a bottle of aquafortis [nitric acid] in your pockets, wax and all other useful adjuncts, and come to me to-morrow about one or two o'clock, and

47

bite in an etching for me, ferociously and expeditiously. Can you?
Will you? – oblige, Yours sincerely, H.K. Browne.[21]

By the time Phiz was hired, Dickens and the publishers had decided
to double the number of pages for each instalment of *Pickwick* to thirty-
two, and to halve the amount of illustrations from four to two. An economic
move on the part of the publishers, it gave Dickens the upper hand with
his illustrator but meant he was often unable to finish writing the text
before a new design was due. He sometimes had to tell Phiz what he had
in mind, making things up on the spot. Phiz sketched away as Dickens
delivered himself of text, and the design would get the go-ahead there

'Mr Winkle's Situation when the Door "Blew-to"', *The Pickwick Papers*

and then. Unlike Seymour, Phiz found suggestions from Dickens helpful rather than hurtful. He also found it easy to lift images from the shelves of his vast visual store, feeling no need, or desire, to waste time hunting down the actual.

If Phiz were not around, Dickens wrote suggestions directly onto the design. For instance, on the initial drawing for 'The First Interview with Mr Serjeant Snubbin', he notes, 'I think the Sergeant should look younger, and a great deal more sly, and knowing. He should be looking at Pickwick too, smiling compassionately, at his innocence. The other fellows are noble.'[22] And on the design for 'Mr Winkle's Situation when the Door blew to', Dickens writes: 'Winkle should be holding the Candlestick above

'Mr Pickwick and Sam in the Attorney's Office', *The Pickwick Papers*

his head I think. It looks more comical, the light having gone out . . . . A *fat* chairman so short as our friend here, never drew breath in Bath. I would leave him where he is, decidedly. Is the lady full dressed? She ought to be.'[23] Phiz scribbles on the edge of the same picture, 'Shall I leave Pickwick where he is or put him under the bed-clothes? I can't carry him so high as the second floor. H.K.B.'

Dickens insisted on seeing every sketch before giving his go-ahead for the plate, almost always making comments such as, 'I think it would be better if Pickwick had hold of the Bandit's arm. If Minerva tried to look a little younger (more like Mrs Pott, who is perfect) I think it would be an additional improvement.'[24] Where Robert Seymour would have taken exception to making changes, Phiz was willing to comply. The pressure to perform upon demand, so damaging to Seymour, was actually exhilarating for Phiz. He welcomed the interplay, and as Dickens did not often interfere with backgrounds and iconography, Phiz had room for creativity, often inserting telling details and visual jokes of his own devising.

But Dickens was then and would always remain what is called today a micro-manager. 'Have you got the second design from Mr Browne – or is it to go to the Steel without our seeing it?'[25] he complained to Chapman and Hall in October 1836. Another instance of his control is evident two months later. He wanted the artist to illustrate his farce, *The Strange Gentleman*. Writing to J.P. Harley, the actor/stage manager, he says: 'I shall be at the Theatre, and will bring the gentleman who illustrates Pickwick with me. If you will leave his name at the Stage Door, he can come round to your dressing room afterwards, and make whatever Sketch he thinks best. It will be a complete scene with two figures.'[26] It is interesting to note that Dickens is pressing the artist to do precisely what Phiz so rarely did with any enthusiasm: that is, to draw from life. The charming little mini-portrait reveals a cosy couple, Harley and the actress Julia Smith in their roles, sitting side by side, holding hands.

Phiz was well acquainted with Robert Seymour's work and wise enough to remain close to the earlier artist's style even as he added idiosyncratic detail and Hogarthian embellishment to Mr Pickwick's world. He also profited greatly from recent advances in technology. The printing process itself had undergone rapid improvements since the early nineteenth century, and he gained an advantage with the advent of steel plates that did not break down as fast as copper. This was vitally important because sales of *Pickwick* rose meteorically from the 400 copies printed for the first monthly part to 40,000 by the end of the book. Even so, steel itself would eventually break down, and Phiz had to make duplicate, and sometimes triplicate, plates for each subject. (In *Phiz Illustrations from the Novels of Charles Dickens*,[27] Albert Johanssen examines the versions of each image, often pointing out that each new plate profited from the opportunity to improve on the original.) When faced with the problem of Seymour's plates breaking down, Phiz copied that artist's designs; in the case of Buss's two illustrations, he redesigned 'The Fat Boy Awake on This Occasion Only' and produced a totally new illustration ('Mr Wardle and His Friends under the Influence of the Salmon') to replace 'The Cricket Match' as soon as he came on board, rather than waiting for Buss's images to break down. This had the effect of making those copies of *Pickwick* containing Buss's illustrations eminently desirable among collectors. 'I am . . . sometimes amused,' says Buss, 'to think how in time to come *future bibliomaniacs* will rave over a scarce copy of *Pickwick* having in it my two unfortunate etchings.'[28]

It is not clear exactly how much Phiz earned for his *Pickwick* etchings. In a letter to Bentley in January 1837, Dickens writes: 'I have spoken to my Pickwick artist. He is delighted at the prospect of doing an etching for the Miscellany. His demand is £5. I suppose it is not too much, considering all things.'[29] This implies that £5 is a bit more than Phiz regularly received for one etching, and an item in the Widener Collection at Harvard, containing several pages of Chapman and Hall's accounts, corroborates this. It includes a payment to Phiz in 1836 of £8, presumably for work on one plate containing two etchings at £4 a piece (that is, the two illustrations for a monthly part). This figure and various escalating amounts for his later Dickens work (six guineas an etching for *Dombey and Son*; seven guineas for *David Copperfield*; and £11.8.6. for *Bleak House* and *Little Dorrit*[30] seem counter to Croal Thomson's sweeping claim that: 'Fifteen guineas was his price at first for an etching and though – as in the Smedley plates – he often took less, he never seems to have asked more.'[31]

After signing a mere two plates as N.E.M.O., Hablot Knight Browne became Phiz. It can be no coincidence that Dickens had just introduced a character called Fizkin into *Pickwick*. That, combined with the artist's gift for etching 'phizzes' (faces) and the public craze for physiognomy, are all good reasons for the pseudonym, but Phiz himself remarks: '. . . I signed myself as "Nemo" to my first etchings before adopting "Phiz" as my *Sobriquet*, to harmonise – I suppose – better with Dickens's "Boz."'[32]

And, most certainly, Phiz and Boz chimed well together.

7

Looking Down, Looking Up, Looking Around

In November 1836, the year of Phiz and Dickens's first great collaboration, Charles Green rose up from the Vauxhall Gardens – Phiz's childhood playscape – and sky-sailed in the Great Balloon of Nassau all the way to Germany. Looking down at the earth from a position in the sky had become a popular and fascinating phenomenon (even if the balloon were tethered), and hot-air balloons make occasional appearances in Phiz's illustrations. It certainly looks as though he took a joy-ride over Epsom, to witness the Derby from a new vantage point, as seen in an extraordinary little sketch he made of a horse and jockey from directly overhead.

Phiz also enjoyed viewing the heavens from the earth, and declared that if there were any way he could make a living at it, he would become an astronomer.[1] He had probably taken up star-gazing at Botesdale with Mr Haddock acting as guide to the sky. But the view of sky was much dimmer in the smut-laden air of London, and instead of gazing up at the stars,

'Off'

Phiz had to content himself with gazing down from his studio on a view which had taken a distinct turn for the better. A delightful young woman had taken up residence at 15 Furnival's Inn, across the courtyard. She was Dickens's bride, Catherine Hogarth; another charming young woman, Catherine's younger sister, Mary, made frequent visits. Because of constant communication between author and illustrator and the to-ing and fro-ing between 3 and 15 Furnival's Inn, Phiz was soon accepted as a member of the family, and often ate dinner with the young couple. He became very fond of Catherine and, like Dickens, found himself captivated by the charming Mary, perhaps even forming his own romantic notions about her.

Following the birth of Charley Dickens on 6 January 1837, the Dickenses moved to larger quarters at 48 Doughty Street (now the Charles Dickens Museum). Their new home was a five-minute walk from Furnival's Inn, and Phiz continued to be included in their social life. Doughty Street was a private road with pretensions of grandeur, having a gate at either end. A gatekeeper, sporting a gold-trimmed hat and mulberry uniform with the Doughty Arms on its buttons, kept his eye on the traffic coming and going. Imagine the sneer on his face the first time the young artist (not known for his sartorial scrupulousness) showed up with a request to be admitted through the gate to visit the street's newest arrivals, Mr and Mrs Charles Dickens.

On 6 May 1837, Mary Hogarth spent the evening with Charles and Catherine at the theatre, where they enjoyed Dickens's farce, *Is She His Wife?*, a one-act comic burletta written firmly in the broad eighteenth-century style, brimming with broad humour and allusions to seduction, adultery, and bigamy. (Also on the bill was J.P. Harley, decked out as Pickwick, performing a song by Dickens about the pleasures of a white-bait[2] dinner.) Mary returned happily to Doughty Street with her sister and brother-in-law, and made her way upstairs to her room at about one a.m., in high spirits and apparently perfect health. Moments later, she uttered a sudden, choking moan, startling Dickens, who fled upstairs to help. He found she had collapsed, still dressed in her evening finery. While he and Catherine remained by Mary's side, desperately trying to revive her, his brother, Fred, ran for the doctor. But neither the doctor's skill nor their kind nursing could help Mary, and she died in Dickens's arms at three o'clock in the afternoon. The doctors later described her condition as heart disease.

Dickens in his sorrow turned to Phiz, insisting that he capture an image of Mary. Phiz was quick to respond. Although Mary lay in a coffin in her bedroom for six days, Phiz, rather than painting the living girl from her corpse, probably locked himself in his studio, using his formidable memory to recall her face. In similar fashion, much later in life, at the request of his good friend and family physician, Dr Westall, whose only son had recently died, Phiz barricaded himself in his studio, refusing to communicate with his family for several days, and concentrated on painting a full-size image of the boy, 'which had considerable merit, and was considered an excellent likeness by the poor lad's friends, and supposed to have no drawback beyond a certain sadness of expression'.[3]

A mystery surrounds the present location of the original painting of Mary, but a watercolour copy by Frederic Kitton can be found in the

Drawing by Phiz, possibly of Mary Hogarth, c. 1837

Charles Dickens Museum (plate 18). This copy is a formal nineteenth-century representation of a lifeless, rosebud-lipped young woman. Recently, however, a drawing by Phiz of a young woman in the same pose as Kitton's watercolour has come to light, included in a batch of sketches said to be of Kate Nickleby.[4] This particular image differs markedly from the other sketches in the collection, being a carefully finished drawing, and, unlike them, has nothing written on it to indicate that it is meant to be Kate Nickleby. Perhaps the strongest clue to its being a likeness of Mary Hogarth is the figurine in eighteenth-century clothing standing under a glass cloche on the left side of the picture, bearing a distinctly Scottish look. Sir Walter Scott, who died just four years before *Pickwick* was born, was a close family friend of the Hogarths. Mary's middle name was Scott, and Phiz offers a figurine as a clue to the identity of the central image. In the absence of the oil painting, it is possible to imagine that Kitton produced his watercolour copy from this very drawing. Whatever the case, Phiz's drawing pays tribute to someone who was 'young, beautiful, and good'.[5]

Dickens grieved extravagantly, Mary's mother was rendered insensible for a week, and Catherine miscarried. Phiz's sadness, undoubtedly profound, was less dramatic, and it was probably his idea, since Dickens was incapacitated by sorrow and unable to write the forthcoming instalments of *Pickwick* and *Oliver Twist*, that a change of scene might do Charles, Catherine, and himself some good. He already had a destination in mind. Waterloo.

It is impossible to say whether Phiz grew up believing himself to be the son of William and Katherine Browne, or if he knew the truth about Kate Browne and Captain Nicolas Hablot. Yet he was bound to be curious about the battlefield where the man whose name he carried lost his life. Waterloo was extremely attractive to tourists, a deadly but glamorous site, the source of countless legends of heroism. Like many sightseers from England, who regularly made pilgrimages to the battleground, Phiz and the Dickenses set off to witness the site of the single most important event of their time.

Writing to his friend (and later biographer) John Forster on 2 July 1837, Dickens was hazy about their destinations: 'We have arranged for a post coach to take us to Ghent, Brussels, Antwerp, and a hundred other places that I cannot recollect now and couldn't spell if I did.'[6] This haziness adds fuel to the conjecture that Dickens left the travel arrangements and destinations in Phiz's hands. Off they went together; Catherine fared well on the voyage to Calais, but poor Dickens only narrowly escaped 'that dismal extremity of qualmishness into which I am accustomed to sink when I have "the blue above and the blue below".' Once restored to land, he completely revived in time to enjoy the afternoon, which he describes in the same letter to Forster:

We went this afternoon in a barouche to some gardens where the people dance, and where they were footing it most heartily – especially the women who in their short petticoats and light caps look uncommonly agreeable. A gentleman in a blue surtout and silken Berlins [woollen gloves] accompanied us from the Hotel, and acted as Curator. He even waltzed with a very smart lady (just to show us, condescendingly, how it ought to be done) and waltzed elegantly too. We rang for slippers after we came back, and it turned out that this gentleman was the 'Boots'. Isn't this French?

. . . Mrs D and Browne beg their best remembrances[7]

Dickens mentions their trip to Waterloo in a letter to Captain Basil Hall, written four years later, on 16 March 1841. Hall had sent him a copy of his sister's account[8] of the death of her husband, Sir William De Lancey, in the aftermath of the Battle of Waterloo. Phiz would have read the courageous, tear-jerking account as it went from hand to hand, and Kate Browne, too, may have read it, empathising with Lady De Lancey's sorrow. Dickens was deeply moved and told Hall: 'I shall dream of it every now and then, from this hour to the day of my death, with the most frightful reality. The slightest mention of a battle will bring the whole thing before me . . . let me say again . . . that the ground she travelled (which I know well) is holy ground to me.'[9]

If their experience at Waterloo was anything like Thomas Noon Talfourd's, it may be that Phiz and the Dickenses had a thoroughly disagreeable time, however holy the ground. Talfourd writes:

The next day we spent in exploring the field of Waterloo; which I heartily wish we had left unvisited. . . . The scene of carnage is changed for one of civil spoliation: for every step is infested with lazy, urgent guides or beggars; some thrusting their physical infirmities, some their false relics, in your face; and some putting forward nothing but their sturdy prayers, ready to be turned into curses; all around you is pettiness, pretence, and plunder. A kindred spirit of mean exaction pervades the miserable hotels, . . . the host charging you the price of chambertin for vin ordinaire you cannot drink; and the waiter is astonished if you do not pay him handsomely for bringing it into the room, as if he had some hand in winning the battle; . . . you are beset with such relics as the skull of a soldier, with teeth of horrid whiteness, to indicate that he fell in the bloom of life.[10]

Phiz and Dickens were above relic-hunting (the sort that Douglas Jerrold immortalises in *Gertrude's Cherries: or Waterloo in 1835*, when Mr Crossbone declares, 'If I can only get the skeleton of a French dragoon for my summer house I shall be happy'[11]) but they were not above revisiting their memories of Waterloo when they created Mr Meagles, the souvenir hunter in *Little Dorrit*.

8

Travels with Boz

A wild and darker course they keep,
A stern and lone, yet lovely road,
As e'er the foot of Minstrel trod.
    Walter Scott, 'Rokeby'

On 11 January 1838, the restless Dickens cast about for a companion to
walk with him through the snow to Hampstead for a meal at Jack Straw's
Castle, a pub about five miles steadily uphill from Doughty Street. Unable
to find anyone willing, he finally persuaded Phiz, that reluctant walker, to
agree to a compromise. (Edgar Browne said his father would never walk
fifty yards if he could throw his leg over a horse: 'I don't think he regarded
himself as quite complete if he was on foot.'[1]) Dickens and Phiz would
tramp the shorter distance to the Royal Exchange and inspect the ruins
of a fire that had broken out the previous day. The walk gave them a
perfect opportunity to discuss their imminent trip to Yorkshire in search

Anthropomorphic train, Charles Lever, *Tales of the Trains*, 1845 of material for the next joint venture, *Nicholas Nickleby*, a discussion they could continue when Phiz dined at Doughty Street two nights later.

Dickens was dead set on exposing the horrors of the Yorkshire boarding schools, and wanted to meet 'a schoolmaster or two'[2] to use as a prototype. He decided to visit Yorkshire with Phiz, and acquired letters of introduction from Smithson, a solicitor friend with Yorkshire connections.[3] Because of his new fame as the author of *Pickwick*, he decided to assume the identity of a Mr Hablot Browne (Phiz was as yet unknown to the public by his real name) and to pretend that he was seeking a school for the son of a poor widow.

Early on the freezing morning of 30 January 1838, Phiz, a notorious slug-a-bed in those carefree bachelor days, tore himself from the arms of sleep, packed his sketching material in his portmanteau, flung on his heaviest clothes, and made his way up Holborn through the icy darkness to meet Dickens in the coachyard of the Saracen's Head. This ancient coaching inn was a celebrated terminus, situated on Snow Hill, near the junction of Holborn Hill and Farringdon Street.

'Snow Hill! . . . The name is such a good one,' Dickens cries in *Nicholas Nickleby*. 'Snow Hill – Snow Hill too, coupled with a Saracen's Head: picturing to us by a double association of ideas, something stern and rugged. A bleak desolate tract of country, open to piercing blasts and fierce wintry storms – a dark, cold, and gloomy heath.'[4] This describes the Yorkshire landscape towards which Phiz and he were about to travel, but the reality of London's Snow Hill was very different. Newgate Gaol lurked nearby like a gigantic memento mori, drawing crowds of the morbidly curious to witness public hangings, and if the imagined Snow Hill represented the landscape ahead of them, Newgate acted as a metaphor for the hell of the Yorkshire boarding schools.

Phiz made it to the Saracen's Head by the skin of his teeth – to judge from Dickens's subsequent efforts at ensuring punctuality on the part of his illustrator – just in time to catch the slow coach to Grantham. This conveyance, wryly known by its regular passengers as 'The Express', offered the collaborators plenty of leisure to observe the peculiarities of their fellow travellers and to soak up material which they later transformed into words and images in the novel.

After a comfortable night in Grantham followed by another day's perilous journey through deepening snow, they arrived at Greta Bridge in Yorkshire. (Which inn they stayed in – the George, the New, or the Morritt Arms – remains the subject of rigorous debate in Greta Bridge.)

Dickens took time the following morning to write his wife a description of their adventures so far:

> . . . As we came further North, the snow grew deeper. About eight o'Clock it began to fall heavily, and as we crossed the wild heaths hereabout, there was no vestige of a track. The Mail kept on well, however, and at eleven we reached a bare place with a house standing alone in the midst of a dreary moor, which the Guard informed us was Greta Bridge. . . . it was fearfully cold and there were no outward signs of anybody being up in the house. But to our great joy we discovered a comfortable room with drawn curtains and a most blazing fire. In half an hour they gave us a smoking supper and a bottle of mulled port (in which we drank your health) and then we retired to a couple of capital bedrooms in each of which was a rousing fire half way up the chimney.
>
> We have had for breakfast, toasts, cakes, a yorkshire pie, [a] piece of beef about the size and much the shape of my portmanteau, tea, coffee, ham and eggs – and are now going to look about us.[5]

Fortified, Phiz and Dickens were ready for the day ahead. They hired a postchaise to travel the four miles through the snow to Barnard Castle, a town famous for its throng of questionable boarding schools. After crossing the bridge over the River Greta and trotting a short distance along the Roman road, they turned right along the River Tees in sight of magnificent Rokeby Hall, a building they would recognise from Sir Walter Scott's epic poem, 'Rokeby'. (Phiz often tucked small volumes of poetry into his pocket.)

In Barnard Castle, they peppered any promising-looking person with questions about the local schools, and admired a handsome grandfather clock in the window of 'Humphreys, Clockmaker'. (Nothing they saw was wasted; this would later be immortalised in *Master Humphrey's Clock*.) They presented their introductions to Dickens's contact, a ruddy, jovial fellow, who warned against letting the widow send her son to any nearby school, going so far as to assert that it would be far better for the child to sleep in a gutter in London than be placed in the care of one of the local schoolmasters.[6] Dickens and Phiz thanked him for his advice and set off again, driving the postchaise five more snowy miles to the village of Bowes in order to corner one of these devils.

On arrival, they sought out Bowes Academy, which Dickens transformed

'The Internal Economy of Dotheboys Hall', *Nicholas Nickleby*, 1838

into Dotheboys Hall. "'The fact is, it ain't a Hall," observed Squeers drily.
. . . "We call it a Hall up in London, because it sounds better, but they
don't know it by that name in these parts."'[7] (The 'long cold-looking
house' still stands, now broken up into apartments.) The man they encoun-
tered there was William Shaw, the prototype of Mr Squeers, the cruel
headmaster, who 'had but one eye, [when] the popular prejudice runs in
favour of two'.[8] It is unclear exactly how much Squeers actually resembled Shaw; Dickens insisted that Squeers was the representative of a class,
and not of an individual.[9] However, in later years when Edgar Browne
asked his father what the original for Squeers was like, Phiz replied that
the representation in *Nicholas Nickleby* was 'not unlike the man'.[10]

An image in a series of loose pen and ink drawings, in the Huntington
Library, shows Squeers with one eye flaring wide and the other firmly
sealed.[11] These fascinating, hurried sketches, in a completely different style
from the sketches for the plates, most resemble Phiz juvenilia, which
implies they were early work rather than extra drawings made later. Phiz
may have made the sketches at Bowes, in the Ancient Unicorn where he

Mr Squeers

Early unpublished sketch for Squeers

and Dickens went to warm themselves; or he could have sketched them at stops on the long coach journey back to London, while Dickens talked through the plot coming to the boil in his imagination.

Shaw became suspicious about the rather foppish Mr Hablot Browne (i.e. Dickens in disguise) with his pointed, journalistic questions, and smelled a rat. The two young men were given a chilly reception and sent packing. Undaunted, they inspected the ruins of Bowes castle and walked around St Giles's churchyard. Dickens describes the scene: 'The country for miles around was covered . . . with deep snow. . . . [T]he first grave-stone I stumbled on that dreary winter afternoon was placed above the grave of a boy, eighteen long years old, who had died . . . at that wretched place. I think his ghost put Smike into my head, upon the spot.'[12] This is the inscription he and Phiz read (still legible in St Giles's churchyard):

HERE lie
the Remains of
GEORGE ASHTON TAYLOR,
Son of John Taylor

of Trowbridge, Wiltshire,
who died suddenly at
Mr William Shaw's Academy
of this place, April 13th, 1822
Aged 19 Years.
Young reader, thou must die,
But after this the judgement.

Phiz, too, was moved and inspired by George Ashton Taylor's ghost. In 'Smike's Escape', one of the Huntington sketches, he draws a wraithlike, terrified Smike, fleeing out of a doorway, arms reaching desperately forward in a bid for freedom. An ominous figure stands in the doorway, while Mr and Mrs Squeers (?) and one or two children eat at a table in the background. This picture is particularly interesting because Dickens does not describe the moment it illustrates in the novel, but says instead: '[Nicholas] looked anxiously round for Smike . . . but he was nowhere to be seen.'[13] It appears that Phiz sketched a moment from the first telling of the tale, a moment

Early unpublished sketch for Smike's Escape

'A Sudden Recognition, Unexpected on Both Sides', *Nicholas Nickleby*

that Dickens later omitted. 'A sudden Recognition', however, vividly depicts Smike's recapture.

After spending two days soaking up atmosphere in Barnard Castle and Bowes and picking the minds of willing informants, Phiz and Dickens set off for York, once again through snow. They took rooms at the Black Swan Inn in Corey Street, and went to a service in York Minster, where they admired the Five Sisters Window in the north transept and first heard the legend of the Five Sisters of York, which they liked so much that they worked it into Chapter 6 of *Nicholas Nickleby*. Its appeal lay in the character of the youngest of the five sisters, Alice, whose joyous personality and early death paralleled those of Mary Hogarth. 'Alice, dear Alice; what living thing within the sphere of her gentle witchery, could fail to love her!'[14] exults Dickens.

Phiz illustrates the moment when the gloomy Benedictine monk visits the sisters in their orchard. The text reads: '[He] descried at no great distance, the five sisters seated in the grass with Alice in the centre, all busily plying their customary task of embroidering.' Phiz, his artist's eye straying from the text, places Alice *standing* in the middle of the group.

'The Five Sisters of York', *Nicholas Nickleby*

Had he left her seated, she would have sunk in the middle, being the smallest of the five; standing, she dominates the scene. Again Phiz strays: Alice is not embroidering. She has discarded her embroidery frame and helps another sister unravel the embroidery thread. Her arms are raised as she enjoys her gesture of kindness. This picture reveals a moment when Phiz's understanding of pictorial composition overrides the exigencies of the text. His gentle tweaking (which occurs throughout the collaboration) did not seem to disturb Dickens. Phiz's image *complements* the text, in the full meaning of the word, and this is the essence of their collaboration.

At the end of a week in the freezing north, Phiz and Dickens were ready to return to the (relative) warmth of London.[15]

Dickens enjoyed Phiz's company. They went on excursions together; they dined together; together they became members of the Shakespeare Club, a group of like-minded men who gathered each Saturday evening at the Piazza Coffee House in Covent Garden to discuss the role of great literature in the publishing climate of the time; and they played battledore and shuttlecock together, the game nowadays called badminton. In an undated letter, Phiz arranges a raincheck for a game, implying that they played on a fairly regular basis: 'I am sorry I cannot have a touch at battledore with you to-day, being already booked for this evening, but I will give you a call to-morrow *after church*, and take my chance of finding you at home.'[16]

In October 1838, Phiz and Dickens began planning another trip, during which they intended to hunt down still more background material for *Nicholas Nickleby*. An entry in Dickens's diary on 24 October declares, 'Looking forward to a fortnight's holiday with Browne. Wales.'[17] After a quick trip to Hatfield together on 27 October, they set off for Wales on the 30th, and Dickens made special arrangements to ensure that Phiz not be late for their departure. A few days before leaving, he wrote a note to J.P. Harley, saying, 'I regret beyond measure that I am prevented from dining with you on Sunday. Browne never gets up in the morning without the application of force, and deeming it prudent to have him here in order that we might not miss the coach in the morning, I have invited him to come on Saturday and stop till we go away on Monday. . . .'[18] Dickens's careful planning paid off. He and Phiz caught the coach from Hungerford Street on time, and made a speedy but extremely cold journey to Leamington.

Part of the reason for leaving town was Dickens's dislike of being anywhere near the scene of a book's publication, and *Oliver Twist* was about to appear in its first bound edition. He would certainly have been 'flush' at this point, after the success of *The Pickwick Papers* and the serialised *Oliver Twist*, and it appears from his scrupulous account of their expenses that Phiz was his guest on the trip, at least in the matter of fares.[19]

They were delighted with Copps's Hotel in Leamington, where they were welcomed with 'a roaring fire, an elegant dinner, a snug room, and capital beds'.[20] The following morning, they travelled by postchaise to Kenilworth, a town that captivated them (the weather must have improved), went on to Warwick, and eventually found themselves in Stratford-upon-Avon, in the room where Shakespeare was born. Phiz, who was Shakespeare mad, may have been the instigator of this break in the journey. They pored over the guest book, looking at autographs of other visitors, and added their own to the list.

The two men were clearly enjoying themselves to the fullest. Dickens writes to Catherine on 1 November 1838 from the Lion Hotel in Shrewsbury:

> We were at the play last night. It was a *bespeak* – The Love Chace, a ballet (with a phenomonon! [sic]) divers songs, and a Roland for an Oliver.* It is a good theatre, but the actors are very funny. Browne laughed with such indecent heartiness at one point of the entertainments that an old gentleman in the next box suffered the most violent indignation.[21]

'The Great Bespeak for Miss Snevellicci', *Nicholas Nickleby*

They had travelled to Shrewsbury via Birmingham and Wolverhampton, where Dickens – and Phiz, too, no doubt – was appalled by the sight of the grim industrial scene, of engines bellowing and spewing out fumes,

---

*A 'bespeak' is a benefit performance, and 'a Roland' is a farce.

Sketches for the 'Cheeryble Brothers' and others

'Mr Linkinwater intimates his Approval of Nicholas', *Nicholas Nickleby*

spreading a blanket of filth for miles around. From Shrewsbury they went on to Llangollen and Bangor, with side trips to Capel Curig and Conway, and then to Chester, Liverpool, and Manchester. John Forster joined them in Manchester, and it was there, at a dinner at the home of Gilbert Winter, that Phiz laid eyes on the affable brothers, William and Daniel Grant of Cheeryble House,[22] men whom he and Dickens would soon immortalise, taking no pains at all to disguise them, as the Cheeryble brothers in *Nicholas Nickleby*. Phiz was clearly delighted with their looks, and made many fluid sketches of them, being much more at home with this kind of loose portraiture than with formal portrait painting.

Dickens suddenly began to worry about how the publication of *Oliver Twist* was proceeding, cut the trip short after nine days, and returned to London by train with Phiz and Forster, for which he once more paid the fares. The railway itself had only been established a few months, and this was the first time Phiz had ever ridden by train. The speed and noise of the journey was disconcerting for someone whose favourite method of transport was horseback, and his subsequent images of trains often contain ferocious anthropomorphism.

Two days later, on 10 November, the pair set off again, this time to Greenwich. Whether they were sightseeing or hunting down material no one knows, but it is a safe bet that they visited the observatory and took refreshment at the Ship, an ancient inn and site of whitebait dinners, before returning to Doughty Street for the evening meal.

The year of 1838 was extraordinarily successful in the long collaboration of Charles Dickens and Hablot Browne, and on 30 November, Dickens celebrated their triumph by spending £5.10.0. at Simmonds, the jeweller, for a gold ring to present to Phiz. He also bought rings for his brother and himself, each of which cost £1.0.0., and thus, in fiscal terms, he demonstrated just how much he valued his illustrator.[24]

9

In the Work Saddle

'Owing to a sudden indisposition,'[1] Phiz was unable to supply illustrations for the May 1839 part of *Nicholas Nickleby*. 'Indisposition' was an odd state for the usually robust Phiz. He must have been so severely ill that he was unable to hold a stylus. But he made up for it by producing four images for the June part.

   With the success of *The Pickwick Papers* and *Nicholas Nickleby*, he began receiving commissions from a wide range of authors. The more illustrations he completed, the more skilled he became, and his early, often ill-proportioned, caricatures gave way to a smoother, defter line as he entered fully into his authors' intentions. This was particularly the case with Dickens, whose blazing inventiveness continued to ignite Phiz's imagination. Michael Steig, author of *Dickens and Phiz*, comments on the way author and artist fed on each other and on the depth and complexity of the result: '[We know] that Dickens was capable of an astonishing range of insight and expression, and that Browne was a literate man, widely read and fully

'Quilp', *The Old Curiosity Shop*, 1840

70

conscious of his predecessors in English graphic art. . . . Even if not a single Victorian reader recognized the complexities of the illustrations they are there, like the complexities of the texts; they are at once an expression of Dickens' intentions and Browne's interpretations, at once a visual accompaniment to the text and a commentary upon it.'[2]

Back in 1837, Phiz had contributed six etchings to *Sketches of Young Ladies*, written by Edward Caswell under the pseudonym 'Quiz'. Quiz's lack of gallantry in his pastiches of young women so offended Dickens that he tried to redress the balance in 1838 by describing the foibles of young men in *Sketches of Young Gentlemen*. Here again he used the pseudonym 'Boz', a name he had first coined when he was working as a reporter and

'The Couple who dote upon their Children', Charles Dickens,
Boz's Sketches of Young Couples, 1840

71

used for his *Sketches by Boz* (later illustrated in book form by George Cruikshank). Phiz provided six etchings for the riposte, and in 1840 he provided yet another six for Boz's *Sketches of Young Couples*. He threw himself into the spirit of these enterprises and created rambunctious etchings to accompany the text. 'The Couple who dote upon their Children' is particularly amusing, and an early example of how much Phiz could reinforce his main image with background details. The subject of the large portrait hanging over the dining room table is six neatly dressed and coiffed children, lined up in a tidy row. The oldest rolls his eyes as he contemplates the chaotic actual dinner scene where children fight and scream, pull hair, answer back, climb on the table, and stuff food in their mouths with their hands. On the wall to the left hangs an ideal portrait of the mother; on the right, the ideal father (looking strangely like George Cruikshank).

This illustration offers an excellent opportunity to look at the differences between Phiz's original sketch and the finished plate. The sketch is flat and hurriedly executed with a blunt pencil, and looks more like a compositional aide-memoire than a satisfying piece of art. The plate, by contrast, is sharp and spiky with life.

Dickens concludes *Sketches of Young Couples* with an injunction to young people about to get married: 'Before marriage and afterwards, let them learn to centre all their hopes of real and lasting happiness in their own fireside; let them cherish the faith that in home, and all the English virtues which the love of home engenders, lies the only true source of domestic felicity . . .'[3] Phiz certainly took Dickens's injunction to heart. In spite of his own fractured background (or perhaps because of it), he became the most steadfast and loving family man.

In 1838, Phiz illustrated his first book for Robert Surtees, *Jorrocks' Jaunts and Jollities*, a compilation of the stories Surtees had earlier published in the *New Sporting Magazine*; and in 1839, he completed the illustrations for *Harry Lorrequer*, the first of many commissions for Charles Lever. His work for these two authors displayed to the fullest his skill at drawing horses. Interestingly, Thackeray was invited to provide additional illustrations for *Jorrocks* in a new edition to be published in 1843; but he demurred, in an act of kindness to his friend Phiz, to judge from the content of his letter to Ebenezer Landells that same year:

My dear Landells,
  . . . With regard to Mr Tattersall and Jorrocks, I think on 2nd thought it will be better that I shd have nothing to do with Mr J – I should

not like to take away work from Phiz; or indeed for my sake be
obliged to follow after him, and copy his invention of the illustrious Great Coram St. Sportsman.[4]

Thackeray obviously had Phiz's interests at heart, and in 1839, after
spending some years in Paris, gave him an excellent suggestion in the
London and Westminster Review: '. . . if we might venture to give a word of
advice to another humorous designer, whose works are extensively circu-
lated – the illustrator of 'Pickwick' and 'Nicholas Nickleby' – it would be
to study well these caricatures of Monsieur Daumier.'[5]

Daumier's work was already in high repute in London and, heeding
Thackeray's recommendation, Phiz carefully examined Daumier's 100 lithographic illustrations of Robert Macaire, which had appeared serially in *Le
Charivari* from 1836 to 1838. The series was the brainchild of Philipon,
editor of *Le Charivari*, and took as its hero a character from the mediocre
melodrama *L'Auberge des Adrets*. The great actor, Frédérick Lemaître, claimed
this raffish character, Robert Macaire, as his own, and turned the dismal
failure of *L'Auberge des Adrets* into a riotous success.

Philipon wrote the long captions for the images (Seymour should have
hired him instead of Dickens to write the captions for the Nimrod Club!)
and Daumier's Macaire lithographs illustrate the antics of wily, thieving
Robert Macaire and his sidekick, Bertrand, as they insinuate themselves
into the worlds of business, journalism, and *puffisme* (an extreme form of
advertising). About the lithographs, Baudelaire in his '*Quelques caricaturistes
français*' declared:

> *Robert Macaire* was the decisive starting point of the caricature of
> manners. The great political war had died down a little . . . The
> *Satire Ménippée* surrendered the field to Molière, and the great epic
> cycle of Robert Macaire, told in Daumier's dazzling version,
> succeeded to the rages of revolution and the drawings of allusion.
> Thenceforth caricature changed its step; it was no longer especially
> political. It had become the general satire of the people. It had
> entered the realm of the novel.[6]

So great was the popularity of the Macaire adventures that G.W.M.
Reynolds, a publisher and author of sensational novels who had spent a
great deal of time in France, wrote a sequel entitled *Robert Macaire in England*.
Reynolds had a penchant for creating sequels to successful books, for

Daumier's Robert Macaire, 1836   Phiz's Robert Macaire, 1839

example: *Pickwick Abroad*, *Noctes Pickwickiana*, and *Pickwick Married*. (He and Dickens loathed each other, a feeling they often aired in their publications.7) Phiz furnished the illustrations for *Robert Macaire*, and his portrayal of Macaire and his assistant Bertrand is clearly based on Daumier's. Phiz, of course, worked on a far smaller scale than Daumier (he came to lithography much later in life) so his Macaire lost something in the translation. Nonetheless, his etchings are full of verve, demonstrating his growing competence, and the hold that Daumier would continue to exert on his imagination.

Between 1837 and 1840, in addition to his work for Winkles, Dickens, Caswell, Lever, Reynolds, and Surtees, Phiz completed many other commissions. In 1838, he provided six etchings for Stephen Oliver's song 'The

Old English Squire', work he must have thoroughly enjoyed because it gave him a chance to show off his skill with hunting scenes, and the hunt would remain his favourite subject throughout life.

That same year, James Grant capitalised on the success of Boz's sketches by writing his own *Sketches in London*, which described places such as theatres, asylums, workhouses, courts, and their various inhabitants. Having used other illustrators for the first three chapters, Grant hired Phiz for the fourth and was so delighted with the result that he employed him for all subsequent chapters and the frontispiece, a total of eighteen plates. Their collaboration was so enjoyable that Grant took care to mention his illustrator in the preface to *Sketches in London*, saying: 'With regard to the Illustrations by "Phiz", which embellish the volume, the Author can speak more unreservedly than he could do of the letter-press. They are among the happiest achievements of the genius of one who, though yet but young in years, is unquestionably, in this particular style of engraving, the first artist of the day.'[8] The inattentive audience in 'A Scene before the Curtain', with its pickpocket and drunken Adam and Eve, rewards particular scrutiny.

'A Scene before the Curtain', James Grant, *Sketches in London*, 1838

In 1839, as well as his illustrations for *Nicholas Nickleby* and *Harry Lorrequer* (thirty-nine and twenty-two plates respectively), Phiz worked on three charming little books, *Solomon Seesaw* by J.P. Robertson; *A Paper on Tobacco* by W.A. Chatto using the pseudonym 'Joseph Fume'; and Douglas Jerrold's *The Handbook of Swindling*. *A Paper on Tobacco* describes various kinds of smokers, and Phiz's frontispiece manages to get three different types into one image: a jaunty Yankee cigar smoker, a pipe-smoking slave, and a smoke-belching steamship in the background. The background image, adding its comment on the foreground, is a good example of how Phiz's iconography often 'speaks' to his dominant theme.

The same can be said for the frontispiece to *The Handbook of Swindling* which purports to be

BY THE LATE

CAPTAIN BARABBAS WHITEFEATHER,

LATE OF THE BODY-GUARD OF HIS MAJESTY, KING CARLOS; TREASURER
OF THE BRITISH WINE AND VINEGAR COMPANY; TRUSTEE FOR
THE PROTECTION OF THE RIVER THAMES FROM INCEN-
DIARIES; PRINCIPAL INVENTOR OF POYAIS STOCK;
RANGER OF ST. GEORGE'S FIELDS; ORIGINAL
PATENTEE OF THE PARACHUTE CON-
VEYANCE ASSOCIATION; KNIGHT
OF EVERY ORDER OF
THE FLEECE;
SCAMP
AND
CU
R.

Mark how the iconography of Barabbas's swindling comments on his portrait! The coins, the jewels, the pocket-watch, the silver plate, the trophy. And mark the features of this glorious filcher! The foxy eyes, the monocle, 'the gash across my nose, from an enemy's sickle when bivouacking in a hen-roost', the extra-long, pointed canine tooth, the elegant hand with its ringed pinky, the white glove, and the whip. But most of all, mark the handwriting: a 'Yours truly' which thumbs its nose at the reader, and a signature to delight graphologists with its complex mess of slants and whirls and slashes and blobs.

Captain Barrabas Whitefeather, Douglas Jerrold, *The Handbook of Swindling*, 1839

In 1840, Phiz's publishers realised that he could provide plates for reprints of earlier, unillustrated books, and Fielding's *Life of Mr Jonathan Wild* was the first of many such ventures. Meanwhile, Dickens, not content with writing enormously successful novels, was consumed with desire to create his own popular journal along the lines of eighteenth-century miscellanies like Addison and Steele's *Tatler* and Goldsmith's *Bee*. He persuaded Chapman and Hall to underwrite a weekly journal, to which he gave the name *Master Humphrey's Clock*, in memory of the clock he and Phiz had seen in the town of Barnard Castle. His intention was to invite other authors to contribute articles, while he flexed his editorial skills. The announcement of the first instalment ticked: 'Now wound up and going, preparatory to its striking on Saturday, the 28th March, Master Humphrey's Clock, Maker's name – "Boz". The Figures and Hands by George Cattermole, Esq. and "Phiz".'[9] *Master Humphrey's Clock* would be published in a dazzling array of formats: eighty-eight weekly numbers; twenty monthly parts; and bound volumes every six months.[10]

Dickens made the expensive decision to have the illustrations dropped into the text, rather than printed on separate pages, so that they would retain the closest possible relationship to his story. This meant that the illustrators had to create their designs for wood instead of steel because wood engravings can be inked and printed simultaneously with the raised typeface, whereas etching plates, with their ink in grooves rather than on the surface, must be sent through a rolling press and printed on individual dampened pages. But the use of wood engravings required that Dickens wait until all the designs were completed before he could work out exactly how much text was needed. Prompt delivery of the illustrations was of the essence.

After initial interest in the journal, the public – counting on another serialised novel by Dickens – became disappointed and sales slumped. Dickens had failed to attract other contributors (or maybe he did not have time to attract them before the first four numbers went to press), and it was left to him to write all the articles. In the fourth number, he began a story, *The Old Curiosity Shop*, and, realising that this was what the public wanted, continued it in the seventh number, after which it became the exclusive content of the journal. The public was, once again, hooked. Sales zoomed up again when *The Old Curiosity Shop* started appearing in regular weekly instalments in *Master Humphrey's Clock*, and Little Nell and Quilp began to exert their hold on the popular imagination.

Because *Master Humphrey's Clock* began life as a popular miscellany rather than a novel, Dickens decided to use more than one illustrator and, in addition to Phiz, asked George Cattermole, Samuel Williams, and Daniel Maclise to join the team. Cattermole was fifteen years older than Phiz, a well-established watercolourist and illustrator. He was distantly related to Dickens by marriage, and Dickens maintained a rather worshipful relationship with his distinguished cousin – in 1838, Cattermole had been offered, but declined, a knighthood for his service to the world of art. He had supplied many designs for the works of Scott and Bulwer, and Dickens decided to lean on him for those illustrations based on the architecture and costumes of the past. Accordingly, Dickens divided up the work: Phiz would be more responsible for people (especially the low characters), active moments, and comic rascality, while Cattermole would embark upon loftier, antiquarian, angelic, and architectural subjects. Daniel Maclise and Samuel Williams waited in the wings for Dickens's call, but in the event they only contributed one drawing each.

Dickens did not initially trust Cattermole to transfer his designs onto the block. For this he called in Phiz, to whom he was giving the added

Phiz's grandfather,
Simon Browne, c.1775.

Phiz's grandmother,
Ann Loder Browne, c. 1775.

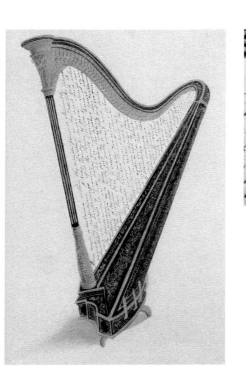

Harp gilded and inscribed in ink
by Simon Browne, c.1770.

Phiz's uncle,
John Henry Browne, c.1830.

Norfolk landscape, John Henry Browne, c.1820.

Phiz's brother-in-law,
Elhanan Bicknell, *c.* 1845.

His sister Lucinda Bicknell,
likeness taken from her death mask, 1850.

The Bicknells' house at Herne Hill.

Phiz's brother,
General Charles Alfred Browne, *c.* 1865.

His brother Octavius as a young man in
Australia, by Georgiana Macrae, *c.*1840.

Octavius around 1870.

His brother Henry Albert, *c.* 1850.

Phiz, 'Impressionistic view of the Country around Banstead', *c.* 1855. Watercolour.

Furnival's Inn, London.
In 1836 Phiz lived at No. 5
and Dickens at No. 15.

Phiz's pen and ink sketch of Dickens.

F.G. Kitton's watercolour copy of Phiz's
oil painting of Mary Hogarth, c.1837.

Robert Seymour, *c.* 1830.

Robert Buss, *c.* 1830.

George Cattermole, *c.* 1830.

Marcus Stone, *c.* 1830.

Charles Lever.

Title page with spelling
error, for Charles Lever's
The Knight of Gwynne, 1847.

'The Letter', *The Knight of Gwynne*, 1847.

responsibility of choosing some of the subjects. He makes this clear in his letter to Cattermole probably written on 21 January 1840:

> I think the drawing most famous, and so do the publishers, to whom I sent it today. If Browne should suggest anything for the future which may enable him to do you justice in copying (on which point he is very anxious) I will communicate it to you. It has occurred to me that you will like to see his copy on the block *before* it is cut, and I have therefore told Chapman and Hall to forward it to you.[11]

While Phiz usually drew his own designs in reverse directly onto the specially whitened end grain of a section of boxwood, he traced Cattermole's images before transferring them onto the wood. Then different woodcutters with varying degrees of proficiency – Landells, Williams, Gray, Vasey, Dalziel – engraved the design, using gouges and gravers before inking the wood in preparation for printing. As many as 100,000 impressions could be made from a single woodblock;[12] however, the gain in quantity of prints was inevitably offset by the loss of character and sprightliness at the hands of the cutters.[13]

The Old Curiosity Shop is a book clearly divided in subject matter between the forces of good and evil. To Phiz was given the privilege of illustrating the forces of evil, incarnate in the figure of Quilp.[14] The artist's work deepened and darkened as he took on the monstrous Quilp, and Jane Rabb Cohen comments: 'The subtle brilliance of Browne's later portrayals of Quilp . . . may have surprised admirers of his comic work. Indeed, the artist now began to display in a positive way the versatility that would enable him to keep pace with Dickens for so long.'[15]

By 1840, when he was twenty-five, courtship, marriage, and physical love were clearly on Phiz's mind. Michael Steig points out many sexual nuances in the illustrations for *The Old Curiosity Shop*, the climax being Quilp, '[who] cavorts through sixteen cuts (excluding one by Cattermole and the more quiescent illustration of Quilp's death), five of which, following the text, have him thrusting himself through doors and windows, often preceded by his tall, narrow hat. In another he is shown having gone through a gateway. Elsewhere he is usually engaged in violent or disreputable behavior.'[16] (Steig is missing something by calling Phiz's illustration of Quilp's death quiescent; it is far and away the most sexually allusive in the entire book!) Steig also points out that even when the artist ventured into Cattermole's territory, he triumphed: 'Phiz was notably more skillful than Cattermole in dealing with human figures close up. . . . Less has been said in favor of his Nell, but compared to Cattermole's, who is either a wax doll or barely visible, Browne makes us believe in the "cherry-cheeked, red-lipped" child Quilp describes so lecherously, and yet the artist never loses the pathos of Nell's situation – indeed, it could be argued that Phiz's Nell is more flesh and blood than Dickens'.[17] Phiz's Nell radiates budding sexuality, and Tony Bareham, a Lever scholar, impressed by the vivacity of Lever's heroines as drawn by Phiz, remarks that the artist manages to make her into 'a sexpot'[18]; while Diana Phillips, likening Phiz's Nell images to Lewis Carroll's photographs of young girls, comments that Nell has 'that twilight look of half-comprehended sexuality'.[19]

'Miss Montflathers Chides Nell' *The Old Curiosity Shop*

After Phiz's first two illustrations for the miscellany, which he signed with his pseudonym, he revealed his true identity, signed his illustrations 'HKB' or, later, 'HB', and presented himself as Hablot Browne on the title page of the first bound volume. (The public was unaware that Phiz and Hablot Browne were one and the same, and enjoyed comparing the work of the 'rival' artists.) So great was Phiz's pleasure in revealing his identity that he began placing his signature on various objects in the illustrations in a sort of 'find the initials' game. They can be discovered on floortile, tombstone, chair brace, suitcase handle, washstand, drum, sideboard, barrel, plate, hitching post, Moses basket, stool, book, and the drapery at the edge of a stage.

Dickens went to enormous lengths to praise Cattermole, even though he was often late with his designs ('Don't forget dispatch, there's a dear fellow . . .'[20] '. . . there is no time to lose'[21]) and was even sometimes incapable of producing an image. Phiz usually stepped in to save the day, and once, during March 1840, probably at the time that he was away getting married, Samuel Williams stepped in to portray Little Nell asleep in the curiosity shop. (Williams was an artist and wood engraver who had already cut some of Phiz and Cattermole's designs onto the block.) The fact that he both designed and engraved the sleeping Nell, and thus had more control over the image, makes it the most beautifully executed illustration in the book. The surprise is that Dickens never used Williams as a designer again, in spite of claiming in a letter of instruction to him on 31 March, 'As Mr Dickens hopes to communicate with Mr Williams on very many future occasions, he will not weary him with any apology for these remarks just now.'[22] What on earth did poor Samuel Williams do that precluded his being pressed into further service as an illustrator? Probably nothing. Clearly, the author was, to some degree, in awe of Cattermole and would do nothing to offend him, and Phiz was, to say the least, spinning merrily along.

From the start, Dickens had also intended to use Daniel Maclise, who had painted the attractive portrait of him for the frontispiece of *Nicholas Nickleby*. That artist's moment finally came towards the end of *The Old Curiosity Shop*, where he provided a powerful and text-enhancing (in spite of a slight case of macrocephaly on the sexton's part) illustration of Little Nell and the sexton at the well. John Harvey explains Maclise's not being used again: '[I]f he had done more, he would have disturbed the balance of complementary roles that was coming to characterize Dickens's use of his two resident illustrators in the magazine.'[23]

'The *works* of the Clock, printers, publishers, designers, engravers, and wood-cutters dine here on the completion of the accompanying Volume next Tuesday at 6 for half past exactly.'[24] So wrote Dickens to his friend, the actor J.P. Harley, on the completion of Volume I of *Master Humphrey's Clock*. Having celebrated the event, author and illustrators then entered the last stages of the novel (which was carried over into Volume II). While

Dickens barricaded himself in his room to write the death of Nell, Phiz was creating the image of the death of Quilp. He produced a masterpiece, working from Dickens's description: '[The resistless water] toyed and sported with its ghastly freight, now bruising it against the slimy piles, now hiding it in mud or long rank grass, now dragging it heavily over rough stones and gravel, now feigning to yield it to its own element, and in the same action luring it away, until, tired of the ugly plaything, it flung it on a swamp . . .'[25] In Phiz's image, the body of Quilp lies with his head

Death of Quilp, *The Old Curiosity Shop*

diagonally slanted towards the bottom of the picture, his mouth a grimace, one hand a frozen claw. The picture reeks of mud, slime oozes underfoot, and a huge piling thrusts priapically towards the sky. It is astonishing that Dickens, the author who wished never to publish anything that would make a young woman blush, did not veto this image, apparently totally oblivious of the enormous phallic symbol thrusting skywards. But those were the years before Freud.

Cattermole's task of illustrating the death of Nell was far more challenging, if not impossible; he had to illustrate abstractions: 'Sorrow was dead indeed in her, but peace and perfect happiness were born; imaged in her tranquil beauty and profound repose.'[26] His design did not satisfy the author at first, as the following letter of 14 January 1841 makes clear:

> My dear Cattermole,
>   I cannot tell you how obliged I am to you for altering the child, or how much I hope that my wish in that respect didn't go *greatly* against the grain.

And then Dickens launches into another impossible request:

> Will you do a little tail piece for the Curiosity story – only one figure if you like – giving some notion of the etherialized spirit of the child – something like those little figures in the Frontispiece. If you will and can dispatch it at once, you will make me happy.[27]

Phiz must have breathed a huge sigh of relief at not being chosen to deal with an etherialised spirit; it was easier for him to deal with the very real, very dead but extraordinarily potent figure of Quilp.

★

When Dickens learned of the death of his first publisher, John Macrone, he was moved to produce a collection of essays and illustrations by famous men as a benefit for Macrone's widow. Because of the pressure of his own work and the dilatory behaviour of some of the contributors, he had been unable to get it off the ground, but in the brief hiatus between writing *The Old Curiosity Shop* and *Barnaby Rudge*, he whirled into action and galvanised those who had not yet fulfilled their pledges. Phiz responded, on a scrap of paper, to the prod:

> My Dear Dickens, – I have just got one boot on, intending to come round to you, but you have done me out of a capital excuse to myself for idling away this fine morning. I quite forgot to answer your note, and Mrs Macrone's book has not been very vividly present to my memory for some time past, for both of which offences I beg innumerable pardons. I think by the beginning of next [week] or the middle *(certain)* I shall have done the plates, but on the scraps of copy that I have I can see but *one good* subject, so if you know of another, pray send it me. . . .
>   – Yours very truly,
> Very short of paper. Hablot K. Browne[28]

Phiz was always very short of paper.

Dickens must have supplied more subjects because Phiz then quickly and generously provided six illustrations – he had originally been asked to provide two – for the benefit volume, which Dickens titled *The Pic-Nic Papers*.

★

'*The clock does not stop, and was never intended to. It goes on but with a new story.*'[29]

Dickens wrote a brief transitional piece between the end of *The Old Curiosity Shop* and the beginning of *Barnaby Rudge* in which he brought back the device he used at the beginning of *Master Humphrey's Clock*, that of speaking in the voice of 'Master Humphrey from his Clock Side in the Chimney-Corner'. But it was left to Phiz to whet the public's appetite with an image of what lay in store. In a tailpiece to Dickens's transition, he pictured Master Humphrey, legs crossed, asleep in his chair, surrounded by little figures, including Mr Punch, some wildly cavorting through the

'Master Humphrey's Dream', *Master Humphrey's Clock*, 1840

air, some referring directly to the forthcoming novel, some referring to the past. This image strikingly resembles Robert Buss's picture, 'Dickens's Dream' (mentioned earlier), created shortly after Dickens's death, in which the author sits, legs crossed, asleep in his chair, while all around him play the creatures of his – and his illustrators' – imagination. Buss may well have had Phiz's image of Master Humphrey in mind when he started to draw 'Dickens's Dream'.

Barnaby Rudge was a novel Dickens had promised to the publisher, Bentley, and had been writing, on and off, for five years. He originally intended to have George Cruikshank, his illustrator for *Oliver Twist*, illustrate it, and in October 1839, he wrote to Cruikshank:

> I am going forthwith tooth and nail at Barnaby, and shall have MS by the middle of the month for your exclusive eye. Meanwhile as many consultations and preliminary explanations as you like.[30]

They must have had a meeting about it because later that month, Cruikshank wrote to Dickens:

> I do not know whether I am correct or not, but the impression upon my mind is that when I saw you last you were in doubt as to having Barnaby illustrated or not, but that you would consider the matter & let me know in a few days – am I right? I have finished all the work I had in hand and have been waiting these last few days.[31]

But the writing of *Barnaby Rudge* had come to a stop, amidst squabbles with the publisher, and Cruikshank was soon snapped up by other authors.

Barnaby's moment came in January 1841 after Dickens's final rupture with Bentley. Having completed *The Old Curiosity Shop*, and being badly in need of another serial for *Master Humphrey's Clock*, he broke what he had already drafted for Bentley into weekly parts. After the book's protracted gestation, he delivered the balance of it in a white heat. Phiz, and to a lesser degree Cattermole, were whirled along with him, Phiz producing about fifty-nine illustrations, mainly of characters, Cattermole producing about nineteen, usually of settings.[32]

Barnaby Rudge opens in 1775 and comes to its climax with the No-Popery Gordon riots in 1780 and the storming of Newgate prison. Jane Rabb Cohen, author of *Dickens and His Principal Illustrators*, comments:

Both author and artists, particularly Browne, met the challenge of providing the greater variety of styles needed for the historical, compared to the allegorical, fiction in the *Clock*. Dickens and Browne continued to exploit their skill at expressing the exaggerated or grotesque to render the crude characters – Gashford, Dennis, and the Protestant mob. They treated the Maypole rustics in their earlier humorous manner. Throughout the first two-thirds of the narrative, however, both men were uncharacteristically restrained. . . . [But] when, at the story's climax, Dickens really let his imagination go in describing the orgiastic riots, Browne readily caught his spirit. His designs, with their tumultuous crowds yet individualized participants, fully embodied the violent excitement of the prose.[33]

Although the new novel had no character of quite the same power and grotesqueness as Quilp, Phiz had plenty of strong material to work from, and he delighted the public with what seemed to be a new-found ability

George Cruikshank, 'The Last Chance', *Oliver Twist*, 1837

'The Secretary's Watch', *Barnaby Rudge*, 1840

to draw his characters on a large scale. In Chapter 11, he created a heavy, spacious image of the sleeping Maypole Hugh which, had it not been signed, might well have puzzled viewers about the artist's identity. But perhaps his most intriguing image in *Barnaby Rudge* is of Gashford on the roof, an out-and-out parody of (or homage to) Cruikshank's 'The Last Chance' in *Oliver Twist*. The villain Gashford, like the villain Sikes, is perched atop a slate-tiled roof. Chimney pots dominate the background in both pictures, as does a stone wall in the foreground. While Sikes holds an actual noose, the text behind the Gashford image stinks of the hangman. Both pictures contain an animal on the roof's peak, but Cruikshank's dog is a generic animal, while Phiz's cat (not in the text) is patently feline. It is a delight to see Phiz doffing his hat to the old master.

John Ruskin, that self-anointed guardian of artistic taste, was appalled by the illustrations. 'Take up,' he commands, 'for an average specimen of modern illustrated works, the volume of Dickens's "Master Humphrey's Clock" containing "Barnaby Rudge". . . . The cheap popular Art cannot draw for you beauty, sense, or honesty; and for Dolly Varden, or the locksmith, you will look through the vignettes in vain. But every species of

Study for Emma Haredale, 1840

distorted folly or vice . . . are pictured for your honourable pleasure on every page, with clumsy caricature, struggling to render its dullness tolerable by insisting on defect.'[34] Phiz took Ruskin's criticism to heart; in the series of extra plates he made for *Barnaby Rudge*, Dolly Varden and Emma Haredale stand out as the most beautiful young women he ever created. Only Grip, the raven, escapes Ruskin's censure. He declares him 'perfect', but then grumbles, 'I am the more angry with the rest because I have every now and then to open the book to look for him'.

The raven certainly had a firm hold on Dickens's affection, and he wanted it based on his own delightful bird. On 28 January 1841, he wrote to Cattermole: 'I want to know whether you *feel* Ravens in general, and would fancy Barnaby's raven in particular. Barnaby being an idiot my notion is to have him always in company with a pet raven who is immeasurably more knowing than himself. To this end, I have been studying my bird and think I could make a very queer character out of him. Should you like the subject where the raven makes his first appearance?'[35]

Receiving no reply to this letter, Dickens tried again on the 30th: 'Now I must know what you think about the Raven, my buck, otherwise I am in this fix – I have given Browne no subject for this No., and time is flying. If you would like to have the Raven's first appearance, and don't object to having both subjects, so be it. I shall be delighted. If otherwise, I must feed that hero forthwith'.

Then Dickens heaped Cattermole with praise for his ability to render etherialised spirits: '. . . I have deeply felt your hearty and most invaluable co-operation in the beautiful illustrations you have made for the last story . . . this is the *very first time* any designs for what I have written have touched and moved me, and caused me to feel that they expressed the idea I had in my mind'.[36]

But even this effusive praise did not spur Cattermole into attempting to draw the raven, and on 9 February 1841, Dickens wrote to Forster: '. . . I am thinking hard, and have just written to Browne enquiring when he will come and confer about the raven'.[37] And this letter was followed the next day by a note to Maclise: 'Browne (who is coming to sketch the raven) dines with me in the study *en garçon* at five. The gay and festive Thompson also joins us. Will you make a fourth? Say yes. All going on famously'.[38]

Phiz spent enough time with the actual Grip to allow him to observe the bird in varying postures. This was lucky because Grip died in March 1841, after crying out 'in a tone of remonstrance and considerable surprise "Halloa old girl!"'[39] Phiz's Grip appears initially, and somewhat insignificantly, in the headpiece to Chapter 6 of *Barnaby Rudge*, but is given pride of place in the tailpiece at the end of Volume II (Chapter 12). Grip continues to make sporadic, Ruskin-pleasing appearances throughout the novel and in the frontispiece to Volume III.

Phiz and Cattermole worked well together, non-competitively, for nearly two years because the spheres of their subject matter were distinct. The younger man carried the heavier load, and stepped in when Cattermole was ill – or flummoxed by avian challenges. Cattermole designed the frontispiece to the first of the eventual three volumes of *Master Humphrey's Clock*, but was ill when the second frontispiece was due. Phiz was called on to create that design, and eventually the third. Having no idea what Volume II would contain in its entirety, he quickly wrote to Dickens:

Will you give me some notion of what sort of design you wish for the Frontispiece for second volume of *Clock*? Cattermole being put *hors de combat* – Chapman with a careworn face (if you can picture that) brings me the block at the eleventh hour and requires it finished by Wednesday. Now, as I have two others to complete

'Barnaby and Grip', *Barnaby Rudge*, 1840

in the meantime, something nice and *Light* would be best adapted to my *palette*, and prevent an excess of perspiration in the relays of wood-cutters. You shall have the other to criticise on Tuesday.[40]

Phiz also created the wrapper design for the weekly numbers, a complex, whirling image filled with allusions to the passage of time.

On receiving Dickens's invitation to a dinner to celebrate the conclusion of Volume II and the beginning of Volume III, Phiz responded:

I shall be most happy to remember not to forget the 10th April. And, let me express a *dis*interested wish, that having completed and established a 'shop' in an 'extensive line of business', you will go on increasing and multiplying such like establishments in number and prosperity, till you become a Dick Whittington of a Merchant with pockets distended to most Brobdignag proportions. . . . I return you the Riots [probably Holcroft] with many thanks.[41]

Master Humphrey's Clock finally stopped ticking in December 1841, at the end of *Barnaby Rudge*. Suddenly, the relentless demands for weekly illustrations ceased, and Phiz must have been greatly relieved because 1841 was one of his busiest years ever; it included work for Frances Trollope (the mother of Anthony Trollope), Theodore Hook, Charles Lever, and W.J. Neale, among others.

With Dickens out of the country, visiting the United States, from January to June 1842, Phiz had more time for other authors and for creating a new cover for *Punch*. He had earlier turned down an invitation from Mark Lemon, the editor of *Punch*, to join the staff at its inception, preferring to wait and see what kind of publication it would become before signing on. According to Edgar, he feared that the paper might be too personal, meaning that its humour might hurt the individuals it lampooned. Obviously the magazine did not overstep the personal in his opinion, and when Lemon again applied to him, he gladly furnished the cover for the new volume, a volume in which he was joined by such luminaries as Thackeray, Sir John Gilbert, Kenny Meadows, and 'Crowquill'. And in 1843, Mark Lemon, delighted by Phiz's comic wood engravings, collected them to illustrate *A Shilling's Worth of Nonsense*.[42] Although Phiz never again had the chance to join the staff of *Punch* as resident illustrator (that honour fell to John Leech), he contributed designs

Cover of *Punch*, 1842

every so often for nearly thirty years, and he and Lemon remained the best of friends.

During the 1840s, Browne also contributed illustrations to other journals, including the *Illustrated London News, Ainsworth's Magazine, Sharpe's London Magazine*, the *Union Magazine, Man in the Moon*, and the *Great Gun*, in the last of which he had ample rein for his favourite occupation: the drawing of horses.

Dickens returned from the United States refreshed by the change of scene and five months' holiday from the task of writing books. He certainly deserved the break – he had produced four major novels in five years, in addition to all other writing. He set to work straight away on *American Notes for General Circulation*, with no illustrations, but before he finished it, his mind had already turned to a novel which he would set, in part, in the country he had just visited. He decided to renew the tried-and-true format of monthly publication, with each part again containing two etchings on steel instead of wood engravings. As soon as word flew round literary circles that Dickens was back at work on a novel, John Leech applied to him, asking the favour of providing at least some of the illustrations. Dickens replied in a rather mysterious manner:

> . . . If it can possibly be arranged with that regard which I feel bound to pay to Mr Browne, I shall be truly happy to avail myself of your genius in my forthcoming Monthly Work. Until I have communicated with him (which I will do immediately) in reference to a project which has occurred to me, I cannot well explain myself further. But I will write to you again and tell you how arrangements stand.[43]

Dickens then approached Phiz in what must have been a somewhat strained encounter. He probably proposed Leech as a co-illustrator for *Martin Chuzzlewit*; Phiz probably dug in his heels. On listening to Dickens's synopsis of the plot, he would quickly understand that this particular book did not divide itself clearly into two forms of artistic subject matter. As he was gradually growing away from caricature and grotesquerie, he could imagine that he and Leech, illustrating similar material, would inevitably become objects of comparison. Leech, who was two years younger than Phiz, was extremely busy with work for *Bentley's Miscellany, Punch*, and for various authors, and had a reputation for not always delivering his work promptly. Phiz could envision himself, once again, picking up after a co-illustrator. Agreeable though Leech might be, '[H]e did what he liked, and it has been for years considerably less than was originally arranged',[44] according to his publisher. Dickens wrote again to Leech two days later:

> I find that there are so many mechanical difficulties, complications, entanglements, and impossibilities, in the way of the project I was revolving in my mind when I wrote to you last, as to render it quite impracticable. I perceive that it could not be satisfactory to you, as giving you no fair opportunity; and that it would, in practice, be irksome and distressing to me. I am therefore compelled to relinquish the idea, and for the present to deny myself the advantage of your valuable assistance.[45]

Dickens had obviously been attracted by Leech's skill and persistence, and as soon as he needed an artist for *A Christmas Carol*, he engaged him to illustrate that eminently successful publication (written during the later stages of his work on *Martin Chuzzlewit*). This decision may have driven Phiz to vent his irritation in a very strange, anti-Christmas polemic – an undated drawing of a great, greasy Father Christmas surrounded by nightmarish images of over-indulgence.[46] Phiz painted the image on a piece of home-made scraperboard and then scratched away the places he wanted gleaming white. Crowned with holly and wearing a heavy, ermine-trimmed robe, Father Christmas dominates the centre of the image. His nose is the nose of a drinker – bulbous, pocky, red; his eyes are bleary; his red lips are stretched wide in a gap-toothed smile; his white hair and beard hang lankly; his right arm, holding a steaming bowl of wassail, is held up high. Over his head, spread-legged, flies Cupid, with his bow in one hand and, in the other, a large clump of mistletoe which he suspends over a naked couple.

Father Christmas is surrounded by food and drink: a huge plum pudding, a slab of bloody roast beef, steaming elder wine, pears, grapes, a large cake, and bottles of spirits. Under his raised arm lurk 'bogies', ghosts, and a skull. A devilish snap dragon (that is, a representation of a toy dragon whose mouth can open and shut), complete with pitchfork and sinuous, arrow-headed tail, stands attendant on his left. (It can be no coincidence that snap dragon is also the eighteenth-century name for gin punch.) But who are the strange figures in the bottom right and left of the picture, apparently wearing halos? Hark the herald angels sing? Surely not. The one on the right is playing a lyre, so this must be Orpheus, signifying a return to the old gods. The one on the left has an Old Testament look, and the instrument he holds could be a shofar.

'A Merry Christmas', 1842. Watercolour on scraper board

Phiz has scraped his signature boldly white on this picture of protest, and titled the whole 'A Merry Christmas'. Can it be a coincidence how much this image satirises that of Scrooge's Third Visitor – right hand raised, plum pudding to the fore – one of John Leech's illustrations in *A Christmas Carol*?

Phiz and Dickens continued to develop side by side in the course of *Martin Chuzzlewit*, feeding off each other's brilliance, working more closely than ever before. Dickens went to lengths to describe certain scenes for Phiz, particularly the American ones, and Phiz responded with care, making special efforts over his sketches, and adding fascinating details to the etchings. He reverted to signing his name as 'Phiz' on the steel plates. In

Chuzzlewit, he created three of his most memorable characters: Mr Pecksniff, of the preposterous quiff; Tom Pinch, in a supreme realisation of Goodness (surprising from the hand of one who was so at ease portraying Evil); and Sarah Gamp, the Ur-midwife, whose trademark umbrella soon became referred to as a 'gamp' by the public.

In 1842, Daumier published in *Le Charivari* an image called '*La Garde-Malade*' (the sick nurse), another of his pictures which stuck fast in Phiz's mind, and it is upon Daumier's sick nurse that the immortal Sarah Gamp

Sarah Gamp, Charles Dickens, *Martin Chuzzlewit*, 1842

is based. The image also seems to have stuck in Dickens's mind. John Harvey comments, '[I]t may be that Dickens had seen the lithograph (perhaps at Browne's house) and found it a useful point of departure for the new comic creation'.[47] Whatever the case, Phiz's midwife bears an extraordinary likeness to Daumier's sick nurse. Thackeray's early injunction to Phiz to study Daumier certainly bore fruit.

'I have a notion of finishing the book, with an apostrophe to Tom Pinch, playing the organ', wrote Dickens to Phiz in June 1844 in his instructions for the frontispiece of *Martin Chuzzlewit*. 'I shall break off the last Chapter suddenly, and find Tom at his organ, a few years afterwards. And instead of saying what became of the people, as usual, I shall suppose it to be all expressed in the sounds; making the last swell of the Instrument a kind of expression of Tom's heart. . . . Tom has had an organ fitted in his chamber, and often sits alone, playing it; when of course the old times rise up before him. So the Frontispiece is Tom at his organ with a pensive face; and any little indications of his history rising out of it and floating about it, that you please; Tom as interesting and amiable as possible.'[48]

This, the depiction of an abstraction, is Cattermole's territory, but the frontispiece turned out to be one of Phiz's most inspired creations, a fusion of Dickens's suggestions and his own imagination and developing skill. Tom Pinch sits at his organ (in another image that presages Robert Buss's 'Dickens's Dream'), gazing reflectively into the past, while all around him circle and stream scenes from the book. How Phiz enjoyed himself! Tom Pinch forms the central image, an image that could stand quite properly on its own, and myriad characters, including anthropomorphised musical notes drawn on manuscript pages, surround him. At the base of the image, little portraits of Pecksniff crowd together in an uncanny precursor to the page of drawings of Mr Dombey that Phiz would soon present to Dickens for his consideration.

A careful study of the crowded frontispiece to *Martin Chuzzlewit* reaps rewards. Phiz took enormous pains with it, and it is possible to claim that it illustrates the moment in which his skill and Dickens's intent are most perfectly fused.

Frontispiece to *Martin Chuzzlewit*

10

Phiz and his Family

At the time of Queen Victoria's wedding to Prince Albert in February 1840, all London went cuckoo about love. 'Society is unhinged here, and I am sorry to add that I have fallen hopelessly in love with the Queen,'[1] Dickens wrote to a friend. Phiz, too, found love unhinging, and a Mr A.W. Venner, writing to Edgar's widow, tells an amusing story about one of Phiz's impetuous courtship attempts:

> Hablot was enamoured of a Miss Griffith, & called upon her father to ask permission to pay his addresses to her. I knew her mother who told me the story, how he called & found her & her husband in the room he was ushered into. The mother was so well preserved she could be scarcely distinguished from the daughter; and Hablot failed to notice she was not the daughter. Mr Griffiths said to his wife, 'kindly leave the room my dear, while Mr Browne tells me his business'. 'No', said Hablot 'it's about her I wish to see you. I wish

'We are seven', letter, 1856

98

to have your consent to pay my addresses to her'. Certainly a disconcerting interview! However, he did not marry the young lady, she
was already engaged to a Captain Varden of the Indian Army, whom
she afterwards married. . . .[2]

Phiz's courtship display finally attracted sixteen-year-old Susannah
Reynolds, the great love of his life, a tiny blue-eyed blonde, born in Essex
on 11 July 1824. Her father was Abraham Reynolds, a Baptist minister,
but according to the marriage certificate her parents were both dead when
she married Phiz. The groom's official father, William Loder Browne, alive
and well in Philadelphia, was also declared dead on the marriage certificate. Susannah's address was given as 5 Burn[3] Street, Stepney, and the
witnesses were Thomas Cheshire and Caroline Jane Bell. Because of the
absence of Browne or Reynolds witnesses, it is tempting to assume that
the wedding was a sudden decision. Thomas Cheshire and Caroline Bell
must have been Susannah's guardians, or acting *in loco parentis*, because
Susannah was a minor and needed permission to wed.

The wedding was celebrated on 28 March 1840 at Holy Trinity,
Marylebone, not far from Phiz's lodgings in Fitzroy Street. Holy Trinity
was designed by Sir John Soane (architect of the Bank of England) and
completed in 1828, twelve years before their wedding. It was one of the
'Waterloo' churches, constructed with the £1 million thanksgiving fund
that Parliament approved to celebrate the deliverance from invasion. It also
served to accommodate the overflow from the popular St Marylebone
Parish Church (which Dickens attended). Many luminaries of the day
worshipped at Holy Trinity, including the Duke of Wellington, W.E.
Gladstone, Florence Nightingale, and J.M.W. Turner (whom Phiz would
have already known from encounters at his sister Lucinda's house in Herne
Hill).

The Brownes were not very religious, although they clearly adhered to
the Christian principles of kindness, forgiveness, and humility. Phiz was
quiet on the matter of his faith. He seldom went to church, but had a
fondness for the New Testament, liking it much better than the Old.[4] He
far preferred to turn the other cheek than to demand an eye for an eye.

Rita Browne comments in her addendum to the family record that
after her marriage Susannah 'seems to have lost touch with her own people,
hardly to be wondered at with such a large family & later on many grandchildren to look after. None of her surviving children know anything of
their maternal relations'.[5] It is more than likely there were no close maternal

relations at all for the orphaned Susannah to be concerned about, and her early marriage to Phiz was a welcome escape from loneliness and guardians into a warm and loving home of her own.

With a parson for her father, Susannah was literate and well read. She was of a cheerful disposition, dearly loved, and proved to be a devoted wife and mother. '[T]he artist's domestic life must be considered to have been eminently satisfactory,' says Thomson. 'In the society of his wife and children – to whom he was fondly attached – his greatest pleasure consisted.'[6] Rita Browne adds that Susannah 'had one marked peculiarity in her inability to get names or quotations correctly. On the late arrival of some guest, wishing to put him at his ease she said – "The first shall be last & the last shall be first, as the old man said in the play."'[7] This reveals Susannah as not only a gracious hostess but a literary eccentric who did not have much time for the Old Man (God) or his organ of speech (St Matthew) – in spite of her clergyman father and her husband's fondness for the New Testament.

Phiz's exuberance at the time of his marriage seems to have rubbed off in his illustrations of Little Nell. As mentioned earlier, he was totally incapable of turning Nell into Dickens's wan 'little creature'.[8] Her horror and fear are palpable, and her coquettishness (never apparent in the text) enchanting. It is tempting to trace the course of Phiz's sexual wooing of Susannah through his images of Nell, especially as it took the Brownes nearly two years after their wedding to produce a child (it took the Dickenses a mere nine months). Seen through Nell, Phiz reveals his young bride as at first fearful of physical intimacy, relenting somewhat, throwing up her hands in horror, and then suddenly becoming coquettish. And it was less than a year after he drew his powerfully sexual 'Death of Quilp' that he and Susannah welcomed their firstborn.

By the time of his wedding, Phiz had already left lodgings in Bedford Place, Newman Street, 68 Warren Street, and 8 Fitzroy Street, while still retaining his studio at Furnival's Inn with Robert Young. He and Susannah continued this pattern of moving from place to place, living rather like hermit crabs, constantly changing their residence as their family grew larger and their fortune ebbed and flowed. Their initial home together was on Howland Street, round the corner from Fitzroy Street, and their first son was born there on 2 January 1842, and given the name Edgar Athelstane, Edgar after his uncle.

Charles Michael, their second son, was born on 5 September 1843, either at Howland Street or at 2 Stamford Villas in Fulham, their next house. The family moved to Fulham for two reasons: Susannah needed fresh air for her health and that of her babies, and Phiz needed physical distance from the demands of ever-present authors and publishers. The house was small, but had a very large dog kennel as can be seen in a sketch on an undated (but most likely mid-1840s) letter Phiz wrote to his brother, Decimus:

Letter to Decimus, mid 1840s

My dear Dec:

    Can you dine with us on Friday? – Bob [Young] and other odd fish – at table.

    Yr. affec. Bro,

    H.K. Browne

Tuesday Evening

2 Stamford Villas[9]

This letter proves that Decimus, the youngest of William Loder Browne's children, then nearing his thirties, had not yet left for Australia, and that he and Phiz stayed on good terms as adults. By this date, most of Phiz's other remaining siblings had already travelled far from home: Emma left England in 1836 to keep house for her brother Charles in Madras, where, at the age of forty-two, she married an officer in the Madras Infantry, Samuel Auchinleck Grant. They produced one daughter, Maggie, when

Emma was forty-six. (Colonel Grant is said also to have had a child by an Indian woman, on whom he settled the then enormous sum of £10,000.[10]) And Gordon was already in New Zealand, where Octavius visited him on his travels between 1839 and 1842.

Back home in Fulham, Phiz and Susannah's third son, Walter Robert Geoffrey, was born on 6 July 1845. He was shortly followed by their first daughter, Kate, in 1846, and by Frederick in 1847, but both those babies died within forty-eight hours of birth. About this time the Brownes decided to move to the country, wisely distancing themselves from the city where 500,000 people were infected with typhus fever in 1847. Phiz's love of horses and desire to have his own was also a key factor.

The move to Thornton Heath, a part of Croydon, then a country town on the London–Brighton road, was an unqualified success. '[M]y mother recovered her natural activity', writes Edgar Browne, 'and from being a person who required waiting upon, became one who looked after everybody else.'[11] She quickly produced two more daughters, Emma Grant, named after Phiz's sister in India, in 1848, and Eliza Mary in 1850. Then Susannah seems to have suffered a stillbirth, to judge from a clue in a letter written by Phiz from Thornton Heath, on Thursday, 26 July (no year, but probably 1853). Its unidentified recipient (Charles Lever?), has obviously been trying to persuade Phiz to join him on a jaunt. The letter reads:

> My dear Sir,
>
> My 'Blessings' have not yet 'increased or multiplied' – Mrs Gamp [that is, the midwife] has arrived – but as yet she sits in solitary dignity and undisturbed tranquillity – over her tea pot – I have waited a day also, hoping to be able to give you some notice that the little event *had* come off – but no – Now, on this unexpected little delay involves another delay of at least a month – before we can make a clearance. I really think (as these are perilous times for trifling with any great questions –) that to avoid a domestic revolution – (and blame me the innocent cause of this detention in Town) you had better yield – surrender Croydon – and be taken whithersoever the rebellious spirits may determine. –
>
> I will – however – drop you a line when the sum in addition is correctly and satisfactorily finished.
>
> Believe me – Yrs. very sincerely
>
> Hablot K. Browne.[12]

The reason to suspect a stillbirth is that none of the Brownes' surviving children had a late July or early August birthdate.

Thomas Hablot arrived safely in 1854, Mabel Anna in 1856, and Gordon Frederick in 1858. On Mabel's birth Phiz wrote to Robert Cole: 'You see I now sing with Wordyworth [sic], "We are Seven!"'[13] Phiz is having fun with Wordsworth's name here, turning him (one might say justifiably) into 'Wordyworth'.[14]

Edgar remarks, 'Our mother, of course, was greatly occupied with household affairs and the upbringing of the last new baby, who might almost be described as a hardy annual. Large families were considered a blessing, and not even an inconvenience.'[15]

Hablot, Susannah, and their quiverful lived in a rather raffish, rambling establishment, actually two tiny houses knocked into one, complete with two of everything on the front side: two front doors, two staircases, two front rooms. The back of the house had been altered and was not twinned quite so strictly, having a kitchen on the south end and a large dining room on the north, above which Phiz had his studio, 'a room held sacred, and supposed to be full of invisible dangers for intruders, like Bluebeard's chamber'.[16] The joint grounds contained stables and outbuildings, and the joint gardens with their acacia and cherry trees ran down to a field where the family's horses were pastured. A pond provided endless entertainment for the children and was an excuse to build Robinson Crusoe's raft, an elaborate structure which took the children weeks to construct and invariably capsized each time they set sail.

If Susannah and the children flourished as a result of the move, Phiz also flowered in that funny, rambling house. He worked happily and industriously in his upstairs studio, disappearing there immediately after breakfast and only reappearing for meals if importuned to do so. And in Surrey, he was able to indulge in his passion for hunting. Although he had managed to hunt as a boy by dint of borrowing horses from others, this was his first opportunity to keep his own animals: a strong saddle-horse for serious hacking and hunting, and a gentle cob for riding around and for pulling the chaise. He kept a donkey for his children, and a goat with its own carriage in which the tiniest Brownes could practise driving. Two Scottish terriers and the inevitable cat made up the complement of animals.

Phiz taught his children to ride, and Edgar remembered one occasion when he was riding the cob and it caught its foot in a rabbit hole and flung him 'outspread like a frog on the hard chalky surface of the downs, not at all mitigated by what appears to be a covering of grass. I recall the sound of the fall, and the universal shake up of every atom of my body, and hearing the Governor's voice, apparently from an enormous distance, asking if I were dead'.[17] The children were allowed to drive the pony-chaise at a very early age, and soon became adept at exploring the country-side and its various farms and churches, going wherever they wanted, trespassing at every turn. Their parents seem to have trusted them completely, relying on healthy appetites to bring them home in time for meals. Edgar claims that the girls had as much liberty as the boys, and they all lived a carefree and happy existence.

When they were not gallivanting over the countryside, the three oldest boys, Edgar, Charles, and Walter, 'lived a good deal in the trees and the sloping roof between our own and our neighbours' stables, . . . free from the embarrassing presence of grown-ups, as pirates or Saracens, or other terrible kinds of men, and we were wont to summon three girls who lived next door, and who were treated as female slaves'.[18] In later years, Edgar ran into one of these girls, then a young mother, and felt 'hideously ashamed' that he had driven her round the garden with a whip.

Another family, with eighteen children, lived nearby, and Edgar says that he and his siblings frequently visited them to prevent them from feeling lonely. The small Brownes, who understood the rules of hospitality, invited them back to their house. It seems that not all eighteen ever arrived at one time, but they could appear in large enough numbers to produce a shortage of chairs. Edgar continues:

> Occasionally the two families made expeditions, accompanied by an extraordinary number of acquaintances and female slaves, carrying bows and arrows, and provisions to an amount suitable apparently for a long voyage, but actually only capable of lasting a few hours. The ammunition was intended for the slaughter of squirrels or any small birds that might be about. I have considerable satisfaction in saying not a single death resulted in spite of all our preparations – we might as well have carried some salt to put on their tails.[19]

Susannah adored her husband, believing he could do no wrong, and the children clearly recognised that their father was the hub of the house-hold. They believed Phiz was their best friend, a man whose good temper invariably prevailed unless the noise-level, particularly of the kind made by young people bleating on musical instruments, became overwhelming. 'When a hubbub became unbearable he would sometimes appear with a hunting crop and lay about him and so restore order, but though there was a great appearance of vigour, and great sounds of cracking of the whip, there was little damage done'.[20] Although Phiz went so far as to hide his children's musical instruments in a huge cupboard, a ruse that was discovered by accident during a ritual spring cleaning, he never objected if they filled the house with their friends 'even if his dinner was put off, or a few squares of the dining-room windows smashed . . . Where there are boys and balls broken panes are a logical consequence, and a glazier was always ready to attend at the shortest possible notice'.[21]

At some point, perhaps because their lease was up, the Brownes moved to a 'villa residence' on Duppas Hill. Phiz loathed the place, mainly because it had no stables, and they soon moved again, this time to Banstead, much deeper into the countryside. Banstead was also closer to Epsom, the site of the famous Derby race, a fact not lost on Phiz. Everyone was happy except visitors from London, among them Charles Dickens, Robert Young, and Mark Lemon, who found the journey rather exacting. These friends had become accustomed to escaping from the city and enjoying Sundays with the Brownes at Thornton House. Stout Mark Lemon, a veritable Falstaff, was a particular favourite of the children because he paid them attention and made them laugh. Dickens, by contrast, did neither. '[He] was not much interested in us. . . . He appeared overwhelming, very splendid as to his clothing, and rather unapproachable'.[22]

Friends had made the easier journey to Croydon either by coach or by the 'atmospheric railway', a short-lived and unreliable transportation experiment in which the cars were pulled by a piston travelling inside a tube between the rails rather than by a locomotive. By contrast, the journey to the Brownes' Banstead house, stuck on a lonely heath miles from anywhere, was another matter altogether, and involved a hair-raising trip over rough and unmarked roads. Gradually, friends visited less and less frequently, except for Robert Young who made work-related calls on his partner once or twice a week. The children were fond of their cheerful and well-read 'uncle', who always brought the latest books from London and introduced the Brownes to authors on the brink of illustrious careers. Edgar comments that Uncle Bob was sincerely attached to Phiz and deeply admired his skill and intellect.

Phiz did not encourage local people to become his friends; he distrusted their motives, fearing they only wished to make his acquaintance because of his fame and his relationship with the literary lions. According to Edgar, Dr Westall was the one exception. 'As he was a doctor, he could penetrate to any room in the house without giving offence, and he was not long in making his way into the studio. How could he be repulsed when he brought tidings of wife and child? Being accustomed to put people at their ease, he soon overcame the Governor's reserve.'[23]

The Brownes' long absence from London finally took its toll on Phiz's finances, and 1855 and 1856 were particularly lean years for the illustrator. 'Out of sight, out of mind' became all too true. Dr Westall, appalled by Phiz's lack of shove in the matter of acquiring commissions, decided to take action and secure a regular income for him. He used his influence to propose Phiz for the position of drawing master at Addiscombe, the East India Company's military college, which Charles Alfred Browne had attended so many years previously. Phiz agreed to an interview (dragging his feet, one feels), but in the end did not get the job. 'I cannot help smiling at the idea of the delineator of Micawber instructing future generals in the drawing of fortresses or the contour of hills',[24] comments Edgar wryly.

Eventually, the Brownes had to face the grim reality of a move back to London. They sadly packed their belongings, not an arduous task for Phiz who had already made a bonfire of letters and sketches, material he considered to be mere rubbish. He seems to have had no sentiment about what he was burning. The loss is disastrous; a written record of the artistic collaboration and bond of friendship between Phiz and Dickens would be a precious thing.

Many years later, when W.J. Fitzpatrick wrote to Phiz for material to include in *The Life of Charles Lever*, Phiz responded:

Living as [Lever] did abroad, our correspondence was generally confined to the etchings we had on at the time. Some years ago when I was about to remove from Croydon, I had a bonfire to lessen the lumber, and burnt a stock of papers containing all Lever's, Dickens', Ainsworth's, and other author's notes, as they were almost solely about illustrations. I did not at the time attach any importance to them, nor did I think anyone else would; but I was afterwards blamed by several autograph collectors for my wilful destruction of what they considered valuable.[25]

S.M. Ellis, Harrison Ainsworth's biographer, also moans about how few letters to 'Phiz' have been preserved:

Dr. Edgar Browne, the artist's son, tells me his father had an enormous mass of letters from Ainsworth, Dickens, Lever, and other writers containing their notes and suggestions for the illustrations 'Phiz' designed for their books. These letters – together with a quantity of Browne's sketches, proofs, etc. – were stored in a large cupboard in his studio. On removing from the house, 'Phiz' – to avoid the trouble of packing them – made a bonfire in the garden of these invaluable papers; and in this lamentable holocaust perished a unique collection of material relating to world-famous books and their authors.

Whether or not Dickens learned about Phiz's fire, he, too, later succumbed to the impulse to rid himself of letters received from others, including, of course, those from H.K. Browne. Since Phiz's letters were often extremely funny, the loss of those that went up in Dickens's conflagration is grating. Dickens describes the bonfire: 'Yesterday I burnt, in the field at Gad's Hill, the accumulated letters and papers of 20 years. They sent up a smoke like the Genie when he got out of the casket on the seashore; and as it was an exquisite day when I began, and rained very heavily when I finished, I suspect my correspondence of having overcast the face of the heavens'.[26] As he watched the last letters burning, he expressed the wish that all the letters he had ever written had burned too. In the case of his letters to Phiz, the matter had already been attended to.

'Give Me Back the Wild Freshness of the Morning!'

Thomas Moore[1]

Into the supper-room we rushed: but what a change was there! The brilliant tables, resplendent with gold plate, candelabras, and flowers, were now despoiled and dismantled. On the floor, among broken glasses, cracked decanters, pyramids of jelly, and pagodas of blancmange, lay scattered in every attitude the sleeping figures of the late guests. Mrs Rooney alone maintained her position, seated in a large chair, her eyes closed, a smile of Elysian happiness playing upon her lips.

Charles Lever, Jack Hinton[2]

Charles Lever loved parties. The riotous gatherings in his early novels are drawn largely from life and attended by loosely disguised friends and acquaintances. When Phiz and Samuel Lover, 'Painter, Etcher, Lyric Poet,

'The Finale to an evening', *Jack Hinton*, 1843

Musical–composer, Executant, Novelist, and Dramatist',[3] visited him in Brussels in 1839, Lover wrote home and noted that they did nothing day and night but eat and drink and laugh themselves sick. Lever in turn told his publisher, 'If I have a glass of champagne left (we finished nine dozen in sixteen days Lover and "Phiz" spent here), I'll drink your health.'[4] The high point of the visit came when, not content with merely knocking back champagne, the three men decided to install themselves as Grand Crosses of the Order of the Knights of Alcantara in an elaborate ceremony which concluded with a musical procession and a grand ballet. Lever was working on his third novel, *Jack Hinton*, at the time, and he and Phiz soon translated their antics into print. At one point in the story, Jack Hinton was, like Captain Hablot, a prisoner on parole, and Hinton's parole town was St Omer, the very town where Mrs Browne and the family lived in 1814–1815. It sounds as though Phiz recounted the story of Kate and Captain Hablot to Lever, and Lever, who enjoyed nothing more than inserting real people and events into his novels, could not resist making this veiled reference.

Phiz's children always looked forward to their father's return from trips with Lever because he came back overflowing with anecdotes about the kind of hilarious pranks that appeal to young people. The charismatic Lever managed to overcome Phiz's natural reticence to the point where the artist dashed headlong with him 'into the spirit of the time and place, and presented all the features of an irresponsible roisterer.'[5] The two men were much alike in cheery optimism, devotion to horses, rough riding across the countryside, and belief in the healing properties of fresh air. Lever was a large, enormously energetic, good-looking man, with a strong jaw, deep-set blue eyes, and beautiful feet. When asked 'What is the nicest thing in boots?' his wife is said to have replied, 'My husband's foot'.[6] His friend, Mary Boyle, commented, 'His conversation was like summer lightning – brilliant, sparkling, harmless. . . . He was . . . warm-hearted, witty, rollicking, never unrefined [or] imprudent, often blind to his own interests – adored by his friends, and the playfellow of his children and the gigantic boar-hound he had brought from the Tyrol'.[7] His biographer, W.J. Fitzpatrick, describes his conversation in more earthy terms, 'In descriptive vivacity every feature took a part, even to his nose, which seemed to enjoy a life of its own; his anecdotes fell like ripe fruit from an overladen tree'.[8] But Lever had a darker side: he was prone to melancholy; inclined to self-pity; lacked confidence in his writing; needed constant reassurance; loathed having jokes turned on himself; procrastinated; and was addicted to whist and roulette.

Sketches of Phiz and Lever, on a page of *The Confessions of Harry Lorrequer*, 1839

Charles Lever was born in Dublin in 1806 to an English father living in Ireland and an Irish Protestant mother. He spent his childhood in a happy home and at private schools where he was known for his fencing skill, the whirl in his waltz, his outrageous pranks, devouring novels, and smoking. 'The iron had not entered his soul like that of his great contemporary – the ill-fed, ill-clad, uneducated, and uncared-for boy . . . engaged at this very time in tying and labelling blacking jars . . .' says Fitzpatrick, referring to Charles Dickens's miserable childhood experience.[9] Lever constructed a little theatre at home where he performed dramas of his own making, designed sets and costumes, and sometimes provided his own musical accompaniment. His father hoped that his son would follow in his footsteps and become an architect, but Charles was more interested in people than in buildings and decided to become a doctor. He studied at Trinity College, Dublin, from 1822 to 1827, taking longer than usual to complete his college education because of his leisure activities, which included 'training horses for a race in the Phoenix, arranging a rowing match, getting up a mock duel between two white-feathered friends, or organising the Association for Discountenancing Watchmen'.[10]

'If I'd ever had Charles Lever in a class of mine, I'd have kicked the blighter out!' says Tony Bareham, a Lever specialist and editor of *Charles Lever: New Evaluations*.[11]

Lever sailed to Canada as an unqualified surgeon on an emigrant ship, and spent the summer of 1829 travelling within Canada and the United States. Wanting to experience at first hand 'the wild freedom of life with an Indian tribe',[12] he disappeared into the backwoods and joined up with members of the Comanche nation. Apparently, leaving them proved more difficult than joining them, and he had to conspire with a Comanche maiden to effect his escape. But he returned safely to Dublin with tales of hair-raising adventures (some probably apocryphal but ripe for inclusion in his novels) and bearing an enormous dugout canoe, which he and a friend launched on the Grand Canal to the amazement of onlookers. He then set off for Germany, where he enrolled in the university at Göttingen and entered fully into the city's boisterous, beery, student life.

Lever finally completed his medical education and began work in 1832 in County Clare where he was fearless in combating the devastating cholera outbreak. When it abated, he moved with his bride, Kate Baker, to Portstewart, near Coleraine, in Northern Ireland, to work as a dispensary doctor. Although prone to prescribing purges for family and friends, Lever was largely a physician of the 'How about a bit of fresh air?' school of medicine. Often, instead of dosing his patients, he suggested that they follow Dryden's advice:

> Better to hunt in field for health unbought,
> Than fee the doctor for a nauseous draught.
> The wise for cure on exercise depend;
> God never made his work, for man to mend.[13]

Charles and Kate Lever settled in Verandah Cottage on Portstewart's seafront, and started the family that would eventually consist of four children – three daughters, Julia ('Pussy'), Kate, and Sydney, and a son, Charley. During his years there, Lever began contributing his first major work, *The Confessions of Harry Lorrequer* (a series of sketches not originally intended to be a novel) in monthly parts to the *Dublin University Magazine*.

Portstewart still has the feel of a nineteenth-century seaside town, and although Verandah Cottage no longer exists, one can stand on the pavement and look at Lever's view of the harbour and the open sea, and imagine him in evening dress 'riding backward and forward through the entire night between the bed of some child that was dangerously ill and a ball given by the officers of a regiment then at Coleraine'.[14] At nearby Coleraine he is said to have jumped his own horse over a horse and cart, a feat that he and Phiz later immortalised in *Charles O'Malley*, Lever's second book.

Lever fell out with the Portstewart medical establishment,[15] and left for Brussels in 1837, where he set up a fashionable medical practice and resumed his extravagant entertaining. Meanwhile, the popularity of the *Harry Lorrequer* sketches encouraged his publisher, M'Glashan, to reprint them in novel form with illustrations. In December 1838 he wrote from Brussels to his friend Alexander Spencer: 'I am very desirous that the illustrations should be by Cruikshank, not Phiz. Pray try to accomplish this for me. . . . I wish above all that he [M'Glashan] could put me in relation with the illustrator for the scenes to be selected as subjects'.[16] Phiz, however, landed the job, perhaps because of the popularity of *Pickwick* and *Nicholas Nickleby*, but more likely because the much sought-after Cruikshank was unavailable. Cruikshank did eventually illustrate one of Lever's books when Phiz was working on *Martin Chuzzlewit*. He writes, 'I regret I was only able to illustrate one of [Lever's] works, "Arthur O'Leary." My engagements on "Jack Shepherd", etc., at that time prevented me from illustrating his other works'.[17] But it may be that Lever realised how much easier Phiz was to work with than the great George; in fact, Lever used Phiz almost exclusively throughout the next two decades (see Appendix 2 for list of works and illustrations.)

Phiz's work for Lever was uneven but always lively, rather like the writing of Lever himself. Both author and artist were full of verve and comic invention in the early swashbuckling romances; straddled the fence between frothy adventure and seriousness in the middle period; and broadened and deepened in the later novels. But *The Confessions of Harry Lorrequer* is still the work for which Lever remains best known. He later wrote that the sketches were penned with little hope of permanence, lightly undertaken, and carelessly thrown together.[18] But the public adored them, and Phiz had a field day. Caught up in Lever's exuberance, he produced images reminiscent of both *Pickwick* and *Nicholas Nickleby* – but far noisier in effect – giving his comic characters huge faces and balloon-like bodies, while reserving disproportionately small heads and svelte bodies for the leading men. Women are an endangered species in this novel, which ends with the totally unanticipated words: 'So passed the last evening I spent in Munich – the next morning I was married'.[19]

'The Supper at Father Malachi's', *The Confessions of Harry Lorrequer*, 1839

Even with Phiz hard at work, Lever was still anxious on several counts, writing to M'Glashan in January 1839:

> H.K. Brown [sic] has not yet written to me, and I regret it the more because if I knew the scenes he selected, I might have benefited by his ideas and rendered them more graphic, as an author corrects his play by seeing a dress rehearsal.
>
> . . . Has Phiz any notion of Irish physiognomy? for this is most important. If not, and as 'Lorrequer' abounds in specimens, pray entreat him to study the Tail[20] when they meet in February: he can have nothing better, if not too coarse for his purpose.
>
> The illustrations in No. 1 are very good, but why is Lorrequer at the supper at Father Malachy's [sic] made so like Nicholas Nickleby? That is unfortunate, and every one sees it at a glance. All plagiarisms in the book, I beg to say, are my prerogatives.[21]

Lever's anxiety about how Phiz would portray the Irish was well founded.

The author was beginning to feel the sting of criticism from Irish nationalists, who assumed that as an Anglo-Irishman he was incapable of writing without ridiculing his countrymen. Unfortunately, Phiz's rollicking illustrations for *Harry Lorrequer* helped to reinforce this impression, and may be the reason Lionel Stevenson in *Dr Quicksilver* blames the artist for the Nationalists' animosity.[22] Phiz's early illustrations of Irish peasant characters resembled those seen on the English stage – drunken, red-nosed troublemakers – the only type to which he had been exposed until he visited Ireland.

The mud of Nationalist criticism still sticks to Lever. This is largely due to an 1843 article in *The Nation*, 'that unique Irish paper', in which the author William Carleton accused him of not only committing every literary vice but also of caricaturing and debasing Irish life.[23] (Phiz, however, escaped Carleton's barbs and subsequently illustrated three books for him, *Traits and Stories of the Irish Peasantry* in 1843, *Tales and Stories of the Irish Peasantry* in 1846, and *Valentine McClutchy* in 1854.) Carleton has been quoted, parrotlike, down the generations by such literary heavies as W.B. Yeats and Daniel Corkery. This is deeply unfortunate. As biographer Edmund Downey says, Lever's sympathies were as Irish as the Wicklow hills.

Lever's reputation also suffered at the hands of Nationalist historians and the adoption of the traditional Nationalist creed, which excluded Anglo-Irish literature and concentrated solely on home-grown writing and writers. How sad it is that none of those historians took time to read beyond *Harry Lorrequer* and *Charles O'Malley*, books that Stephen Haddelsey, author of *Charles Lever: The Lost Victorian*, claims 'simultaneously made and blasted Lever's reputation'. Haddelsey continues, 'One would like to believe that if *Lord Kilgobbin* [Lever's last novel] had received the same attention as *Harry Lorrequer*, from both readers and critics, we would be far less likely to find modern critical authorities of Declan Kiberd's weight rolling out the tired old clichés.'[24]

Again and again, Lever returned to Ireland for the source of inspiration, and at the end of his life, he expressed a heartfelt wish: 'If any nation is to be judged by her bearing under calamity, Ireland – and she has had some experiences – comes well through the ordeal. That we may yet see how she will sustain her part in happier circumstances is my hope and prayer, and that the time be not too far off!'[25]

Lever moved much of the action in his second novel, *Charles O'Malley, the Irish Dragoon* (1841) to the Continent at the time of the Peninsular War and the Battle of Waterloo, drawing on what he calls the 'inexhaustible store of fun and buoyancy within me'.[26] Indeed, Lever is at his funniest in this book, and the public was particularly captivated by Lever's answer to Dickens's Sam Weller, the irrepressible Mickey Free, complete with striped waistcoat. Lever writes: 'Of Mickey Free I had not one, but one thousand types. . . . in my late visit to Dublin [I chanced] on a living specimen of the "Free" family . . . The fellow was "boots" at a great hotel in Sackville Street; and he afforded me more amusement and some heartier laughs than . . . a party of wits'.[27] Phiz was completely at home rendering a Samlike Mickey, but other images in this novel are thin and hurried (not surprising with Little Nell breathing down his neck). Lever invited him to Brussels for this reason, suggesting he travel there with Samuel Lover, who was going to paint his portrait. While Lover worked, Lever could describe to Phiz the gang of wild characters springing to mind for his next novel, *Jack Hinton*. Working together proved productive; the illustrations for *Jack Hinton* are far more carefully conceived and wrought than those for *Harry Lorrequer* and *Charles O'Malley*. By the time Phiz left Brussels, he and Lever had secured not only their artistic partnership but a lifelong friendship.

Phiz's images for *Jack Hinton* (1843) include twenty-six complex steel plates and nine powerful wood engravings. One of the most memorable illustrations, 'Farewell to Tipperary Joe' represents a real person, who collected 'rent' from stagecoach passengers. About him, Lever wrote:

When he learned . . . that I had put him in a book, he made it . . . the ground of a demand on my purse; and if the talented artist who had illustrated the tale had been accessible to him, I suspect that he, too, would have had to submit to the levy of a blackmail, all the more heavily as Joe was by no means pleased with a portrait which really only self-flattery could have objected to.

Hablot K. Browne never saw him, and yet in his sketch of him standing to say his 'good-bye' to Jack Hinton at Kingston, he has caught the character of his figure and the moping lounge of his attitude to perfection.[28]

On the one hand, Phiz found Lever easy to work with because he was given a far freer rein than he had with Dickens; on the other, Lever was often late providing copy. Once he got going – he dallied at length before starting to write – he poured out torrents of words at breakneck speed. Phiz had to scramble to complete the etchings, and if Lever skimped, he skimped too. Getting to press was a major problem as Lever lived abroad

'Farewell to Tipperary Joe' *Jack Hinton*, 1843

for most of his writing life; the printer was in Dublin or London; Phiz was tucked away in Surrey during much of their partnership; and although Lever took advantage of the Diplomatic Bag, manuscript deliveries were often delayed and, on one occasion, lost.

With his reputation as a writer assured, Lever gave up medicine for what he felt would be a more lucrative profession, a decision which gave him twinges of regret in later life,[29] and which may have been prompted by rising gambling debts. In 1842, he returned to Dublin as editor of the *Dublin University Magazine*, a magazine which owed much of its success to him. He settled five miles outside Dublin, at Templeogue House, a large mansion reeking of history and hauntings, in which James I is reputed to have spent the night after the Battle of the Boyne. During Lever's years there (1842–1845), Phiz visited him several times. Like Lucinda Bicknell's home at Herne Hill, Lever's establishment presented an ideal, with its high walls, waterfalls, grottoes, and avenues, and may have been one of the goads that spurred Phiz to leave the city for the countryside in 1849.

Here was a house which offered plenty of space for parties, stables for Lever's twelve horses – named after the horses in his novels – and wonderful gardens for his children to frolic in. Dublin's literary circle thronged around the Lever's generous table, and friends arrived from England, including Phiz and Thackeray. When Phiz visited, Lever and he would saddle up and disappear, rough riding across the countryside. They may have ridden as far as Lever's old haunts at Portstewart and the Giant's Causeway because several of Phiz's illustrations of the area show a clear understanding of their geography. After this visit to Ireland and his exposure to its land-scape and people, the artist could no longer be accused of treating the Irish anything but sympathetically.

Like Phiz, Lever believed in putting his children on ponies before they could walk, and a narrow spot on the Dodder is called 'Pussy's Leap', a title which must commemorate the moment when that daughter first jumped her pony over the water. Fitzpatrick remarks; 'He was fond of his children, braced and beaming, he daily rode out with two of them on ponies, a stout cob sometimes falling to his share. Attended by this tiny escort, and followed by a belted groom, he might be often seen travers-ing the streets of Dublin, where all four, attracting every eye, were famil-iar figures. The flowing auburn hair of his daughters, so ample that it well-nigh seemed to cover the pony, was in itself striking.'[30]

Again like Phiz, Lever adored his wife. He read his novels aloud to her and she pruned them as they went along.[31] She influenced some of his later heroines (often named Kate) who were plucky, full of personality, and loving – a far cry from Dickens's limp and vapid creatures. Kate Lever's only flaw seems to have been a passion for clothes, and Lever is said to have sweetened her with new dresses if they ever had a spat.

Lever's fourth novel, *Tom Burke of 'Ours'*, was published in 1843. A major turn occurs with this novel; even though his writing remains spirited and ebullient, his content becomes more serious and he develops a fuller emotional range. *Tom Burke* supplied Phiz with an extraordinary variety of subject matter: Napoleon in six locations (including Egypt); lots of horses; sword fights; beautiful women; a heroine who dies in battle; a peeping Tom; pigs, sheep, and a goose in full honk. 'Peeping Tom' is the first of several erotically charged illustrations Phiz provided for Lever.

Tales of the Trains (1845) is a slim volume containing fourteen wood engravings. The subject matter allowed Phiz to flex his comic muscle, even as he offered social comment on the effect of the railway on the country-side. *Nuts and Nutcrackers* (also 1845), is a high-spirited but tiny volume of essays, one of the only works in which Lever and Phiz can be justly accused of caricature. It contains six neat steels by Phiz, including 'Honourable

'Peeping Tom', *Tom Burke of 'Ours'*, 1843

Members', in the half man/half animal style of Charles Le Brun,[32] and fifty-two(!) wood engravings.

St Patrick's Eve (1845), Lever's impassioned plea against absentee landlords, contains a mixture of etchings and wood engravings, in which, surprisingly, the wood seems more lively than the steel; the finest wood engraving is the '. . . huge fellow, without legs, [who] rode upon an ass, his wide chest ornamented by a picture of himself, and a paragraph setting forth his infirmities. He, with a voice deeper than a bassoon, bellowed forth his prayer for alms . . .'[33] Lever had been impressed by the success of Dickens's Christmas books, and *St Patrick's Eve* is his attempt to capitalise on a religious festival while showing sympathy for his less fortunate countrymen and his hope for their future. His friend Thackeray praised

'The Honourable Members', *Nuts and Nutcrackers*, 1845

'The Beggar', *St. Patrick's Eve*, 1845

the little book in the *Morning Chronicle* on 3 April 1845, and spoke highly of Phiz's work: 'Great praise must also be bestowed upon the charming, faithful, and picturesque designs with which Mr Brown [sic] has illustrated this brilliant little volume.' Thackeray's use of the word 'faithful' confirms both the new truth of Phiz's images of the Irish people and his fidelity to Lever's text.

With Lever complaining of overwork and fatigue – he had started work on his next novel, *The O'Donohue* – Thackeray advised him to do justice to his writing by giving up the editorship of the *Dublin University Magazine* and moving to London. Lever agreed to a change of scene, but chose the Continent instead. Off he went with his family, first to Germany, where he continued to work on *The O'Donohue*, subtitled *A Tale of Ireland Fifty Years Ago*. It seems that the further he travelled from Ireland, the more clearly he understood the country of his birth and the problem of his countrymen.

From Reider Schloss, a castle Lever rented at Bregenz on Lake Constance, he wrote 'wish[ing] to see in his new home the pleasant face of "Phiz", with whom cheery days had been passed, and to hear some literary gossip "from the big village".'[34] He invited Phiz on a ramble through Switzerland and the Tyrol, promising to drive him everywhere himself with his own nags. Poor Phiz, weighed down with work, popularity, and the birth of his third son, had to decline.

> I wish I could accept it, but, alas! 'Heigh-ho Harry,' I can't. I have just taken a sort of holiday, and now must buckle on my harness again, and work! work! work! I will do the pretty for 'The O'Donoghue' title page. I am in dreadful poor-law-union state of inanition regarding literary news. Of course, you read or heard of Dickens's theatricals?[35] Bulwer, for want of something else to do, is blowing the trumpet for the water doctors! 'To what strange uses,' etc. He must either have water on the brain or a cataract in his eye.[36]

The few existing letters between Phiz and Lever clearly demonstrate their camaraderie. Here is Phiz again, after apologising to Lever for the extraordinary title awarded to one of the more serious illustrations in *The O'Donoghue*:

> When I saw it I was convulsed with laughter. I do not know whether to attribute the mistake to the carelessness, stupidity, inebriety, or the practical-joking peculiarities of the writing engraver. I think it is a

'Mercy on us! The Leddies are Coming', *The Knight of Gwynne*, 1847

compound. Orr sent to me for a title to the plate; and as I was rather at a loss how to name the child, I wrote on a slip of paper thus: – 1. 'Mark recognizes an old acquaintance;' or simply 2. 'The Glen;' or (addressing Orr) 'anything else you like, my little dears' – meaning that Orr might give a better if he could; and behold! the writing engraver makes a Chinese copy of the whole![37]

The error is available for all to see, bound for ever into the first edition of *The O'Donoghue*.

The novels that follow teeter between the comic dash and conversation of his early work and the more serious plotting and construction of his later novels; Phiz's work expresses the same ambivalence. But of all the Lever novels, *The Knight of Gwynne* (1847) reveals Phiz's range to the fullest. His comedy shines in 'Mercy on us! The Leddies are coming!' where Lever's dugout canoe suddenly reappears; 'The Letter' (plate 23) is another example of the erotic Phiz and a nice nod to Hogarth's 'After'; his delight in anthropomorphism, which shows up time and again in his work, has him adding faces and presence to 'two abrupt and jagged masses of rock' in 'Foster's Warm Reception at the "Corvy"'; and the title page (plate 24) could be a representation of Portstewart itself. Phiz etched 'Chales' for Charles on this image, which was never changed in later editions because the plate as a whole was so pleasing.

Every so often Phiz's comic streak threatens to undermine Lever's serious intent, for instance in 'The Camanches' in Lever's next novel *Con Cregan* (1849), where Lever writes:

[W]hile yet the 'yellow-glory' of the hour bathed the earth, we saw the cane wigwams of the 'Camanches,' as they stood at either side of a little river . . . Some squaws were seated on the banks, and a number of children were sporting in the stream . . . Some mustangs, seemingly fresh caught, were picketed in a circle, and a few boys were amusing themselves, tormenting the animals into bounds and curvets . . . The soft influence of the hour – the placid beauty of the picture – the semblance of tranquil security impressed on everything – the very childish gambols – were all images so full of home and homelike memories, that we halted and gazed on the scene in speechless emotion.[38]

Hardly serene. Seven wild-eyed horses are rearing and bucking, while

The Camanches

'The Camanches', *Confessions of Con Cregan*, 1849

one (very evidently a stallion) tries to mount the horse next to him. Another attempts to take a nip from a neatly rounded haunch, even as its owner prepares to kick back with both rear hoofs. The children on the bank and in the river could be part of any of Phiz's seaside scenes, apart from the token feathers they wear, while in the background are classical female figures – one bearing an amphora, another combing her tresses – suitable on the Portland vase, except for the feather and papoose sported by the most dominant figure.

In *Con Cregan*, Phiz is all over the map (and off it when G.H. Thomas takes over the wood engravings in the later chapters). He provides twenty-nine steels, including two ineffectual dark plates, and twenty-one wood engravings before Thomas is employed. Pressure of work is undoubtedly the reason for the substitution.

Phiz used *Roland Cashel* (1850) as a vehicle for perfecting dark plate technique (described in reference to *Dombey and Son* in the next chapter). In spite of the experiments, *Roland Cashel* contains some masterful images, especially 'Bravo Toro', with its chiasmus of brilliantly drawn bull and horse. The book is also a vehicle for some of Phiz's most sexually allur-ing females, possibly in reaction to the steady stream of images of Dora and Agnes for *David Copperfield*, on which he was working concurrently.

Charles Lever and his family continued their peripatetic existence for

'Bravo Toro', *Roland Cashel*, 1850

several years, providing daunting communication challenges. They finally settled in Italy, first in Como and then Florence. In 1851, Lever became Vice Consul in La Spezia, from where he made frequent visits to the charming casino up in the hills at Bagni di Lucca.

In *The Daltons* (1852), Phiz relinquishes dark plates, and his illustrations revert to being easily recognisable. As always, he was sensitive to an author's effort; Lever was dashing off *The Daltons* with little struggle, so Phiz did the same.

The Dodd Family Abroad (1854) is an entirely epistolary, comic novel, to which Phiz's illustrations are well suited but seem thin – hardly surprising since it overlapped with *Bleak House*, a book guaranteed to drain the most vigorous artistic invention.

By 1856, the year *The Martins of Cro' Martin* was published, Phiz had picked up energy again – and so had Lever, after a visit to Ireland, where he set the novel. Lever's enthusiasm for his old homeland was catching, and Phiz had plenty of opportunity to recall the scenes he had witnessed himself. His old inventiveness returned in plate after plate of crowd scenes and Irish landscape, and in his realisation of Lever's most impressive heroine, Mary Martin. However, the illustration 'Sir Lucius', Phiz's attempt to render 'an animal of surpassing symmetry, in all the pride of high condition',[39] is a surprising failure for one so adept at drawing horses. Poor Sir Lucius is surpassingly asymmetrical and suffers from severe curvature of the neck and a tiny head. Perhaps Phiz was trying so hard to be George Stubbs that he confounded himself.[40]

At times, as with *The Dodd Family Abroad*, Phiz's energy flagged. The etchings for *Davenport Dunn* (1859) are disappointing, except for nine compelling dark plates. This may have something to do with Phiz's working concurrently on *A Tale of Two Cities*. It was also the year of his return to London.

Lever was busy with Foreign Office work in La Spezia during the writing of *One of Them* (1861) for Dickens's magazine, *All the Year Round*. His lack of attention to the illustrations in *One of Them* affected Phiz, whose work is listless; the recent arrival of his ninth child might also partly explain this. All the pictures are horizontal, except the frontispiece and title page, even when the subject matter insists they should be vertical; it is as though Phiz did not even have enough strength to turn the plate.

The illustrations for *Barrington* (1862) are even thinner, but Lever was pleased enough with the book to dedicate it to Dickens. Phiz clearly had Dickens on his mind, too, because his Aunt Dinah is remarkably like Aunt Betsey in *David Copperfield*. When Dickens received *Barrington* and saw the tired, derivative illustrations, he must have been more than ever convinced that it was time for a new look for his novels. In 1863 he hired Marcus Stone to illustrate *Our Mutual Friend*.

Phiz marked the end of his twenty-six-year collaboration with Charles Lever in 1865 when he illustrated *Luttrell of Arran*. The book clearly took his fancy because his illustrations are lively and inventive. He took particularly kindly to the maid, Molly Ryan, who in one image bears a huge basket of fish and looks for all the world like a Hogarthian shrimp girl; another image, 'Molly sees the Ghost of the Master', shriekingly recalls 'Tom Smart and the Chain', the drawing with which John Leech applied for work on *The Pickwick Papers*. After *Luttrell of Arran*, Lever changed publishers and wrote several books without illustrations. Whether this was his decision or Blackwood's is unknown, but the latter seems likely. He did, however, include illustrations in *The Bramleighs of Bishop's Folly*, and his final novel, *Lord Kilgobbin* (1872), has illustrations by Luke Fildes who had worked on Dickens's last book, *The Mystery of Edwin Drood* (1870).

In 1867, the Levers made their final move, to Trieste where Charles was appointed Consul. Life in Trieste depressed Lever, and his love of homeland never died. On his occasional visits to Ireland, he would stop in England on the way to see his friend Phiz, remembering the good old days. Gout and heart disease – the physical disease and the dis-ease caused

'Molly sees the Ghost of the Master', *Luttrell of Arran*, 1863

by despair over the death of his wife – took their toll, and Lever died in
Trieste on 1 June 1872. In 1878, Lever's complete works were published
in the Harry Lorrequer edition, and Phiz was charged with providing
designs for four wood engravings in each of the seven works that had not
previously contained illustrations.

Which was the more successful partnership, that of Phiz and Lever or
Phiz and Dickens? Certainly the best work for both authors is equally
fine, but more of the Lever plates reflect the rush with which Phiz had
to work, the consequent loss of detail, and the lack of a vigilant eye on
the part of the author.

On his final trip to Dublin, Lever dined at his old haunt, the University Club. 'Standing to receive cordial greetings,' Fitzpatrick tells us, 'his back leaning against a chiffonier on which some books lay, he sadly remarked that many once-familiar faces had gone. "You have still some old friends *at your back*," observed a friend, pointing behind Lever. The old author turned rapidly round, and found to his surprise "Lorrequer", "O'Malley", "Jack Hinton", and "Tom Burke". . . . Somebody having praised "Lorrequer", Lever merely said, "A poor thing – but how well Browne illustrated it!"'[41]

12

Work, Work, Work

'[The *Daily News* will] extinguish, but at the same time enlighten the *Times*, spifflicate the *Chronicle*, pull down the *Standard*, strip the *Herald*, smash the *Courier*, gouge the *Observer*, and astonish *John Bull*,'[2] wrote Phiz to Lever about Charles Dickens's new venture in 1845. Dickens was anxious to branch out into directions other than novel writing after sales of *Martin Chuzzlewit* had not fulfilled his expectations. He liked the idea of editing an important liberal newspaper, and just such a one had been waiting in the wings. Joseph Paxton had conceived the idea as early as 1840, and with the funds of various railway proprietors, the *Daily News* became more than a pipe dream. Dickens was hired as editor, and gathered a stable of prominent leader-writers. However, he was ill suited to the daily grind; after three months he handed over the editorial reins to John Forster but continued to supply the occasional short piece.

Wanting to minimise his living costs – he had six children by this time – Dickens decided to move to Switzerland in June 1846. The difficulty in

Letter from Charles Dickens to Phiz, 1856[1]

communicating between Lausanne and London (and then, making matters worse, Surrey) was tremendous, but seemed only to fuel Dickens's desire to supervise the pictures for his new novel, *Dombey and Son*. Through Phiz, he was determined to realise an abstraction – the theme of pride – that he was threading through the novel.

If this were not difficult enough for the artist, the author's long-distance determination created inevitable delays and discord. Dickens first sent the subjects for illustration to Forster in London; Forster forwarded the sketches to Phiz, who executed the sketches; Phiz then delivered them to Forster to forward to Lausanne for Dickens's comments. Only after Dickens had approved them, titled them, and communicated his desires to Forster, who sent the information along to Phiz, could the artist begin work on the plates. Nor was this a simple process. Cohen explains: 'First, his London partner, Robert Young, prepared the ground and sent each plate to Browne in the country in a specially constructed box; then the artist etched it and forwarded it back to Young in the city who did the biting-in while another assistant did the lettering for the title.'[3]

Illustrating for Dickens and Lever while they were living on the Continent was difficult enough, but the length of time it took for plates to be exchanged between England and America made working for American authors virtually impossible. Nonetheless, Phiz took on the challenge when he was asked to illustrate Cornelius Mathews's *The Career of Puffer Hopkins* (1842), a work which Edgar Allan Poe described as 'a clever satirical tale somewhat given to excess in caricature'.[4] Mathews was well aware of the problems inherent in illustrating at a remove and comments in his preface: 'It will be perceived that a portion of the text is illustrated by H.K. Browne, Esq., (PHIZ) of London. In justice to the artist, it should be added, that the distance, at which he labored from the author, has caused him to depart, in some particulars, from the conception it was the author's purpose to embody. As they are the first and only designs procured from that gentleman for America, the author ventures to add, that he regards them, with this reservation, as eminently ingenious and spirited.'[5] The challenge of fitting image to text at such a long distance proved so great that *Puffer Hopkins* remains the only work illustrated by Phiz for an American in its first edition.

When Phiz first started work on *Dombey and Son*, he was energised and keenly interested in the new project. The quality of his illustrations always rose in proportion to interest in a book and its author. In spite of the complexities enforced by distance, all went smoothly at first, and Dickens was pleased with his efforts. '. . . Browne seems to be getting on well. He will have a good subject in Paul's christening,'[6] wrote Dickens to Forster on 30 August, and the same day he sent a letter to Thomas Mitton, declaring: '. . . The first No. is considered very good indeed. So much so that Browne, who is generally the most indifferent fellow in the world, couldn't help writing me a long letter about it, and saying how pleased he was. I have taken immense pains, and think it strong.'[7] Again, a week later, Dickens writes to Forster: 'Browne is certainly interesting himself and taking pains. I think the cover is very good; perhaps with a little too much in it, but that is an ungrateful objection.'[8] Indeed it was ungrateful, considering that Dickens, in a letter to Forster, recommended that John Leech pay special attention to the Dombey cover when illustrating that year's Christmas book, *The Battle of Life*. He wrote, 'I should like each part to have a general illustration to it at the beginning, shadowing out its drift and bearing: much as Browne goes at that kind of thing on Dombey covers.'[9]

Dickens considered *Dombey and Son* a more serious book than his earlier works, and was filled with what Forster referred to as his nervous dread of caricature. The dread that his central, prideful character would be caricatured at the hands of his illustrator led him to suggest to Forster that Phiz use a living model for inspiration. 'The man for Dombey, if Browne could see him, the class man to a T, is Sir A— E—, of D's. I do wish he could get a glimpse of A, for he is the very Dombey.'[10] Forster was never able to contrive a glimpse of Sir A— for Phiz, but the illustrator, well aware of Dickens's anxiety, forwarded to Switzerland a sheet containing twenty-nine potential Dombeys, including the 'rather bold – rather red – handsome well-made – pompous stern – close shaved – close cut & stuffy formal'.[11] Once Dickens had indicated his preferences, Phiz set to work to illustrate pride personified, and even went to the trouble of sending Dickens two sketches of Mr Dombey for the second plate, one seated and one standing. Dickens chose Dombey seated, the one Phiz preferred, and approved the sketch.

Dickens loosened his hold on the illustrations of the second number a little, and Phiz slipped back into a more boisterous, humorous style, a bad misjudgement which caused Dickens to rant to Forster that the plates were so dreadful that they made his legs curl up in distaste.[12] Worse was yet to come. On 4 November, Dickens wrote to Forster: 'The best subject for Browne will be at Mrs. Pipchin's; and if he liked to do a quiet, odd thing, Paul, Mrs. Pipchin and the Cat, by the fire, would be very good for the story. I earnestly hope he will think it worth a little extra care.'[13] Phiz did,

Studies for Dombey

indeed, take extra care and produced one of his most charming etchings, but intense pressure of time meant Dickens did not look at the sketch before it was etched and went to press. On first seeing it, he raged to Forster:

I am really *distressed* by the illustration of Mrs. Pipchin and Paul. It is so frightfully and wildly wide of the mark. Good Heaven! in the commonest and most literal construction of the text, it is all wrong. She is described as an old lady, and Paul's 'miniature arm-chair' is mentioned more than once. He ought to be sitting in a little arm-chair down in a corner of the fireplace, staring up at her. I can't say what pain and vexation it is to be so utterly misrepresented. I would cheerfully have given a hundred pounds to have kept this illustration out of the book. He never could have got that idea of Mrs Pipchin if he had attended to the text. Indeed I think he does better without the text; for then the notion is made easy to him in short description, and he can't help taking it in.[14]

The editors of Dickens's letters are quick to point out that he was hardly fair to Phiz and that the text does not say Paul is looking or staring *up* at her. They comment: 'His "little arm-chair by the fire", evidently visualized by Dickens as a low chair, but not further described, was taken by Browne, excusably, as a child's "high chair"; . . . Mrs. Pipchin is sufficiently witch-like, and certainly not young, though not old enough to please Dickens and not "stooping" as in the initial description. The real trouble no doubt was that the author had a clear picture in his memory of a particular person, Mrs Roylance.'[15] (Mrs Roylance was the old lady in reduced circumstances who boarded children, including Dickens himself while his father was in prison.)

Paul and Mrs Pipchin', *Dombey and Son*, 1847

'Paul and Mrs. Pipchin' became a popular image with the public, and in August of 1847, John Leech made it notorious in a cartoon for *Punch*. He replaced Paul's face with that of John Russell, the prime minister, and put Sir Robert Peel in Mrs Pipchin's chair, having dressed and coiffed him to look like Mr Dombey.[16] Eventually, Phiz's illustration even managed to worm its way into Dickens's affection; when *The Story of Little Dombey* (an abridged edition of *Dombey and Son*, arranged by the author for his public readings) was published, its cover bore a wood engraving of the image that he had so excoriated, that of Paul in his chair by the fire.

It was fortunate for Phiz, who could be easily hurt, that Dickens used Forster as a sounding board so the author's immediate and sometimes

John Leech, Lord Russell as Paul Dombey, *Punch*, 1847

unreasonable anger went through the filter of an intermediary. Phiz was not the only object of Dickens's ire. John Leech, too, was castigated in a letter to Forster regarding his illustration of Marion with Alfred Warden in one of Dickens's Christmas books, *The Battle of Life*:

> When I first saw [Leech's illustration], it was with horror and agony not to be expressed. Of course I need not tell *you* my dear fellow, Warden has no business in the elopement scene. *He* was never there. In the first hot sweat of this surprise and novelty, I was going to implore the printer of that sheet to be stopped, and the figure taken out of the block. But when I thought of the pain this might give to our tender-hearted Leech; and that what was such a monstrosity to me, as never having entered my brain, may not so present itself to others, I became more composed.[17]

In his instructions dated 6 December 1846, Dickens decided to write a short synopsis for Phiz of the scene to be illustrated, the one called 'Dr. Blimber's young gentlemen as they appeared when enjoying themselves'. He points out that Doctor Blimber only takes ten young gentlemen in his school – boys who, weighted down by learning, have 'blown before their time'. He asks Phiz to illustrate the atmosphere of weariness among the boys, saying, 'All the young gentlemen have great weights on their minds. They are haunted by verbs, noun-substantives, roots, and syntactic passages.'[18]

What was going on in Phiz's head that caused him to depart so dramatically from Dickens's clearly prescribed request for ten boys and arbitrarily add an extra seven young gentlemen? Was he just carried away by the fun of it, or was he making a carefully timed jab at Dickens's despotism? He certainly did enjoy himself with the image, and went so far as to include, from his own imagination, four lively urchins whose antics mock the dull seriousness of Dr Blimber's seventeen scholars; a high-flying kite expressing the freedom the scholars do not have; and a cameo sketch of a donkey ridden by a very young child and a clownishly capped man exuding a whiff of self-portraiture. Strangely enough, Dickens voiced no objection to Phiz's deviation from the specified number of scholars, and wrote to Catherine that 'Browne's plates are much better than usual'.[19]

By March 1847, Dickens was back in England, thus solving the illustration-from-a-great-distance problem. He and Phiz were once again at work in their old back-and-forth collaboration. On 15 March, he wrote to the artist at his studio, a letter that escaped Phiz's conflagration. Dickens

claims that the sketch for 'Major Bagstock is delighted to have that opportunity' is admirable and 'the women quite perfect'. He requests that the
Native, although dark brown, be in European costume. Then he continues in a more social vein: 'I shall propoge[20] to you, a Trip to Leamington
together. We might go one day and return the next'.[21] He concludes the
letter by telling Phiz about William Hall's funeral, and reminisces about
the time they all drank claret in the Counting-house at the time of Queen
Victoria's visit to the city. It is a charming, affectionate letter from one
friend to another.

The critic Queenie Leavis saw *Dombey and Son* as a significant mile-
stone in Phiz's development, and argued that the major illustrations to that
novel 'represent a great enlargement of the powers of an artist who had
hitherto been most at home in Hogarthian satire and figuring the mean,
the ridiculous, the pretentious, the contemptible and the depraved'. She
continues: '"Phiz" has now shown himself equal to the demand . . . to
make clear to ["unintelligent readers"] who is being satirized and who is
to be taken seriously; more delicate distinctions are being required in
Dombey and a greater range of feelings than merely to chronicle fierce and
violent actions or comic overthrows'.[22] What she is recognising is Phiz's
new-found ability to represent abstraction.

In *Dombey and Son* Phiz first tackled the challenge of representing darkness, threat, and sorrow by using a new technique. His task was to illustrate the following lines: 'As [Carker] paused, . . . looking over the gloomy
flat where the slender trees marked out the way, again that flight of Death
came rushing up, again went on, impetuous and resistless, again was nothing
but a horror in his mind, dark as the scene and undefined as its remotest
verge.'[23] For the illustration, 'On the dark road', Phiz turned the plate
horizontally and used a ruling machine, which pushed a bank of needles
across the wax ground on the plate, creating a background of narrow
stripes, akin to mezzotinting. (The technique is sometimes referred to as
'machine-tinting'.) He then drew into dark areas to make them blacker
and produced a variety of greys by stopping-out other areas. To retain
dazzling whites, he burnished away the ruled lines and stopped-out those
areas completely on the first and all subsequent visits to the acid.

Phiz's use of a ruling machine was a divergence from the more popular
aquatint[24] method used by other etchers. He may have disliked aquatint's
time-consuming use of resin, a messy substance which, if inhaled, could
injure the lungs. With his ruling machine he created tones with less
nuisance. (After his experiments on Lever's *Roland Cashel* (1850), he no

longer used the ruling machine for light topics; the brights were never bright enough.)

'On the Dark Road' is one of the most completely successful of all Phiz's images. A long, slow diagonal slices down from receding poplar trees in the upper right to the coach and standing figure of windswept Carker, and moves on down through the coachman (who provides an opposing diagonal with his whip) to the four horses racing towards the bottom left of the picture. Phiz took enormous technical care with the plate, and its atmosphere of menace is enhanced by the addition of details: a black bird, a dark pool, a lowering sky, a leaning finger-post, and the rolling eyes and hot breath of horses.

'On the Dark Road', *Dombey and Son*

Dombey and Son became a favourite with the public, and enjoyed print runs of up to 34,000 copies per part. Thackeray, who was concurrently writing *Vanity Fair* (of which just 5,000 copies per part were printed) flung himself into the offices of *Punch*, and shouted: 'There's no writing against such power as this – one has not a chance! Read that chapter describing young Paul's death: it is unsurpassed – it is stupendous.'[25] One cannot help wondering whether, if Phiz had illustrated Thackeray's novel, sales of *Vanity Fair* would have been more vigorous. The artist was then at the height of his popularity.

In all, Phiz completed thirty-eight etchings, the wrapper design for the monthly parts, the vignette title page, and the frontispiece for *Dombey and Son*, a total which was his standard contribution for novels that appeared in twenty parts. Dickens finished the book in Brighton in March 1848, and Phiz took his sketch for the frontispiece (always the last illustration in a Dickens novel) to Brighton for Dickens's approval, where they would have enjoyed sea breezes and congratulating each other on completing the novel.

Dickens gave Phiz permission to produce extra illustrations for *Dombey and Son* (as in the case of *Barnaby Rudge*). The artist designed four portraits – Little Paul, Edith, Florence, and Alice – and these were engraved on steel plates by Edwards and Knight, under the supervision of Phiz and Robert Young. Dickens was delighted with the portraits, especially the one of Paul. Phiz presented him with the original sketches and set about painting the one of Little Paul in his nightshirt as a gift for him. Dickens responded ebulliently on 13 June 1848:

> A thousand thanks for the Dombey sketches, which I shall preserve and transmit as heirlooms.
>
> This afternoon, or Thursday, I shall be near the whereabout of the boy in the flannel gown, and will pay him an affectionate visit. But I warn you, now and beforehand (and this is final you'll observe) that you are not a going to back out of the pigmental finishing of said boy, for if ever I had a boy of my own, that boy is
> MINE!
> And, as the Demon says at the Surrey [a circus]
> I claim my Victim.
> Ha! Ha! Ha!
> At which you will imagine me going down a sulphurous trap, with the boy in my grasp – and you will please not to imagine him merely, in my grasp, but to hand him over.
> For which this is your warrant and requirement.
> CHARLES DICKENS[26]
> Witness
> William X Topping
>   his
>   Groom

With the success of the first four portraits, Phiz decided to speculate further, and prepared a further eight images of characters from *Dombey and Son.* They were published in sets, in green wrappers, by Chapman and Hall, at the cost of two shillings, and such was their hold on the public imagination that Phiz's portraits found themselves hanging on the walls of homes all across the country.

To celebrate the conclusion of *Dombey and Son*, Dickens held a dinner on 11 April 1848. His guests included Phiz (illustrator), Thackeray (rival), Macready (actor), Jerdan (writer, editor of the *Literary Gazette*), Forster (loyal friend), Beard (reporter), Lemon (editor of *Punch*), D'Orsay (cosmopolitan dandy), Evans (publisher), Frank Stone (portrait painter, illustrator, good friend, 'tedious bore'[27]), Ainsworth (literary lion, with whom Phiz would have conversed about their recent collaboration and planned their next), George Hogarth (journalist, father-in-law), and Henry Burnett (actor, singer, brother-in-law) – a mixed bunch from the various walks of Dickens's life, all of whom Henry Burnett entertained with song after dinner. It is no surprise that Macready comments that the occasion was 'strangely assorted. Still dear Dickens was happy, and I was very, very happy to see him so. God bless him.'[28]

Phiz had known Harrison Ainsworth, ten years his senior, from at least the time of *Nicholas Nickleby* when Ainsworth gave him and Dickens an introduction to his friend James Crossley in Manchester. The Ainsworth–Phiz collaboration was amicable and the friendship enduring. The artist first provided illustrations for Ainsworth in 1844, when he contributed to a work titled 'Revelations of London' in *Ainsworth's Magazine*. ('Revelations of London', containing Phiz's etchings, was eventually completed and published in volume form as *Auriol*, in 1865.) In 1847, Phiz was called in to provide two additional plates for a new edition of *Old St Paul's*. 'Excellent illustrations', cries Thomson, adding, 'The remaining etchings by another illustrator [Franklin] do not add much to the value of the book.'[29] Ainsworth hired Phiz again to illustrate a new edition of his novel, *Crichton*, in 1849, a book for which Thackeray had proposed himself as illustrator as early as 1837. 'I'll do anything that's possible to heighten the charms of your immortal book the admirable Crichton,' Thackeray wrote to Ainsworth, 'and with this noble purpose this little scrap I write on, to say I'll do you drawings such as never man had sight on; and neat vignettes wh: all the world will surely take delight on.'[30] Ainsworth obviously recommended him to his publisher, Macrone, but Thackeray lost his nerve when he tried his hand at etching the designs. 'I tried them on the Copper, but what I did was so bad, that I felt mortified at my failure,'[31] he wrote to Macrone, and the publisher decided not to commission him. It is tempting to imagine that Phiz repaid an artistic debt by inspiring Daumier's 'Man on a Rope' (at least a little) with his frontispiece for *Crichton*.

Ainsworth was an enormously attractive man with a sunny temperament, curly brown hair, brilliant eyes, and a rosy complexion. As a boy he had a consuming passion for making and exploding fireworks; as an adult, he loved crackerjack conversation. His cousin, Edward Harrison, likened his beauty to that of a woman. Samuel Carter Hall claimed that Ainsworth, the 'Adonis of booksellers', was the best kind of gentleman his native city of Manchester ever sent forth,[32] and Henry Vizetelly noted, 'He was somewhat of a fop in dress . . . and made an unnecessary display of the many rings he wore, but his manners were singularly pleasant, and there was not a particle of deceit.'[33] Phiz and Ainsworth collaborated happily, always making sure that illustration and text went hand in hand.

But Phiz was not the exclusive property of Charles Dickens and Harrison Ainsworth. He was in demand to illustrate both classic and contemporary authors, and one of the strangest books he ever worked on was *Fanny the Little Milliner* by Charles Rowcroft (1846). The title page claims 'With illustrations by Phiz', and indeed he did begin, in a style which much resembles his work for *Dombey and Son*. However, opposite page nine can be found an illustration entitled 'The Explosion', signed not by Phiz but by Thomas Onwhyn. It is as clear a realisation of a newly escaped fart as is possible to imagine, and has absolutely no relationship to the text whatsoever. How it came to be there (printer's error? printer's joke? Onwhyn's ambition to oust Phiz?) is a mystery, but the result was that Phiz contributed just four illustrations, and it was left to Onwhyn to complete the final six – a task in which he made no further deviations but remained woodenly faithful to the text.

Phiz may already have been irritated by the other man's treading on his territory. Onwhyn was rather a shady character who had illustrated pirated editions of *Pickwick Papers* and *Nicholas Nickleby*, published by Grattan in 1837 and 1838 respectively, in which he signed his images 'Sam Weller'.

During 1849 and 1850 Phiz was hard at work on *David Copperfield* for Dickens, *Roland Cashel* for Lever, and *Crichton* for Ainsworth, as well as creating dozens of images for other books and magazines. One of his most interesting departures from novel-illustrating appeared in the form of a handsome volume entitled *A Practical Guide for the Tailor's Cutting Room: Being a Treatise on Measuring and Cutting Clothing in all Styles, and for Every Period of Life from Childhood to Old Age* by J.A. Couts. Charles Sessler, the

Philadelphia bookseller, describes it thus: 'With 27 very clever full page designs for fashion by Phiz (13 of which are finely handcolored) and numerous other illustrations. . . . The artist while he has carefully delineated every seam, etc. of the garments of his figures, has at the same time, succeeded in giving a series of life-like and characteristic sketches of society and manners.'[34] It is delightful to see Phiz operating on a large scale, wittily bringing out character in figures which might otherwise be merely clotheshorses, and adding backgrounds to illustrate the environments in which the military uniforms, livery, and day clothes would be worn. The background details in 'The Consultation' are particularly intriguing. The

'The Consultation', J. A. Couts, *A Practical Guide for the Tailor's Cutting Room*, 1849

patient, humpbacked but exquisitely tailored by Couts, is seeking advice from his doctor, who himself suffers from a displaced hip but is also exquisitely tailored. The patient's top hat and 'Gamp' (with a neatly bearded head as its handle) rest on a chair beside the splay-legged table, while a bust with roving eyes and several medical tomes rest on the table. On the wall in the background hang two pictures, one of John Hunter (1728–1793), the physiologist and surgeon who specialised in operating on distorted joints; the other is of Jesus healing the sick. Above the door of the medicine cabinet stands a bust of Galen, the physician and celebrated medical writer of the classical era, while on the floor lies a copy of the *Lancet*, the cutting-edge British medical journal.

Dickens began writing *David Copperfield* in February 1849, after a mighty struggle to name a hero who began his literary existence as Thomas Mag, became David Mag, and was finally transformed into David Copperfield. The author had recently tried to write the beginning of an autobiography, which he cast aside, but Forster suggested that he continue to use 'I' rather than 'he' in writing his new novel, thus giving himself easier access to remembered material. *David Copperfield* thus became by far the most autobiographical of Dickens's works, and Forster also pointed out that his hero's initials, D.C., were the reversal of C.D. Certainly the novel could not have been dearer to Dickens's heart, and it would become his 'favourite child'.

Author and illustrator set to work, and on 4 May 1849, Dickens wrote to Phiz:

> I send you the second chapter. The proofs have been delayed, I find, by Bradbury's illness, and Hivins's [Evans] absence.
>
> Will you come and dine here tomorrow week, at $\frac{1}{4}$ before 7? We shall have two or three people to dinner, and perhaps a little good music in the evening. Ever faithfully, CD[35]

It is evident here and earlier that Phiz's wife, Susannah, was not included in Dickens's dinner parties. Whether this was because it never occurred to Dickens to invite her; or because Susannah found it impossible to leave her growing brood; or because she was perhaps related (at least in Dickens's mind) to G.W.M. Reynolds, the author who had so pilloried Dickens in *Reynolds's Miscellany*, and was hence *persona non grata* at his table; or because she simply did not enjoy being in the heady company of Dickens and his friends – is anybody's guess.

On arriving at the party, Thomas Carlyle delighted Dickens by quoting Mrs Gummidge in response to a question about his health: 'I am a lone lorn creetur' and everythink goes contrairy with me.' But his wife, Jane, in an acid commentary about the evening, tore strips off the Dickenses for their extravagant entertainment with its pyramids of figs, raisins, and oranges, and candles rising out of huge bouquets of artificial flowers. The old poet, Samuel Rogers, was also a victim of her tongue, being described as someone 'who ought to have been buried long ago, so old and ill-natured he is grown'.[36] Mrs Gaskell, in a letter to her friend Anne Green, was altogether kinder about the evening and its principal players:

> . . . There were numbers of people in the room. Mr Rogers (the old poet, who is 86, and looked very unfit to be in such a large party,) Douglas Jerrold, Mr & Mrs Carlyle, Hablot Browne, who illustrated Dickens' works, Mr Forster, Mr and Mrs Tagart, a Mr Kenyon . . . In the evening quantities of other people came in . . . Frank Stone, the artist, Leech & his wife, Benedict the great piano-forte player, Sims Reeves, the singer, Thackeray, Lord Dudley Stuart, Lord Headfort, Lady Yonge, Lady Lovelace, Lady Dufferin, and a quantity of others whose names I did not hear. We heard some beautiful music. Mr Tom Taylor was there too, who writes those comical ballads in Punch. . . . There were some nice little Dickens' children in the room, – who were so polite, and well-trained. We came away at last feeling we had seen so many people and things that day that we were quite confused; only that we should be glad to remember we had *done* it . . .[37]

Because of the crush of people (not exactly the two or three friends that Dickens had advertised in his invitation to Phiz) this was probably one of those evenings where the artist installed himself in a quiet corner or peered from behind curtains,[38] quietly gathering images for his visual store.

David Copperfield almost seemed to write itself, and by the end of July, Dickens was ready for a break at the seaside and a chance to get away from the importunities of Robert Seymour's widow, who was claiming that her husband was the mind behind *Pickwick*, and hoping for remuneration. The Dickens family left en masse for the Isle of Wight, and may have visited the Brownes in Surrey on their way. It is possible, too, that 'Aunt Kate' was also visiting the family and gave Dickens a present. He wrote to 'Miss Browne' shortly after his arrival at Bonchurch:

Mr Charles Dickens presents his compliments to Miss Browne, and begs to thank her sincerely for her extremely pretty gift. He is very proud of that mark of her remembrance, and assures her that he accepts it with the utmost pleasure.[39]

At Bonchurch, the author soon surrounded himself with an array of guests, including his artist friends: Phiz, Leech, Frank Stone, and Augustus Egg. Leech commemorated the event with a drawing of a picnic and the arrival there of an 'enormous wopps', which threw the party into much consternation. Most of the characters are recognisable, and Phiz appears

John Leech, 'Awful Appearance of a "Wopps" at a Pic-nic', *Punch*, 1849

to be seated front and centre with his back to the artist, evidenced by the particular kind of flat hat that he pictured in many of his self-portrait sketches.

If *Copperfield* were indeed autobiographical, Phiz was uncannily able to enter into the spirit of Dickens's real memories. He managed to capture Micawber's grandiose and improvident nature – based on Dickens's own father – in a manner that Dickens called 'uncommonly characteristic and capital'.[40] Phiz seems to be literally under Dickens's skin, and Cohen

'Restoration of Mutual Confidence between Mr and Mrs Micawber',
David Copperfield, 1850

remarks: 'Not since *Pickwick* had Dickens been so openly appreciative of
Browne's efforts. Never again would he be so pleased with the artist or
with himself'.[41]

The two men worked particularly hard on the image called 'I make
myself known to my Aunt,' and Phiz produced a series of sketches, both
vertical and horizontal, for Dickens's consideration, marking them with
questions: 'So?', 'So?', 'or − so − so?' Their final choice was inspired, and
in the plate, Phiz matched Dickens's intent and, within a single image,
depicted the past, present, and future of the hero.[42] A neat trick, indeed,
especially as Phiz also manages to include images from his own present
to accompany Dickens's imagined past: a house in the country and boys
on donkeys cavorting in the background.

Occasionally Dickens wrote too close to reality when portraying some
of his characters. One such was the dwarf, Miss Mowcher, whom he originally planned to portray as a malevolent character. The real dwarf was
Mrs Seymour Hill, a manicurist and chiropodist. She had absolutely no
trouble recognising herself, and wrote immediately to Dickens, threatening legal action and declaring: 'I have suffered long and much from my
personal deformities but never before at the hands of a Man so highly

'I Make Myself Known to my Aunt', *David Copperfield*

gifted as Charles Dickens . . . Now you have made my nights sleepless
and my daily work tearful'.[43] Dickens was mortified, and quickly
responded that, while the likeness had something to do with her, it was
based far more on someone else. He promised to change the character
so that the reader would remember her with affection, a promise that he
kept. Mrs Hill was mollified. Phiz's illustration, with its twinkling eyes
and impressive feathered hat (merely a bonnet in Dickens's description)
did not upset Mrs Hill.

Edgar Browne met Mrs Hill when he was a boy, at the home of his
uncle, John Moxon. '[At] Hanover Terrace . . . I saw the only Dickens
character that I ever beheld quite complete with my own eyes . . . the

etching was remarkably like her, though I do not think my father ever saw her . . . She was driven on her professional rounds in a very narrow little brougham of a kind known as a pillbox, because it was patronised by doctors. I am sorry to say I contributed to a slight accident which she suffered when she was visiting professionally at Regent's Park. I had been concerned with one or two friends in an assault and repulse on the stairs with peashooters; as the little creature came down the stairs, she slipped on some of the peas, and sat down very suddenly and alarmingly. We restored her with a glass of sherry, and she sat on the lowest stair rocking her body to and fro, saying as a sort of refrain between the sips, "You see the body is so long, and the legs so short, and stairs are difficult," all quite in the genuine Dickens manner.'[44]

'I Make the Acquaintance of Miss Mowcher', *David Copperfield*

'My lamp burns low, and I have written far into the night', wrote Dickens on 21 October 1850, as he neared the end of *David Copperfield*. 'Oh, my dear Forster, if I were to say half of what *Copperfield* makes me feel to-night, how strangely, even to you, I should be turned inside-out! I seem to be sending some part of myself into the Shadowy World.'[45] Phiz, too, may have felt strangely torn about concluding work on a novel he had illustrated with so much imagination and confidence, but as he drew his final image, the vignette for the title page, he illustrated not shadows but the pleasures of life drawing him back to reality: an open sky with scudding clouds, seagulls whirling, the warmth of a fire burning in a little home, and, best of all, a girl child like his own little Emma. This image is a reminder that Phiz occasionally had the upper hand. Contrary to Dickens's

'Little Emily' *David Copperfield*

description of a beached but upright boat, Phiz overturned the boat-that-became-a-house in the service of artistic composition.

In the gap between *David Copperfield* and *Bleak House*, Phiz produced on his own account two albums of pictures 'suitable for framing.' The first, *Home Pictures*, depicts sentimental, domestic scenes, where the walls, screens, and furniture are absolutely crammed with paintings by – Phiz! The second album, *The Five Senses*, appeared in a large format which sold for five shillings plain and seven shillings and sixpence coloured, and was decidedly more robust than the demure *Home Pictures*. It depicts mischievous

'Feeling', Phiz, *The Five Senses*, 1851

boys performing various pranks which demonstrate the senses of seeing, hearing, tasting, smelling, and feeling. Once again, Phiz probably drew on his own family for inspiration: his first three children, Edgar, Charles, and Walter, were the right age to be prototypes of the boys in *The Five Senses*.

'Feeling' is amusing to 'read'. On the left stands a desk, bearing an inkwell, a book, and the first volume of a dictionary. Above it, an arm wielding a birch is about to mete out punishment. Graffiti have been carved into the side of the desk, and the names include Jones, Brown, S. Smith, Tomkins, HKB, and R.Y. (Robert Young). Leaning against the desk is a caricature of the schoolmaster, which may be the cause of the punishment about to be inflicted on the main subject, an anxious young boy. He has dropped his Latin book, entitled *Gradus ad Parnass* [sic],[46] and his slate lies in smithereens. Other possible reasons for his punishment are the tops and marbles scattered on the floor. The young mischief-maker holds his hand out for the birch, while eleven others pupils watch the action out of the corner of their eyes. One of them, suffering the pain of toothache, has a swollen left cheek and his head tied up in a scarf. Another is highly amused by the fate of the wrongdoer; he, too, has drawn the wrong kind of image on the back of his slate. Phiz has placed a door, a map of Russia, and a hat rail in the background, and has been unable to resist the temptation to insert a face on the cap on the right.

Also between *Copperfield* and the publication of *Bleak House*, Phiz illustrated children's books by Ann Hawkshaw, Julia Maitland, and Harriet Myrtle. These books were sentimental and inspirational and left him little room to exercise his humorous muscle. However, in 1854, in Mary and

'Ponto and the Spectacles', Mary and Elizabeth Kirby, *The Talking Bird*, 1851

Elizabeth Kirby's *The Talking Bird*, he created one of his funnier images for children, that of 'Ponto and the Spectacles'. Phiz's output of work for children (as opposed to his images *of* children) is relatively small, unlike that of his son, Gordon Browne, who became a prodigious illustrator of children's books.

At the same time, during the hiatus, Phiz contributed several frontispieces to reprints of the works of Bulwer-Lytton, and illustrated Smedley's *Lewis Arundel* and Lever's *The Daltons*, as well as providing images for works by the Irish writers Sheridan Le Fanu and Samuel Lover (his companion on his early visit to Lever in Brussels). Sheridan Le Fanu (1814–1873) was born in Dublin, and was, like Phiz, of Huguenot descent. He worked with Charles Lever on the *Dublin University Magazine*, later becoming its editor. Lever's biographer, W.J. Fitzpatrick, calls Le Fanu 'a truly formidable competitor' who more than once caused Charles Lever 'to look to his laurels'.[47] Le Fanu's novels were sensational, terrifying, and wildly imaginative, and in *The Fortunes of Colonel Torlogh O'Brien* he holds nothing back from his descriptions of torture, violent death, and simpering love. Phiz's illustrations for this book are described by Thomson as being 'repulsive from their disagreeable and shocking subjects', and two scenes in particular are 'far too horrid for illustration, and they are the more painful because the artist seemed to have gloried in his labour on them.'[48]

Phiz revelled in the storytelling capabilities of his Irish authors: Lever, Lover, Le Fanu, and Carleton. Even though his Irish crowd scenes can sometimes look like London or Yorkshire crowd scenes, his imagination catches fire when given subjects such as 'A Legend of Knockmany' in Carleton's *Tales and Stories of the Irish Peasantry*.

In November 1851, Dickens began *Bleak House* and so firm were his ideas for the novel that he was able straight away to give Phiz a clear outline for the wrapper of the monthly parts. Phiz laced the image with satire, and in his hands the wrapper became the playground of judges and lawyers cruelly using their clients as pieces in games of chess, battledore, and blindman's buff. Dickens was filled with righteous anger against the labyrinthine wranglings of the law courts, and in *Bleak House* he railed against a society that so thoroughly exploited its people. With Phiz by his side, he took on the forces of chaos and darkness. Phiz produced some typically memorable scenes and characters, like Jo the Crossing Sweeper, Mr Guppy and the Smallweed family. But during the course of the novel, his vision so deepened and darkened that it became impos-

'A Legend of Knockmany', William Carleton, *Tales and Stories of the Irish Peasantry*, 1854

sible to believe that the man who designed *The Pickwick Papers* could be the same man who created what are referred to as the *Bleak House* 'dark plates'.

Dickens had not fully appreciated the mood created by Phiz's dark plates – the aforementioned one for *Dombey and Son* ('On the Dark Road') and another for *David Copperfield* ('The River') – and Phiz refrained from using them in *Bleak House* until about two thirds through the book. Then suddenly recognising that the dark plate technique would be perfect for conveying the deepening crises Dickens was unfolding, he could restrain himself no longer, and as soon as he produced the illustration for 'The Ghost's Walk', it became clear that dark plates complemented the text.

'Jo the Crossing Sweeper', *Bleak House*, 1852–3

He went on to contribute nine dark plates in the last third of the novel, and a tenth for the frontispiece.

At least one critic felt that Phiz had gone overboard, and took him to task for 'The Black Art' in satirical fashion (while taking side swipes at Ruskin, Gothic medievalism, and the recently founded Pre-Raphaelite Brotherhood). Writing in the magazine *Diogenes*, in September 1853, he noted 'the very marked progress Mr Hablot K. Browne has been making in an entirely new style of art', as the illustrations to *Bleak House* became darker and darker by the month:

Now this is entirely as it should be. None of your nasty pre-Raffaelite

'Mr Guppy's Entertainment', *Bleak House*

'The Smallweed Family', *Bleak House*

rubbish, drawing every figure, every tree, every brick wall, just as they look in reality, – as if Art had nothing better to do than copy Nature! . . . The genuine artist may now take pre-eminence above the simple draughtsman. No longer need his mighty spirit stoop to the indignity of learning drawing: but with the simplicity that ever forms a part of grandeur he need only dip his finger in the ink-stand, blacking bottle, or what else may be at hand, then dash it any how, with true poetic frenzy, on the paper . . . [49]

'The Black Art' was not entirely Phiz's fault. The publisher had taken to reproducing his images by lithography (in which designs are copied onto stone with a greasy material and printed impressions taken from them), a method which did not require Phiz's intervention; however, the mechanically ruled, close lines of the dark plates blotched so badly when transferred to stone that lithography was clearly unsuitable. Phiz was naturally upset about a method of reproduction for which he was not responsible, and expressed his anger in the following undated letter to Dickens, in which the first page is missing:

. . . any want of care in the etching – but to the care in the printing. I am told that from 15 to 25,000 are monthly printed from lithographic transfers – some of these impressions, when the etching is light and sketchy, will pass muster with the uninitiated – but, the more elaborate the etching – the more villainous the transfer – bearing about the same relative resemblance to the plate impressions as the coarse illegible type of the cheap pirated edition of a popr. work does the well-printed page of the real Simon.[50] – I believe you are quite unconscious of the great difference in the impressions – and of the manifest injury they are daily doing me, or you would in justice to me, and in fairness to the public endeavour to do away with the necessity for this wretched printing by supplying me with hints (at least) of the subjects a clear month in advance – Otherwise there must be complaints to the last chapter – and this monthly stoning (which may be very fine sport to Messrs. B. & E.) will be the death of
    Yours sincerely
    Hablot K. Browne.
Charles Dickens, Esqre.

I shall endeavour to procure some impressions to give you ocular demonstration of what I mean.[51]

It would have been impossible for Phiz NOT to create dark plates for *Bleak House*, as they perfectly convey an atmosphere in which evil institutions dominate the lives of the powerless. Harvey claims that 'Browne's small fugitive figures reflect . . . the novel's general intimation of the pitiable helplessness and isolation of hounded human beings',[52] and Cohen points out that six of the dark plates have no human figures at all, and in the four that do, only one figure is discernible. She continues: 'The insignificance of the characters in the artist's plates sensitively reflects their insignificance in the author's narrative, which depicts a society whose institutions dwarf, isolate, and too often destroy members. As Dickens increasingly abandoned his usual satiric devices, finding them insufficient to portray his society, so Browne gradually had to dispense with the traditional methods and subjects of graphic satire.'[53]

In the course of working together on *Bleak House*, Phiz and Dickens apparently remained on friendly terms, even though the devilish remarques in a sketch for the final dark plate, 'The Mausoleum at Chesney Wold' (plate 31), might intimate otherwise. Dickens did not rant to Forster about any mistakes in the illustrations, and Phiz seems to have thrown himself wholeheartedly into his work, even though his line in the conventional plates was not quite as crisp and fresh as it was in, say, *Martin Chuzzlewit*. In the summer of 1853, Dickens, who had been ill, went to Boulogne to recover his strength and to complete the last few instalments of *Bleak House*. He obviously missed his artist, as we can see in the letter he wrote to Phiz on 29 June:

First, I beg to report myself, thank God, thoroughly well again. I was truly sensible of your hearty note, and of the right good will with which you fell to work at the plates under those discouraging circumstances.

Secondly, I send the subjects for the next No. Will you let me see the sketches here by post.

Thirdly, I am now ready with four subjects for the concluding double No. and will post them to you tomorrow or next day!!!!!!!!!!!!!!!!

Fourthly, I wish you would so contrive your arrangements – if so disposed [sic] – as to come and pay us a visit here. I don't know whether you know Boulogne well; but, well known, it is a very capital place, with quite as much that is quaint and picturesque among the fishing-people and their quarter of the Town, as is to be found (if you'll believe me in a whisper) at Naples. We purpose remaining here until the middle of October – have a queer Doll's house of many rooms – and really beautiful gardens. I think you would like it and be amused, and would find much worthy of note and afterwards useful in these parts. Now I have in contemplation, on Monday the 22nd August to do the best French dinner that can be done in these regions to celebrate the conclusion of *Bleak House*. Unto which festival, Bradbury, and Evans, and Lemon, stand pledged to come over. Can you not, on such good notice, arrange to come with them, and to remain after them – taking a good week or fortnight of fresh air and change. We shall be truly delighted to receive you. Consider, O man of business, and at your leisure reply.[54]

Phiz apparently wrote accepting the invitation, and Dickens responded a week later in one of his most playful moods:

> Boulogne, Mecreday, Juil-ly 6, 1853
>
> Mon cher Brune,
>
> If I express myself, not altogether in the perfect English of your country, pardon me for tout-ce que je fais. J'ai si longtemps demeuré – on the continent – que j'ai presqu'oublié my native tongue.
>
> My friend, il me parait – that the esquisses seront – admirable – when they shall be finished according to your so wonderous power of art. I them return – ci-enclos. Yet I am enchanted of the hope you give me – de vous recevoir chez moi à Boulogne! There is a great deal of wind here, almost all the days. Madame et Mademoiselle themselves remember of that Englishman, Brune the immortal, and to him send a thousand friendships.
>
> Receive
>
> My Amiable Brune
>
> The assurance of my distinguished consideration,
>
> Votre tout dévoué, Dickens[55]

In the end, Phiz could not go to the dinner. The reason was probably the 'discouraging circumstances' resulting in Susannah's delivering a stillborn infant at the end of July. Phiz would certainly not have wanted to leave his grieving wife at that point.

Critics believe that Phiz's illustrations for Dickens's next novel were inadequate and unnecessary, that author and artist had diverged, and Phiz had been left behind.[56] Cohen claims: 'Browne's greatest problem was that by now Dickens usurped his very function. The author had always written unusually pictorial prose. In *Little Dorrit* his writing became so graphically suggestive yet selective that it needed little visual help.'[57] Brian Rosenberg enlarges on Cohen's theory; he suggests that the illustrations 'do not succeed because they cannot succeed, that any attempt to translate into visual form so unvisualizable a text is doomed to failure or at least to creating a sense of disjunction between linguistic and pictorial images.'[58] Even Phiz's most loyal champion, Michael Steig, admits that 'definite lapses of technique are in evidence in some of the conventional plates, and seven of the eight dark plates occur in the first half of the novel; not one of the eight includes a single emblematic detail, consistent with a general reduction in Browne's use of such conceptual techniques.'[59]

Readers may be surprised, therefore, to find two pleasant landscapes included in *Little Dorrit*, 'Floating Away' and 'The Ferry' (plate 32). The view of the ferry at Twickenham, just beyond Richmond Bridge, was one Phiz knew well, and he may even have prepared the sketch while visiting the kindly Moxons at The Lodge. These pictures are all the more surprising because they are found in what Paul Schlicke calls 'The most sombre and oppressive of Dickens's novels . . . organized around a pervasive central symbol of imprisonment.'[60] It seems as though Phiz took the opportunity to let a little fresh air flow through the gloom.

During the months of composition, Dickens was constantly restless and often irritable. Having given Phiz a somewhat freer rein in the two preceding novels, he reverted to controlling minute details of the illustrations. In October 1855, he described to Phiz what he wanted on the wrapper for *Little Dorrit*, and then dashed off to Paris, from where he wrote to W.H. Wills, his manager:

> . . . Will you give my address to B & E without loss of time, and tell them that although I have communicated at full explanatory length with Browne, I have heard *nothing of or from him*. Will you

add that I am uneasy and wish they would communicate with Mr.
Young, his partner, at once. Also that I beg them to be so good as
to send Browne my present address.[61]

He continued to exert a firm grip, writing to Phiz on 8 November 1856,
although his 'All right' seems to be ceding a point:

> All right. Please keep Clennam, always, as agreeable and well-looking
> as possible. He is very good in the Flintwich scene here. Mrs.
> Clennam's expression capital.[62]

He followed up this letter with another on 6 December:

> Don't have Lord Decimus's hand put out, because that looks conde-
> scending; and I want him to be upright, stiff, unmixable with mere
> mortality.

'Little Mother', *Little Dorrit*, 1855–7

'Mr Flintwich has a mild attack of irritability', *Little Dorrit*

Mrs. Plornish is too old, and Cavaletto a leetle bit too furious and wanting in stealthiness.[63]

And on 10 February 1857, he wrote:

In the dinner scene, it is highly important that Mr. Dorrit should not be too comic. He is too comic now. He is described in the text as 'shedding tears' and what he imperatively wants, is an expression doing less violence in the reader's mind to what is going to happen to him, and much more in accordance with that serious end which is so close before him.

Pray do not neglect this change.[64]

Little Dorrit has many memorable illustrations – of Dorrit and Arthur Clennam and Maggy, 'Little Mother', of Mr Flintwich at his most excitable. But Phiz's finest work was always created when the subject matter intrigued him. *Little Dorrit* did not. Only 'Damocles' (plate 33), the last dark plate Phiz created for Dickens, truly fired his imagination. In it he revisits his own 'Tom-All-Alone's' in *Bleak House* and Hogarth's 'Gin Lane'. He pictures the moment when Blandois is holding what Steig calls 'the Damoclean sword of blackmail' even as a building crumbles around him. Steig continues: 'It is of special interest that Phiz includes such indications of the imminent collapse as the stone falling from the eaves and the mangy cat apparently fleeing the house, because the text contains no direct suggestion of what is about to happen. . . . It is thus one of those cases where the novelist left an important fact to be dealt with in the illustration, which thereafter will become an integral part of the novel.'[65] 'Damocles' is a rogue image, lurching back to earlier times when Phiz's art fused perfectly with Dickens's imagination.

If only their twenty-three-year collaboration could have ended with that image, that cunning rendering of an author's intent. But it was not to be; there was still one book to come.

13

1859

Phiz lived in the Surrey countryside for twelve years, away from the stresses of city life and the long arm of demanding authors and publishers. In the country, he worked happily at his own pace, and when tired of needling away at the narrow world of illustration, saddled up his hunter and went for a brisk ride. But as the years passed new commissions dwindled to almost nothing because he had been outside the city's artistic ring fence too long. The years 1855 and 1856 were particularly lean. Things looked better in 1857 with the publication of Ainsworth's *The Spendthrift*, Augustus Mayhew's *Paved with Gold*, Dickens's *Little Dorrit*, and Hook's *Precepts and Practice*, as well as illustrations for re-editions of the work of Fielding and Smollett. The surge of work must have raised the Brownes' hopes of remaining in Surrey, but the next year, 1858, was disastrous. Apart from Ainsworth's *Mervyn Clitheroe*, it brought Phiz a mere smattering of uninspiring work.

London changed considerably during the Brownes' absence. Its population increased, its suburbs continued to swell in an inexorable westward

'In the Bastille', *A Tale of Two Cities*, 1859

march, and grandiose schemes for metropolitan redevelopment were afoot; it was also becoming cleaner and safer. Railways revolutionised travel which meant less horse manure in the streets; the advent of better plumbing and drainage meant fewer open sewers and flying slops; and thugs and pickpockets were less in evidence because of the Metropolitan Police patrolling the streets. But there was more than just physical change; the artistic, literary, intellectual, political, and scientific worlds were abuzz. The year 1859 alone saw the publication of Charles Darwin's *On the Origin of Species by Natural Selection*, Karl Marx's *Critique of Political Economy*, J.S. Mill's *Essay on Liberty*, Tennyson's *Idylls of the King*, George Eliot's *Adam Bede*, Edward Fitzgerald's *The Rubáiyát of Omar Khayyám*, and Charles Dickens's *A Tale of Two Cities*, the last novel Phiz illustrated for him.

Dickens was busy with his readings, arranging lucrative deals with publishers in America, setting up an office for his new weekly magazine, *All the Year Round*, spending time with Ellen Ternan (the young woman with whom he was infatuated), and commuting between Tavistock House and his new home, Gad's Hill, in Kent. He spent most of 1859 working like a fiend on *A Tale of Two Cities*, which he was publishing in weekly instalments in *All the Year Round* without illustrations. ('The small portions drive me frantic,'[1] he complained to Forster.) The book also appeared in illustrated monthly parts, on which Phiz worked throughout 1859. It was published by Chapman and Hall in volume form in its entirety, with the illustrations, in December 1859, a month after Phiz returned to London.

As early as September 1857, Dickens had written to his friend, the philanthropist Angela Burdett Coutts, about his first inspiration for *A Tale of Two Cities*: 'Sometimes of late, when I have been very much excited by the crying of two thousand people over the grave of Richard Wardour, new ideas for a story have come into my head as I lay on the ground, with surprising force and brilliancy'.[2] The more complex and challenging his life became, the more his inspiration flourished. In March 1858, he asked Forster, 'What do you think of this name for my story – *Buried Alive*?'[3] In April he wrote to W.H. Wills, 'I have been so hustled by a crowd of cares since I came home',[4] and in May he wrote to Angela Burdett Coutts, 'I believe my marriage has been for years as miserable a one as ever was made'.[5] In June he confided in Edmund Yates, 'If you could know how much I have felt within this last month, and what a sense of Wrong has been upon me, and what a strain and struggle I have lived under, you would see that my heart is *so jagged and rent and out of shape*, that it does not this day leave me hand enough to shape these words.'[6] No wonder Dickens considered calling his book *Buried Alive*.

Gone was Phiz's colleague who, at the time of their collaboration on *Bleak House*, had written jokingly in Franglais to '*Mon cher Brune*'. In his place was a man determined to reinvent himself. Dickens's personal revolution mirrored the people's revolution in *A Tale of Two Cities*. Like a snake sloughing off old skin, he was shedding his past and fighting for a new life. He shed decorum and fell in love; he shed his wife and angrily dismissed those friends who showed her any sympathy; ruthlessly and acrimoniously, he shed his publishers, Bradbury and Evans; he shed restraint and plunged headlong into an exhausting but enormously profitable series of readings; and slowly, in a deadly, tacit dismissal, he shed his loyal illustrator, Phiz. Dickens, the new man, wanted a new look – or no look at all – for his books.

Phiz's design for the cover of the monthly parts of *A Tale of Two Cities* was fairly well received. London with its icon, St Paul's, lies at the top of the image; Paris with its icon, Notre Dame, lies at the foot. London, with the Thames and its ships, speaks of prosperity; Paris, with its guillotine and maddened crowd, speaks of revolution. The rest of the illustrations for the monthly parts were denounced, the detractors criticising Phiz for not moving with the times. They also claimed that the etchings were hastily executed, that Phiz was ill at ease with period costume, and that the images did not add fire to the fury of revolution.

Why such a falling off in his work for Dickens, if this is indeed the case? Michael Slater has commented that people are far too harsh about the *Tale of Two Cities* illustrations, many of which are 'spirited and exciting'.[7] This excitement is certainly true in 'The Spy's Funeral' and 'The Sea Rises', but both of these are Ur-Phiz images. They could just as well have appeared in Lever, Ainsworth, or Dickens's novels from the 1840s, and Dickens may have found Phiz's self-reference and refusal to move with the times aggravating. Michael Steig, however, claims that the most plausible reason for the falling-off is that Dickens himself was no longer concerned with illustration and provided fewer interesting subjects than usual. He concludes that 'it is conceivable that Browne simply found *A Tale of Two Cities* less inspiring than Dickens' other books'.[8] The truth is Phiz may not even have read it. Dickens gave him scant guidance, and Phiz replied in kind by dashing off the sort of illustration he could do with his eyes shut – because he was angry with Dickens. *All the Year Round* containing the weekly parts without illustrations sold briskly, but sales of the illustrated monthly parts of *A Tale of Two Cities* were sluggish.

'The Spy's Funeral', *A Tale of Two Cities*, 1859

'The Sea Rises', *A Tale of Two Cities*, 1859

By 16 October 1859, Dickens had nearly finished the book and wrote to the publisher, Edward Chapman, 'The suggestions for the frontispiece and title, you shall have from me to send to Mr Browne, on Monday 24th of this month. The Dedication and Preface I will send straight to the Printer's at about the same time. I have not yet seen any sketches from Mr Browne for No. 6. Will you see to this without loss of time. . . . Will you also be so kind as to arrange with Mr Browne for the final plates for the book, so that he may not delay it?'⁹

Gone is the jolly banter and the scrupulous attention to detail. The usually prompt Phiz is procrastinating. But the subject for the title page – the last image he ever drew for Dickens – Dr Manette in his cell at the Bastille, catches his imagination. Of all the plates in *A Tale of Two Cities*, this is the most resonant, the most poignant, and the most expressive. Dr Manette is seen through an arch which frames the picture, and represented sitting on a pallet; he is old, tired and hunched-over. Under the pallet sits a ewer. Huge iron chains hang from the walls, whose stone blocks are crushingly enormous. The illustration itself could well be called 'Buried Alive'. The curve of the arch, the curves of Dr Manette's head and back, the curves of the chains, and the curve of the ewer with its promise of water, speak of the endless cycle of life, and curl us back in memory to a similar image, 'Fagin in the condemned Cell', Cruikshank's penultimate plate for Dickens, which in turn reminds us of 'The Dying Clown', Seymour's final, tragic image for Dickens. But the memory of Seymour snaps us back to the beginning of Phiz's happy collaboration with Dickens, to the curve of Mr Pickwick's stomach and to Sam Weller's smile. Phiz's career with Dickens had gone full circle.

A few years later, Phiz commented about *A Tale of Two Cities* in a letter to his son, Walter:

A rather curious thing happened with this book. Watts Phillips, the dramatist, hit upon the very same identical plot: they had evidently both of them been to the same source in Paris for their story. Watts's play ('The Dead Heart') came out with great success, with stunning climax, at about the time of Dickens's sixth number. The public saw that they were identically the same story, so Dickens shut up at the ninth number,¹⁰ instead of going on to the eighteenth as usual. All this put Dickens out of temper, and he squabbled with me amongst others, and I never drew another line for him.¹¹

Edgar calls the coincidence one of the strangest in the history of literature. 'Whether the authors evolved the plot entirely from their own imagination (which seems unlikely),' he ruminates, 'or whether an idea was put into their heads by some obscure *feuilleton* dealing with the central incident, and the preliminary stages reconstructed from the imagination to lead up to the climax, it is equally wonderful.'[12] Dickens could hardly accuse Watts Phillips of stealing his plot and dramatising it (something which happened regularly at the hands of others, much to his irritation), because Watts Phillips was writing ahead of him. And Dickens certainly did not want to be accused of stealing Watts Phillips's plot. This annoying coincidence could only have added to Dickens's irritability during 1859.

The breakdown of the working relationship of Phiz and Boz was less a sudden rupture than a gradual, widening rift. Dickens was distracted by the escalating demands in his life. Convinced that those who were not for him were against him, he would have placed Phiz in the latter camp because of his close friendship with Mark Lemon, Catherine Dickens's champion. And tender-hearted Phiz would have loathed Dickens's treatment of his wife. Dickens may also have been irritated by the fact that Phiz was illustrating for the new periodical, *Once a Week*, Bradbury and Evans's direct competition for Dickens's *All the Year Round*. Other illustrators for *Once A Week* included Keene, Leech, Millais, Frederick Walker, Tenniel, Du Maurier, and Holman Hunt, some of whom also took sides with Bradbury and Evans in opposition to Dickens. Thomas Hughes, author of *Tom Brown's Schooldays*, went so far as to declare to the editor, Samuel Lucas, in 1859, 'I shd be very glad to help you, for I am disgusted with Dickens and his set & think he and they have behaved like snobs as they are'.[13]

No falling off or lack of development in Phiz's work occurred in the late 1850s for authors with whom he was not angry. The illustrations for Augustus Mayhew's *Paved with Gold* (1858) are full of exhilaration, variety, and detail. 'A Midnight Picnic' could be no better depiction of an author's intent. Mayhew writes, 'The moon was up, and shining brightly, and from under their shawl-covered resting-place they could hear the music of the vigorous violins, and see their companions stepping it like fashionable fairies on the green sward'.[14] The viewer *hears* the image: a tall fiddle-player dominates the scene; the dancers' dresses swish out; the wind whistles at scarves and shawls; and on the skyline donkeys bray and race about (recalling those donkeys that so tried the patience of Betsey Trotwood in

David Copperfield). In a more sombre image, 'The Asylum for the Homeless', Phiz illustrates Mayhew's 'Nearly every shade and grade of misery, misfortune, vice, and even guilt are to be found in the place',[15] and creates a chilly, densely populated version of the grey and vacant 'Tom-All-Alone's' of *Bleak House*. But 'The Meeting at Stonehenge' is the most powerful illustration in the book. It is a night scene, heavy with clouds, but in the foreground four young boys huddle around a campfire, warding off terror, while above them the huge circle of dark, thrusting blocks looms over their bright little circle. It is hard not to imagine that this image was Thomas Hardy's inspiration for his own Stonehenge scene in *Tess of the D'Urbervilles*.

In Ainsworth's *Mervyn Clitheroe* (1858), image after image has the moon casting an eerie, watery light. Trees dance and take on threatening, human characteristics; lightning rips down from the sky; and the title page (plate 29) manages the extraordinary feat of bringing to mind at one and the same time Phiz's own image of the death of Quilp and Gericault's 'The Raft of the Medusa'.

Writing to the artist, in February 1858, concerning the designs for *Mervyn Clitheroe* Ainsworth had said: '. . . I hope the present subject will suit you. "The Conjurors Interrupted" will be effective if I am not mistaken. Pray tell your plate-printer to send me proofs early (no matter how wrought) that I may prevent any variations between text and the illustration'.[16] In 'The Conjurors Interrupted' (plate 30) text and image are inextricable, and the subject certainly suited Phiz, licensing him to anthropomorphise trees and shrubs. The text reads: 'The spot selected for the ceremonial seemed suitable enough. It was a part of the lawn furthest removed from the hall, and screened by a group of shorn trees, which, by a little stretch of imagination, might be taken for men and animals suddenly transformed by the power of enchantment. On the right was a gigantic bear reared on its hind legs, and with outstretched paws prepared to close with a huntsman, who was attacking it with an axe. Behind was a gigantic figure, with a long beard, probably meant to represent a Druid. Then came an evil angel with wide, outspread wings. Then a grotesque figure. Then a Faun playing Pandean pipes, with goats skipping before him; and lastly, a cock crowing on a tree'.[17] Phiz set to work enthusiastically, turning trees and shrubs into menacing, sentient beings.

Phiz worked for another American author, Harriet Beecher Stowe, in 1859, illustrating the English edition of *The Minister's Wooing*. George Cruikshank had earlier illustrated an English edition of *Uncle Tom's Cabin*, and he, Phiz, Leech, and Gilbert were responsible for the wood engravings in *Uncle Tom's Cabin Almanack* in 1853. Mrs Stowe visited England that year and attended the Lord Mayor's Banquet where she sat directly across the table from Charles and Catherine Dickens. She was struck by how young-looking Dickens was, and commented, 'They are both people that one could not know a little of without desiring to know more', and went on to describe Catherine as 'a good specimen of a truly English woman; tall, large, and well developed, with fine healthy colour, and an air of frankness, cheerfulness, and reliability. A friend whispered to me that she was as observing, and fond of humour, as her husband'.[18] Mrs Stowe's happy recollection of meeting the Dickenses may have reminded her of their link with Phiz and convinced her to hire him to illustrate *The Minister's Wooing*. She may also have met Phiz himself on her visit to England and seen the watercolour of Eva and Topsy he had prepared for Robert Young to engrave. Unfortunately, Phiz was not exactly at home illustrating the American south.

Another strange connection with an American writer occurred in 1859. In this case, the poet Emily Dickinson's admiration for an image by Phiz got the better of her. Edward Dickinson, her father, had acquired a copy of *Master Humphrey's Clock*, the compendium volume containing *The Old Curiosity Shop* and *Barnaby Rudge*, in spite of his opinion that Charles Dickens and all the modern literati 'joggled the mind' and were nothing compared to the writers of his boyhood.[19] Although her father disapproved of her enjoying novels, Emily read *The Old Curiosity Shop* and was clearly inspired by two particular illustrations. The first, by Phiz, appears in Chapter 54 and depicts Little Nell and her grandfather resting on the ground after beautifying the graveyard (one of the tombs bears the initials HKB), while the bachelor, seated on a stile, admires their handiwork. Emily was, apparently, so moved by this image that she drew a rectangle around the figures of Little Nell and her grandfather, and then snipped along the rectangle until they came loose in her hand.

Using a needle and red silk thread, she stitched the image to the top of a page of pencilled writing. Then she turned to the last illustration in *The Old Curiosity Shop*, Cattermole's apotheosis of Little Nell. Drawing another rectangle to encompass the entire picture, she snipped that image from the text, and stitched it to the bottom of the page. The two pictures embellish the following poem:

A poor – torn Heart – a tattered heart,
That sat it down to rest –
Nor noticed that the ebbing Day
Flowed silver to the West;
Nor noticed night did soft descend,
Nor Constellation burn –
Intent upon a vision
Of Latitudes unknown –

The Angels, happening that way
This dusty heart espied –
Tenderly took it up from toil,
And carried it to God –
There – Sandals for the Barefoot –
There – gathered from the gales
Do the blue Havens by the hand
Lead the wandering sails.[20]

Edward Dickinson's handsome copy of *Master Humphrey's Clock* was published in Philadelphia by Lea and Blanchard in 1840, and bears his bold signature inside its front cover. Emily must have been confident that her father, having sneered at Dickens, would never consult the volume again, thus making it possible for her to take her scissors with impunity to the book, to Charles Dickens's text, and to Phiz and Cattermole's images.

Optimistic about his financial prospects on returning to London at the end of 1859, Phiz settled with his family in a pleasant, five-storeyed terrace house with a pillared entry in Horbury Crescent, halfway between Holland Park and Notting Hill Gate. The household contained the domestic staff in addition to Phiz, Susannah, and their five youngest children, from eleven-year-old Emma down to one-year-old Gordon (destined to become a famous illustrator in his own right). Edgar, seventeen, was living with Aunt Kate (technically his grandmother), who gave him room and board and paid part of his expenses at medical school, the rest being made up by his uncle in India, General Charles Alfred Browne. Charles Michael, sixteen, was in military training at Addiscombe (following in General Browne's footsteps); and Walter, fourteen, was at Bruce Castle, a boarding school in Tottenham,[21] where his two older brothers had preceded him, and where the headmaster was Arthur Hill, brother of the more famous Sir Rowland Hill of Penny Postage fame. (Dickens had considered Bruce Castle for his oldest son, but Angela Burdett Coutts overruled him and Charley was sent to Eton at her expense.[22]) The Hills were passionate liberals; they eschewed tyranny and bullying, and demanded kindness and public spiritedness. 'Let gentleness my strong enforcement be,' was Arthur Hill's motto.[23] The fact that Phiz and Susannah chose this school is an indication of their own philosophy, and it was upon similar principles that they ran their own large household. Arthur Hill was a determined Shakespearean, which would have pleased Phiz.[24] He was continually learning plays by heart and reciting them for his students, adding stage directions. He also encouraged the boys to put on their own plays, and Edgar says: 'One of my brothers and myself were valued as scene painters, and produced some surprising results in distemper'.[25]

The hoped-for flood of commissions that Phiz counted on failed to materialise. Apart from thirty etchings on steel for Charles Lever's latest novel, *One of Them*, he found himself having to work almost exclusively on wood, never his favourite medium. Edgar comments on this: '. . . Browne was never so successful on wood as on steel. . . . In drawing on wood he was obliged to use a very hard pencil, and to depend on the point alone, so that his work resembled a coarse kind of etching, and very often had to suffer from translation at the hands of the engraver, who substituted for a lively line a mechanical one, and treated spaces of shade by cutting in tint. To the end his work on wood suffered from these drawbacks, and he lost greatly in translation, as Dickens himself does when translated into French'.[26]

The age itself conspired against Phiz. The Pre-Raphaelite era was dawning, and their 'truthful' wood engravings and lithographs designed on a grand scale began to eclipse the small, detail-filled etchings of the earlier illustrators. Photography, too, was gaining ground, adding its stamp of truthfulness to the body of illustration. Suddenly, this new accuracy was regarded as being out of reach of artists such as Phiz, Cruikshank, Doyle, and Leech. The illustrations of Millais, Rossetti, Holman Hunt, Charles Keene and other newcomers were all the rage.

Even without much work on book illustrations, Phiz managed to cobble together a pretty good living during his first few years back in London. He acquired work on several periodicals, including *Punch*, painted watercolours, continued to illustrate for Charles Lever, and began publishing his own work, finding a ready market for his hunting prints. Loosened from the grip of Dickens's demands, he bounced back brimming with ideas. He went so far on his own account as to publish a hilarious broadside, *The Times Such as They Are*, a parody of *The Times*, printed in a similar format to the newspaper but containing nearly 150 illustrations,[27] in which he skewered the fads of the day, poked fun at the social contract, and advertised crackpot nostrums and inventions.

14

Can You Forgive Him?

'[My father] lived so entirely in his work and a world of imagination, that it is impossible to describe him in the ordinary terms,' wrote Edgar. 'Politics he had none, though when questioned at election times he said he was a Liberal, more, I believe, because he liked the sound of the words, than from any clear idea of its political significance. He certainly had a holy horror of Radicals. Cobden and Bright[1] he considered humbugs – why, I do not know. He took sufficient interest in the outer world to read *The Times* in the evening, but his interest lay in general events and not in politics.'[2]

Phiz's reading *The Times* in the evening rather than the morning relegates the act to leisure activity; his priority in the morning was work. Edgar also points out that his father lived his life the way he wanted, paid absolutely no attention to public opinion, considered himself quite ordinary, revealed none of the instinct of the social climber, had little ambition, and had no desire to make money beyond what was necessary for daily expenses.[3]

'Arabella with Sea Monster', 'Rattlebrain', *Sir Guy de Guy*, 1864

'No doubt [Phiz] was an exceedingly bad manager of his money or he might have always remained comfortably off. In fact he was the sort of man it was no use to help',[4] complains C.G. Browne, who obviously has no patience with Phiz when it comes to money matters. His remark may be driven by the fact that his father, Phiz's brother Octavius, bailed Phiz out during particularly lean times to the tune of £120 a year. Yet apart from this irritation, C.G. Browne admired the artist, while thoroughly disliking his collaborator: 'It is impossible to conceive of two men more utterly unlike than Dickens & Browne; the former was a noisy perpetual talker who shouted every-one down at dinner, dressed & behaved like a thoroughly common man – which he was – while Browne was the very quietest, most retiring, shy & modest gentleman one could meet.'[5]

Phiz was always full of ideas for new ventures which might bring in some cash, but he was totally impractical. He would produce huge albums of drawings accompanied by the merest sputter of text, albums that were a publisher's nightmare and could not possibly pay their way. When a publisher turned down such an item, it never dawned on Phiz that he might revise or prune it. Instead, he lobbed it straight into the wastebasket, or used the reverse side of the paper for new sketches.

Thomson also comments on Phiz's fiscal ineptitude: 'He never knew what he earned or what he spent, and would for many years take no thought of it. When he wanted money he applied to any publisher who happened to owe him something, and it was unlucky for the employer if he could not instantly settle the account; for Browne never would, or perhaps never could, understand why he should not have his money the very day his work was completed'.[6] And Edgar weighs in again, 'He never realised that he was being exploited, as was often the case. That there was a struggle going on for place and profit, and that there were people fully disposed to give him a push downwards for objects of their own, never occurred to him'.[7] Phiz sometimes had a few hundred pounds in the cupboard, which anybody else would have invested, but he usually ordered what he wanted on credit, and then went to work to pay for it.

Even John Forster recognised Phiz's fiscal ignorance and decided to lend him a hand in the matter of price. In an undated letter without an address, he writes:

My dear Browne, –
. . . I enclose you a cheque – you charged too little for the design of the cover. I took the liberty of changing the five guineas into

eight guineas, and you will find the cheque hereto corresponding.

This liberty I am sure you will excuse, and believe me, my dear Browne, always sincerely, John Forster.

Just received the plates. Send me word what you think the writing underneath should be.[8]

A friendly feeling always existed between Phiz and Forster. Phiz referred to him as a 'little Doctor Johnson', although, as Edgar explains, the 'great Doctor's lucidity was wanting [and] it was rather in the matter of laying down the law that the resemblance lay'.[9]

Making money, having money, keeping money was always a tricky matter for the Brownes, and members of the family dealt with the issue in different ways. The paterfamilias, wicked William Loder Browne, never made enough to satisfy his wife, so he absconded to Philadelphia, leaving her to depend on the kindness of relatives and the influence of friends; of their children who survived, Kate used her income from teaching to support her mother and, later, Edgar when he was a medical student; amiable Emma married up the social ladder, in India; priggish Henry Albert acquired his living at Toft through the influence of Viscount Galway; lovely Lucinda married up; Charles Alfred left England and earned money in India, but spent it all supporting causes, including his family in England; the adventurers, Gordon, Octavius, and Decimus sought their fortunes in the Antipodes; and Phiz supported himself with his talent as long as he was able, before following Katherine Browne's method and relying on family members to help him out. He often repaid the kindness of others with drawings and paintings.

Most people's eyesight becomes less sharp in their forties, and it is possible that Phiz's vision began to dim sometime during the end of the 1850s or early 1860s, thus making it more difficult for him to produce detailed work on steel. As the 1860s progressed, he received fewer and fewer commissions. In 1862, apart from etchings for Charles Lever's *Barrington* and some wood engravings for a little book called *Snowflakes* by M.E. Edwards, precious little in the matter of book illustration came his way. In 1863 he had no book publications and depended on his work for periodicals and money from Octavius. Nor were Phiz and Susannah's woes merely financial; they were desolated in 1864 by the death of their last baby, Arthur John. The little boy was buried in Brighton, which suggests that Susannah took him there for the benefit of his health.

Friends rallied round. Mark Lemon hired Phiz to illustrate *Tom Moody's*

Phiz, 'The Country Manager rehearses a Combat', *c.* 1839. Oil.

Phiz, small oil painting, possibly illustrating *The Vicar of Wakefield*, *c.* 1845.

Harrison Ainsworth, *c.* 1830.

LONDON & NEW YORK.
GEORGE ROUTLEDGE & SONS.

Title page for Harrison Ainsworth's
Mervyn Clitheroe, 1858.

'The Conjurors Interrupted', *Mervyn Clitheroe*, 1858.

Sketch for 'The Mausoleum at Chesney Wold'
in *Bleak House*, 1852–3. Black crayon.

'Damocles', *Little Dorrit*.

'The Ferry', *Little Dorrit*, 1857.

Phiz's eldest son Edgar Athelstane and daughter-in-law Alice Domenica, *c.* 1867.

His second child,
Charles Michael, *c.* 1880.

'Ayah', pen and ink drawing by Charles Michael Browne, *c.* 1880.

His third child Walter, *c*.1865.

His fifth and sixth children
Emma and Eliza, *c*. 1865.

His tenth child, the illustrator
Gordon Browne, *c*. 1920.

Robert Young, *c.* 1885.

Fred Barnard, *c.* 1890.

Luke Fildes, *c.* 1910.

Emily Dickinson's manuscript page
with her cut-out of Phiz's illustration
from *The Old Curiosity Shop*, *c.* 1859.

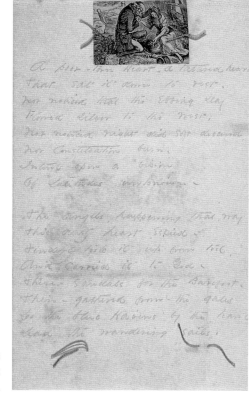

Phiz, self-portrait
resembling Prospero,
c. 1887.

Phiz's widow Susannah, with her grandchildren by Charles Michael and Josephine, *c.* 1890

Phiz having his head 'taken off', *c.* 1874.

Phiz's grave in the Extra–Mural Cemetery (part of the Lewes Road Cemeteries), Brighton.

Tales, and the writer George Halse lent him a hand in a venture which eventually appeared in book form as *Sir Guy de Guy* by 'Rattlebrain'. Phiz's idea had been to produce a book called *The Adventures of Pott,* written by himself in rhyming couplets, for which he had already produced scores of drawings. Thomson describes what happened: 'The artist carried the sketches to Mr George Halse, and asked his advice in the matter. Mr Halse having some experience in literary undertakings, saw at once the merits of the designs and the poverty of the accompanying verses. He suggested an alteration in the projected work, made a selection of forty from the series and, at the artist's request, wrote poetical letterpress to go with the work . . . The title and the scheme of the book as published were entirely Mr Halse's, who utilized the drawings so far as possible, and when they were unsuitable the designs were altered to suit the text. The *Athenaeum* at the time called the book "a remarkably brilliant example of its kind."'[10] The book describes the monstrous adventures of Guy Straggles and his doughty Arabella (undaunted by her crinoline), and it gives full rein to Phiz's wild imagination.

The Victoria and Albert Museum owns a photographed copy of some of Phiz's original pen and ink drawings and the typescript of 'The Adventures of Guy Straggles by Rattlebrain and Phiz – An Extravaganza', but Phiz's text for *The Adventures of Pott* has been lost forever.

It is hard to see why Anthony Trollope chose Phiz to illustrate *Can You Forgive Her?* The only reasons that make sense are the artist's availability and the fact that the author's mother had died in October 1863. Phiz had illustrated *Charles Chesterfield* for Frances Trollope back in 1841, and Trollope may have chosen the artist out of sentiment. It was a predictably unhappy choice because Trollope was only too well aware that illustrations by Phiz would stamp him with the mark of Dickens. About their collaboration, N. John Hall, author of *Trollope and His Illustrators,* remarks, 'Trollope and Browne were as ill-attuned to each other as Dickens and Browne had been suited to each other'.[11]

As soon as Trollope saw the first design, he was angry that Phiz's work did not resemble Millais, his first choice of illustrator. He renewed his efforts to hire Millais, but that artist was adamant. Phiz then completed twenty illustrations, but signed none of them. As Phizzes, they are comfortingly familiar, but as illustrations for Trollope, they are distractingly Dickensian. Mr Micawber, Nicholas Nickleby, and Mr Dombey are barely held in check, and Phiz's high spirits seem ready to break out at any moment and overtake Trollope's more serious intent. Could anything be

'"I have heard" – said Burgo', Anthony Trollope, *Can You Forgive Her?*, 1864

E. Taylor, 'Lady Glencora at Baden', *Can You Forgive Her?*

more resonantly Phizzy than the illustration 'I have heard – said Burgo', complete with its grand hunting scene (by Phiz, of course) in the background?

Working for Trollope was an unpleasant experience, and Phiz disliked the author from the start. To compound the problem, *Can You Forgive Her?* coincided with the moment he realised he would never work for Dickens again, a time when everyone wanted Millais, or failing that (for Millais was very expensive), the Millais 'look'.

Trollope wrote *Can You Forgive Her?* in two volumes. He let Phiz go at the end of the first volume and hired Miss E. Taylor of St Leonards in his place, and she illustrated the whole of the second volume. Her work was in no way reminiscent of Phiz's. She modelled herself on Millais, although she had nothing of his depth and texture, and while she drew on a much larger scale than Phiz, her figures were sometimes ill-proportioned. *Can You Forgive Her?* thus becomes rather a fascinating book, a historic example of early Victorian illustration in Volume I, and a sudden jump to the more heroic, truthful style of the 1860s in Volume II. It is fair to say that neither Phiz nor Miss Taylor succeeded in doing justice to Trollope. Perhaps he should never have considered illustrations at all. Interestingly, in this present age, his work translates remarkably well into television, as the recent production of *The Way We Live Now* so clearly demonstrates.

When Phiz was suggested as illustrator for the next novel, *The Claverings*, Trollope did not spare his sharp tongue:

> I think you would possibly find no worse illustrator than H. Browne . . . he will take no pains to ascertain the thing to be illustrated. I cannot think that his work can add any value at all to any book.
>
> I am having the ten last numbers of Can You Forgive Her illustrated by a lady. She has as yet done two drawings on wood. They are both excellent, and the cutter says they will come out very well. She has £5:5: – a drawing for them. Why not employ her? . . .
>
> But of course the question is one for you to settle yourself. As for myself I can never express satisfaction at being illustrated in any way by H. Browne.[12]

Charles Lever, on the other hand, had no hesitation in recommending Phiz in the following letter to John Blackwood on 14 June 1864:

I looked forward eagerly to your promised letter about O'Dowd. No one could do an imaginary portrait of a foreignised Irishman – all drollery about the eyes, and bearded like a pard – better than Hablot Browne (Phiz), and I think he could also do *all* that we need for illustration which would be little occasional bits on the page and tailpieces. If he would take the trouble to *read* the book (which he is not much given to) and if he would really interest himself in it (not so unlikely now as he is threatened with a rival in Marcus Stone) he could fully answer all our requirements. I would not advise any regular 'plates', mere woodcuts in the page, and an occasional rambling one *crawling over the page*. What do *you* think?[13]

For all his amiability and willingness, Phiz appears to have had a passive-aggressive streak. There was no artistic reason why his illustrations for *A Tale of Two Cities* and *Can You Forgive Her?* should have been so humdrum when his work for other authors was still interesting. He clearly found it distasteful to work for uncongenial writers, and took an instant dislike to Trollope's high-handedness. One might conclude that Phiz was cutting off his nose to spite his face, but money matters never stopped him from doing precisely what he wished.

It is easy, at first, to believe the received wisdom about the shy, quasi-slave to Dickens. But Phiz turns out to be a thoroughly independent man; confident in his talent; strong enough to confront Dickens, although sensitive to slights; witty and phenomenally optimistic. He seems in character most to resemble Edwin Lutyens, the architect. Full of energy, Lutyens adored puns, was fiscally incompetent, doodled constantly when he was not actually drawing plans, could be charming but suffered mood swings, was painfully shy, adored the countryside and gardens, was devoted to his wife whom he failed to understand, went his own way absolutely – and bore grudges.[14]

In Phiz's case, slights produce a mental block rather than a grudge; he responds with a kind of obstinacy, which dams his illustrative powers. And in areas other than work, he shows signs of getting his own way absolutely, as in moving to Banstead to be closer (naturally!) to Epsom. But what about Susannah – how did she manage to stay sane, a lone Reynolds in a crowd of Brownes, living a life of feast or famine, with new babies year after year, and a husband in thrall to illustration?

Deep love, mutual respect, and lots of laughter seem to have carried the day.

15

Milestones and Adventures

Phiz watched as Dickens published *Great Expectations* without illustrations in weekly instalments in *All the Year Round* during 1860-1861 – although the American serialisation in *Harper's Weekly* included designs by John McLenan – and without illustrations in the first bound edition. But he noticed that the author reverted to illustrations in *Our Mutual Friend*, by way of doing someone a favour. After Frank Stone died in 1859, Dickens took the rest of his old friend's family under his wing, and gave Frank's son, Marcus, a leg-up in the publishing world by recommending him to Chapman and Hall. The publishers used the younger Stone for supplementary illustrations in the Library Edition,[1] including images for the first illustrated *Great Expectations*. Dickens then invited Marcus Stone (plate 21) to provide forty wood engravings for *Our Mutual Friend*. Phiz got wind of this, and wrote irritably to Robert Young:

'Toddles'

Marcus is no doubt to do Dickens. *I* have been a 'good boy', I believe. The plates in hand are all in good time, so that I do not know what's 'up', any more than you. Dickens probably thinks a new hand would give his old puppets a fresh look, or perhaps he does not like my illustrating Trollope neck-and-neck with him – though, by Jingo, he need fear no rivalry *there!* Confound all authors and publishers, say I. There is no pleasing one or t'other. I wish I had never had anything to do with the lot.[2]

Phiz's eight surviving siblings were now well into their adult years. Kate went 'away'[3] for a while to teach professionally, then returned to live with her mother; Henry Albert preached, took a great interest in Bible societies, gardened, refused to speak to the rest of his family, and married three times (his third wife was forty-eight years his junior); Lucinda produced eight children, most of whom inherited the Brownes' artistic talent and gift for languages to an extraordinary degree.[4]

Charles Alfred progressed steadily in the Madras Army, and by the end of his forty-four-year military career had become a Major-General. Because of his administrative and linguistic skills, his superiors kept him off the battlefield. He underwent a religious conversion, putting faith into action by starting a number of Sunday schools and becoming secretary of the Church Missionary Society in 1833. Charles was hospitable to a fault and his house in Madras became known as 'Bachelors' Hall'. Even after his marriage his home remained a haven, where ladies, hitherto rigidly excluded, were welcome. In addition to sending financial help for the education of his nephews and nieces, he regularly shipped crates of gifts back to England. He seems almost too good to be true, but a single sentence in *Reminiscences of Christian Life* offers a tantalising glimpse of something unexpected: '. . . he amused himself by getting almost his entire body tattooed with pictures of wild animals'.[5] A roisterer? Perhaps, but not necessarily; if he could not draw, he appreciated talent, and this was possessing art in the most intimate way possible.

While Phiz sought his precarious fortune in an artist's studio in England, his brothers, Octavius, Gordon, and Decimus were determined to make good, even if it meant travelling to the other side of the world. Even though Octavius and Gordon's lives were completely different from Phiz's, they were sustained by the same irrepressible spirits and courage.

Gordon was ten years older than Phiz. He preceded Octavius to Australia in about 1826, and worked in Sydney as a merchant until 1828, when he sailed to New Zealand, where a mere handful of Europeans lived at the time. He established a settlement at Whitianga on the north island for the procuring of Kauri tree spars, which were much in demand because of their tall, strong, straight trunks. Gordon was extremely industrious, but the solitude was profound and eventually led to the breakdown of his mind. His life was brightened in 1835 by a visit from his soldier brother, Charles, who because of ill health had been advised to take a break from his work in India and seek a change of scene. And in May 1839, when Octavius set out from England intending to seek his fortune in Sydney, Gordon induced him to visit him in New Zealand first. Octavius found Gordon in extraordinary difficulties and was soon sucked into the vortex of his mental and fiscal disasters. After paying off debts and making sure that Gordon was as comfortable as possible, Octavius unsuccessfully sought work in Australia before returning to England in 1842. Gordon died in New Zealand in 1844, and was buried at Waikari, Bay of Islands. In the burial registry his age is given as 'about 50 years'. Gordon was actually only forty.

In 1847, Octavius returned to Australia, accompanied by wife and children. This time it seemed everything he touched turned to gold. Eventually overwork and the strain of having too many irons in the fire caused his health to break down. With the lesson of Gordon's decline still fresh in his mind, he decided to sell up, and in 1854 returned to England after handing his business over to his brother, Decimus, who had newly arrived in Melbourne.

Lovely, strong Lucinda died in 1850. 'She had always enjoyed excellent health until she was attacked by enteric fever . . . [which] proved fatal in less than 14 days', mourns C.G. Browne. And Katherine Browne, the materfamilias, died in 1856, and was buried beside her beloved Adelaide in Merton.

Charles retired to England in 1864, following the death of his wife. On the evening of 14 February 1866, he left the office of the Church Missionary Society in Salisbury Square and collapsed in the street. He died on the way to hospital, and Phiz was called in to identify him. All the remaining family, including the long-estranged brother, the Reverend Henry Albert Browne, gathered for the funeral, and Charles was buried in the catacombs of West Norwood Cemetery.

Henry Albert had attended no family events since cutting himself off – not even his mother's funeral in 1856 – but Charles's deeply felt Christianity must have impressed him. One year later, almost to the day,

Edgar Browne, Phiz's oldest son, married Henry Albert's youngest child, Alice Domenica, his first cousin. Charles's funeral was probably the scene of their first encounter. How vengefully Alice repaid her father for all his years of disapproval of Phiz and his family!

Births made up in some measure for losses caused by death. With the arrival of Phiz and Susannah's last two children, Beatrice Alice in 1860 and Arthur John in 1862, the Brownes had a complement of six sons and four daughters; and Phiz never tired of sketching babies and children.

But what about Kate? By the early 1860s, her health had begun to deteriorate. She died of 'internal cancer' on 3 September 1862, at the age of sixty-nine. Long before her death, she placed funds for her funeral expenses in the hands of her cousin, John Moxon, and left her entire estate, about £1,000, to Phiz's children, except Edgar, for whom she had already provided. She was buried in a grave plot shared with the Moxon family in West Norwood cemetery.[6] If her tomb were ever opened, a little gold ring bearing the words '*Je t'aime*' would probably come to light.

She may never have known that Nicolas Hablot survived the Battle of Waterloo. In spite of grievous wounds, his extraordinary constitution pulled him through. His injuries are listed on his service record: in addition to the sabre chop to his right index finger at Montmirail, he received a wound from a musket ball that crossed his chest just below the left nipple, another ball to the left thigh, and a sabre wound to the right thigh, all at Mt St Jean (Waterloo) on 18 June 1815.[7]

Severely injured and with his emperor no longer in command, Captain Hablot retired from the army and moved to Carignan, where his cousin, Phocien Hablot, was mayor. On 16 October 1816, he married eighteen-year-old Anne Thérèse Augustine D'Estenay of Carignan, seventeen years his junior.[8] He had no further children. The Army granted him a half pension for the loss of his index finger. (He would have earned a full pension for the loss of a limb.)

Because no established town cemetery existed when Hablot died in 1836, it is likely that he was buried on his own property. In 1969 his tombstone was inadvertently rooted up by pigs in a back garden owned by Jean Lavorel. It was broken in two, but the inscription was legible:

Nicolas Hablot
ancien officier
des grenadiers
de la vieille garde
décédé
le 8 février 1836[9]

The stone has disappeared again, but a clue remains to its whereabouts. When Anne Thérèse died in 1855 she was buried in Carignan's large, new cemetery, which opened a few years after her husband's death. Her inscription proudly claims her to be the widow of Captain Nicolas Hablot. Anne Thérèse's stone, originally upright, has fallen onto the bed of her grave; it now rests firmly on another slab, obscuring any lettering – but the lower stone is broken into two halves.

16

Poleaxed

I did not die, of course – and I was never in any pain – but, physically speaking, I'd been poleaxed. My left leg was immobilized and my left arm hung from its socket like a dead rabbit.

Robert McCrum, *My Year Off*[1]

In 1867, something terrible happened to Phiz. To the modern eye, it has the hallmarks of a stroke, although everyone who writes about Phiz seems to have a different theory. Edgar, his doctor son, refers to it as a severe illness in which he lost the use of his right thumb, and part use of his right leg; Buchanan-Brown posits it was 'a form of polio, contracted when bathing, since the immediate effects were almost total paralysis of the right side and blindness of the right eye'; Steig calls it 'an illness [that] left Phiz partially paralyzed'; Kitton calls it his 'crippled condition'; M.H. Spielmann calls it 'his stroke of paralysis'; Cohen refers to it as 'paralysis, which, Micawber-like, he persisted in calling "rheumatics"'; Allchin calls it 'the

'An Old Stager'

first intimation of his failing powers' and refers to Phiz as being 'stricken with paralysis'; C.G. Browne calls it his 'difficulties'; and Thomson rambles at length, but inconclusively, on the subject: '[Browne] sustained a severe shock of a kind of paralysis. . . . said to have been partly caused by his having slept in a draught in a seaside house, but from a medical description of the disease there appears to have been some blood-poisoning. . . . Dr Westall, in whom he had implicit faith, attended him, but it is possible that the serious nature of the disease was not understood until its sad results were seen'.[2]

Phiz's health until this point had been superb. Apart from the brief sickness in 1837 when one monthly instalment of *Nicholas Nickleby* had to appear without illustrations, he was extraordinarily fit, in marked contrast with Dickens who constantly complained of being laid low by one thing or another. This is understandable; Phiz worked at home or in a studio, alone; Dickens, particularly during his years of public readings, travelled widely, constantly surrounded by crowds of people.

The apparently sudden onset of Phiz's serious illness seems to rule out a degenerative disease like Parkinson's; polio is unlikely because of Phiz's age – he was fifty-two at the time; and blood-poisoning is an old-fashioned, blanket term for a mysterious, undiagnosed ailment. What is clear is that he went to the seaside – possibly Margate – in 1867 for a breath of fresh air, slept in a draught, and later became partially paralysed on his right side. Although he suffered some transient damage to his right eye, his speech appears to have been unaffected.

'After five months of great suffering [Browne] sat up and began to draw,' claims Thomson. 'He was not really convalescent, but his active nature asserted itself, and he persisted in working, in spite of advice to the contrary. His perseverance was little short of madness. When he first began, the perspiration would pour off him after half an hour's exertion, and then he had to lay by his work and rest again. He refused to go to the seaside, asserting that his health was returning and that he had a great deal of back-way to make up'.[3] And Edgar remarks: 'In his usual optimistic fashion he considered his feebleness as rheumatism, and though he could not close his thumb over his pencil, he continued to draw, holding his pencil between his fingers alone. He also adopted a new material, housemaid's blacklead, with which he made many designs; the solid he used for his outlines and then rubbed the powder on with his finger as shade'.[4]

Edgar insists that with the exception of the partial paralysis, his father enjoyed very good health until just before his death in 1882,[5] whereas

Letter from 'Margit'

Thomson says that within six months he was reduced to 'a broken down old man. He left the sick room with white hair, pallid complexion, and a partial paralysis of the right arm and leg'[6] – a claim refuted by Phiz's correspondence during 1867. The paralytic episode must have occurred early that year because by September he was gainfully employed at the *Sporting Gazette*, as he made clear in a letter to his son, Walter, whom he nicknamed 'Doctor':

> Blenheim Crescent
> Sept., Satirday, 3 o'clk. p.m. A.D. 1867
>
> My Dear Dr.,
> I have nearly bursted my heart out, and proved, that my soul or soles (*I* have two) is'nt – or an't – immortal, – by wearing on 'em out running to and fro after yr. *Balmorals*[7] – Bootless errands! The wretched slave (of awl) has but just brought them! I bristle with wrath! and could welt him! – but – no – I won't – he may want his calf's skin whole, to mend his own *Bad-morals!!* . . . I rush! I fly! to the Gt. W.R. Station! – !!!
> I sink – breathless into the arms of the astounded clerk – point to the boots –
> *My-mouth* faintly whispers *'Wey-mouth'* in his pen-adorned *Ear!!* and – and – 'Bless me! where am *I*?' – and, and – I wish – you may get 'em!

"I rush! I fly!", 1867

. . . If you visit Portland again, make a note of any peculiarities of spot – convict dress, &c. – as I have a touching bit of horse-y sentiment (!) connected therewith, which will do for *Spg. Gazette*. – I should think you ought to find painty bits – within walking distance – say – right or left ten miles? Yrs. affecty., Dad[8]

Another letter, written to his friend George Halse on 30 December 1867, shows that Phiz has continued to mend. His writing is perfectly legible and the letter contains drawings similar in style to those in earlier letters.

Dec. 30 67.

My dear Sir,
Thanks for procuring me the Onions.
'Onions,' some Sage of old Thyme has said, '*is strength*' – they have given *us* strength to attack with renewed vigour a piece of Xtmas Beef – before which our exhausted masticators were beginning to quail. I call it my Case of Family Pills and use them as Digestors – & it is astonishing with what apparent gusto they are swallowed – far different to the ordinary bolus – in fact they take them down with the same ease & avidity that young blackbirds do worms! –
With best wishes for the New Y [drawing of ear],
Yrs. very truly, H.K. Browne[9]

Although Phiz was again moving around without assistance, in good

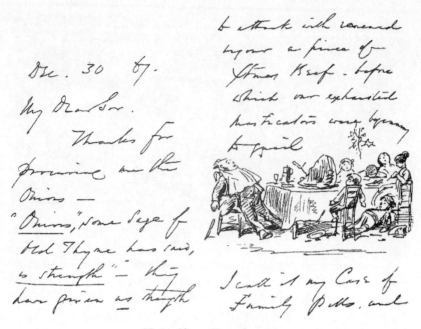

'Onions' letter, December 1867

spirits, and able to write and to create rough sketches, he was no longer capable of executing work that required fine lines and a delicate touch. The illness had damaged his hand so badly that he never really recovered his early dexterity, and his designs no longer brimmed with complexity and originality. But even such a severe, debilitating illness could not dampen his will to draw, and many of his post-1867 drawings, while broad and clumsy compared to the elegance of his work in the 1840s and 1850s, show verve, swing, and rollicking humour.

17

London's Great Outing

A trip to the Derby – 'the snow-storm Derby' – on 22 May 1867 may
have been the most important factor that spurred Phiz back to health.
The weather did not cooperate, but the race was exciting enough to wake
the dead.

Phiz was never a betting man. It was the horses rather than the race
that captivated his interest. 'He disliked gambling', says Edgar, '[If] he won,
he did not like taking the money, and if he lost, he was still more annoyed'.[1]
The family had become accustomed to going to the Derby when they
lived in Surrey. Phiz would ride over to the racecourse at Epsom, and the
rest of the family, travelling by chaise, met him there. They congregated
on a knoll commanding the view of the starting post, and as soon as the
horses were off, galloped to the next vantage point for the view of
Tattenham Corner. 'We had a sort of picnic in the chaise', wrote Edgar.
'Thus we had a long day in the open air, full of a sense of rush and
motion, crowds and festivity, and a feeling of taking part in an important

The Derby Carnival, 1869

national event, without being brought into contact with the blackguardism that abounded in the crowd.'²

Eight days before the 1867 race, the favourite, Hermit, broke a blood vessel in his nose and was not expected to run; his jockey was contracted out to another horse. But after careful nursing and the last-minute hiring of Johnny Daley, a gentle, intelligent Newmarket lad, as replacement jockey, Hermit appeared at the course to run. He looked like a doubtful starter, hanging his head, shivering, tucking his tail between his legs, and trembling as Daley mounted him.

The day was freezing cold; icy winds and a mixture of sleet and snow blew across the racecourse as the horses gathered at the starting gate. After ten false starts, they were off. The crucial moment came when the field turned at Tattenham Corner. Hermit was in the second pack, and at that point Daley brought him forward, making a long run on the outside. The sensitive chestnut suddenly caught the spirit of the occasion; Daley coaxed him on, and Hermit sprang to life. He lengthened his stride, surged towards the finishing post, won the race, made a fortune for his owner, and became a symbol of courage in adversity.

One of the most trying results of Phiz's paralysis was his initial inability to ride a horse but, characteristically, he began drawing horses and even writing about them as soon as he was able. In 1868, he produced *Racing and Chasing*, fifty large drawings in a handsome album, reproduced in colour by graphotype, a process in which the image was drawn onto a chalk block with a glue-rich ink. When the chalk between the lines was brushed away, it left an image in relief, and the block was then turned into a relief block in metal by a double process of electrotyping. Phiz also arranged to have some of these drawings – the ones that referred to the Derby – published in a sixpenny edition, which he called *London's Great Outing*. And in 1869, he produced *The Derby Carnival*, a sixpenny publication for sale at Epsom at the time of the race, adding his own text to the drawings. Phiz's writing is full of his joy at being at the course again. Here are a few excerpts:

'Look at the horses as they curvet³ and stride about. What graceful attitudes! what noble carriage! their skin sheenier than satin, their speed rivalling the wind and water! How they arch their proud necks, as though conscious of their noble lineage! Why, a Derby favourite is attended by a court almost as numerous as that of a German "sublimity", . . . How strange that these noble creatures get enveloped in such an atmosphere of mystery and fraud! . . . Racehorses seem to have the power of entirely upsetting man's calm judgment and common-sense. . . . Truly, in horseracing, like in love and war, everything seems fair. But all this does not make these thoroughbreds less beautiful. . . .

'There are legends that they make the salad there in vats and mix it with wooden spades, that the crust of the pies would cover square roods of land, and that the liquor would float a frigate. . . . Fortnum and Mason are popularly supposed to be up all night for the last week, packing savoury pies, and tinfoil-capped bottles, and tender chickens in capacious wickerwork receptacles – and all because it is the Derby. . . . Mr Dickens, I believe, has stated in print that if he were to enter a horse for the "Derby", he would call him Fortnum and Mason. . . .

'What an incalculable amount of money must be staked every year! what legions of bets must be laid! Scarcely a busman in London but has a little "pot" upon the big race; not a groom or stable-help but anxiously awaits the result. And how soon the result is known in town! The wire takes it swiftly to the telegraphic centres, and soon the news spreads; conductor shouts to conductor, cabman passes it on to cabman, and soon from Brompton to Bethnal-green, from Camden-town to Camberwell, the magic name is known'.[4]

Hooray for the Derby! Phiz's love of horses had him up and going again, drawing horses, writing about horses and, as soon as he was able, riding horses.

18

Family Fun, Good Friends, and Hard Times

Phiz had a successful career as an illustrator but later in life, it appears, he and his professional partner[1] found it increasingly hard to make ends meet because they wasted so much time laughing. I like the whole story.

Alec Guinness[2]

Phiz's firstborn, Edgar, inherited his father's artistic ability, and became a capable watercolourist. He also designed Christmas cards and playbills for the many amateur productions that took place at his home in Liverpool. In his professional life, he changed his focus from general medicine to ophthalmology and became a pioneer in the field of cataract surgery, thus making good use of the family's Huguenot talent for the tiny. Edgar's own eyesight was said to be so good that he was still able to perform operations after the age of seventy without the aid of eyeglasses. He and Alice

'A Surprise'

Domenica produced six children at regular intervals from 1868 onwards, and named their first son Hablot John Moxon, thus covering many bases.[3]

Phiz's days were brightened by the illustrated letters he received from his second son, Charles Michael, in India. Charles had a successful career in the 12th Bombay Infantry. He was a more flamboyant and less religious character than his namesake uncle, relishing amateur theatricals, gymkhanas, and illustrated jokes. In 1873, he returned to England on leave and married Josephine Nicholson, Henry Albert Browne's niece by marriage, a wedding at which Phiz's daughters, Emma and Eliza, were bridesmaids.

Charles Michael wrote for several papers in India, published a series of humorous sketches called *Bombay Ducks*, and recorded much of his life in India in pictures. His work is full of grotesquerie and caricature, and C.G. Browne tells the story of a gaffe when General Sir George Graves (the prototype for Kipling's 'snowy-haired Lothario, Lieutenant General Bangs'[4]) was visiting:

> [Sir George] was putting up with the Brownes during an Inspection Tour, dinner was very late much to the old man's annoyance. He became very irritable & more so when looking into an Album he found a caricature of himself as 'General Bangs that most immoral man'. The atmosphere became very strained, when by a lucky chance his eye fell on a picture by 'Phiz', with whom he had travelled in Italy & Ireland & his delight in meeting Phiz' son made him forget the caricature.[5]

This is the only mention of Phiz's ever having visited Italy. Graves and he may have met while staying with Charles Lever in Dublin, and together visited Lever in Italy at a later date.

Like Phiz, who designed a set (for *Nicholas Nickleby*[6]) in his early days, Charles Michael tried his hand at set design and is given special mention in September 1878 in the *Pioneer*, a Bombay newspaper: 'The scenery was well got up especially the very pretty "Drop Scene", painted by Captain Browne. The subject being the Fairy Queen reclining in a golden boat, steered by a cherub and drawn by a team of swans, other fairies floating aloft. The back-ground appeared to be a bit of Canara scenery, probably a reach of the "Kala Nuddee" near Sirsi.' His acting ability in *The Porter's Knot* was also singled out for praise: 'The part of Samson Burr was done to perfection by Captain Browne [who] certainly exhibits dramatic talent of an order not often shown by amateurs.'[7]

Walter ('My Dear Doctor') studied art at the Heatherly School in London and with Léon Bonnat in Paris. He made commercial art his profession, and worked for several illustrated magazines, including *Punch*. M.H. Spielmann recounts that *Punch* hired Walter through his father's influence with Mark Lemon, and although his work was 'young', Walter might have stayed with *Punch* if he had not accepted a delusive offer of work for *Fun*, thus closing the door in his own face.[8] From then on he worked on news-drawing and book-illustration. He married Constance George, whom C.G. Browne calls 'a very beautiful woman with the real Titian hair' and their son, Reginald, was born in 1870.

When Walter was studying in Paris, he received a wry, undated letter from his father, which throws light on why Phiz was often hard up. If he had cash on hand, he was generous to a fault – and he was still paying school fees:

My Dear Doctor,
   I send the Tenpounder, may it reach you in safety! . . .
   I am (at *present*) *on* a Sporting Paper – supported by some high and mighty Turf Nobs, but, I fear, like everything I have to do with, now-a-days, it will collapse – for – some of the Proprietors of the Paper are also Shareholders, &c., &c., in the Graphotype Co. . . . I hate the process – it takes quite four times as long as wood – and I cannot draw and express myself with a nasty little finiking brush, and the result when printed seems to alternate between something all as black as my hat – or as hazy and faint as a worn-out plate. – If on wood, I should like it well enough – as it is – it spoils 4 days a week – leaving little time for anything else. O! I'm a'weary, I'm a'weary of this illustration business.
   Tom[9], is just off to the R.A., as it is not likely I shall go much before it's close. I will get him to write you a critical description of all the wonderful works in Turps, Varnish, and 'Hile'. [Oil]
   Yr. affectionate Dad, H.K.B.[10]

On another occasion, Phiz responds humorously but bitingly to a request from Walter, who is beginning to sound like a sponge:

Really, my dear Walter, I thought you *did* know better than to disturb my devotional frame of mind on this blessed Sabbath morn by forwarding me such a thoroughly worldly and evil-thought-producing thing as a wretched milliner's bill!!! — The wretch must wait — he gorged £5 not long before I left home. — The greediness of some men!!¹¹

The nerve of Walter! £5 for hats would be a considerable sum at that date.

In September 1868, Walter went to stay with his cousin, Ada Bicknell, and her family in Devon. He brought her a letter from his father; in it Phiz's *joie de vivre* seems back in full force:

> My dear Ada,
>
>   I had hoped to have sent you down by Walter proofs of yr. Graph: drawing — but the wretches have disappointed me — I think the manager is making holiday, out of town like everybody else — so I must send them by post — as soon as I get them.
>
>   . . . Tell the boys [Ada's sons] that Walter is dotingly fond of cricket, & that he will play at it *all day* with them, and go without his dinner, if *they* will! —
>
>   He is also a splendid monkey and could swing by his tail, if he had one — but we Brownes lost ours two generations back — more's the pity — because as Acrobats we should doubtless have made a mint more money than as Artists — I mean Painters — for are not Acrobats Artists also?
>
>   He is also a prodigious Elephant — a most magnificent Tiger — 'Tiger, Tiger, burning bright' — and as a Lion 'he will roar you an t'were any nightingale' — nonetheless, 'he is a gentle beast & of good conscience.' —
>
>   With love to all — Always yours affectionate uncle, H.K. Browne¹²

Phiz followed this up with a letter to Walter:

> . . . I hope you are not belying the *good* character I have given of you to the boys — and are doing Elephant, Tiger, and Rhinoceros to their perfect satisfaction — though, considering yr. predecessor [i.e. Phiz] — it will test your utmost powers, not to be a wretched failure . . . Good Night.
>
>   Yr. affectionate Dad, H.K.B.¹³

In 1865, the Brownes had moved to Blenheim Crescent, and in 1872 they moved yet again, with their four daughters and their servants, the short distance to 99 Ladbroke Grove (now 239), a brand-new house which, with wry humour, Phiz dubbed 'Bleak House'. It was certainly in an exposed position, being at the end of a row of houses, but its bay windows and five storeys offered the Brownes plenty of light and space. By this time, Phiz's two older daughters, Emma and Eliza, were in their twenties. Emma made a speciality of painting on china, and Eliza wrote poems and stories. Mabel, the third daughter, also became a writer, and published essays; Beatrice, the youngest girl, inherited her father's love of animals. She was a staunch supporter of the RSPCA which presented her with an award for her services. It is strange that only one of the Brownes' four daughters married – Eliza wed Captain James Ingram of the Merchant Marine – and none had children. Judging by the photographs, ill looks were not the cause. Rather, the lack of suitors was probably the result of their father's penury and the emigration drain. Young men were leaving England in droves to find their fortunes in the wide reaches of the Empire.

One of his daughters (it is unclear which) describes Phiz's life at Ladbroke Grove, where newspaper-reading has taken over the prime early morning spot:

> About half past eight he would come down to breakfast, read the newspaper, and then regularly disappear into his own room until dinner-time. After dinner he generally remained in the dining-room reading, and if not reading he would be sure to be working. He was seldom idle, and even his evenings were spent in reading or working.

Phiz's favourite author was Shakespeare, and he often carried a play in his pocket. He preferred *Cymbeline* to all others, that paean to steadfast love, full of generous spirit and the wonders of the vast outdoors, where everyone is at the mercy of circumstances, emotions, and events.

His daughter continues:

> He was much affected by the weather, and gloried in bright sunshiny days; a dreary, wet, gloomy day had a most depressing effect upon him, and in Ladbroke Grove Road he frequently went to bed in the afternoon, unless he drew down the blinds and lit up the gas to shut out the gloominess. He was most simple in his ways and life, and hated affectation of any kind, most careless of dress or

personal appearance, and did not care in the least what he looked like, or what people would think of him, never studying Mrs Grundy.[14]

Phiz was not particularly interested in food, and ate sparingly. He loathed being waited on and fussed over, and never complained, even if he felt ill. He loved all kinds of animals. 'If he found the cat in his armchair,' continues his daughter, 'he would never disturb her, however tired he was, but would inconvenience himself for her sake, saying, "Let her be, poor pussy, she likes that chair."'

He was unimpressed by money and status and was as polite to beggars as to the rich. He loved the grandeur of nature and often reminded his children how splendidly the sea broke on Ireland's west coast. 'He was interested in astronomy too, and said he should like to be an astronomer, if he were a rich man and hadn't to work for his living.'[15]

One cannot help wishing that Susannah had been included in this description because so little is known about her. She seems to have appeared out of nowhere and led such a thoroughly domestic existence that even Edgar spends precious few words on her. Apart from mentioning that his mother adored his father and she returned to health when the family moved to the country, his only other comment about her is that she had lovely hands which acted as models for the sculptor, Patrick Park.[16] However, Rita Browne comments that Susannah was cheerful and much loved, and Phiz's drawing of her in a letter to an unknown recipient makes clear the humour inherent in their relationship. It also reveals how well Susannah kept her waistline after having delivered thirteen children (including the three who died at birth). The text of the letter reads:

Oct. 6, 1860

My Dear Sir,

My Better half is charmed with my Head! and thinks it quite a Caput-al likeness – she carries it about up stairs & down stairs, all over the House, to test different light & – till I think she must be trying to experiment in <u>pol</u>arization of Light. – I suggest she had better wear it as a Shawl Brooch –

I think I must make a sketch of her as Herodias walking about with John the Baptist's Head in a charger – (to some, perhaps, it might suggest a tempting dish of Calf's Head!) – But with all this shew of affection, she has just declared her determination to hang me! and grumbles because I am (of course) rather slow in providing a nail for the horrid purpose!

The preparations are now going on!!!! – I feel quite resigned to my sad fate – (thank you!) and only hope that I shall be strung up in the most approved Jack-Ketchy manner.

I remain (for 5 mins. more only!)
Yours Very Truly, H.K. Browne[17]

Susannah hanging Phiz, 1860

Phiz refers in another letter with self-portrait sketch to his head being taken off – in this case, he probably means he has had a portrait photograph taken. The letter is clearly a response to a fan:

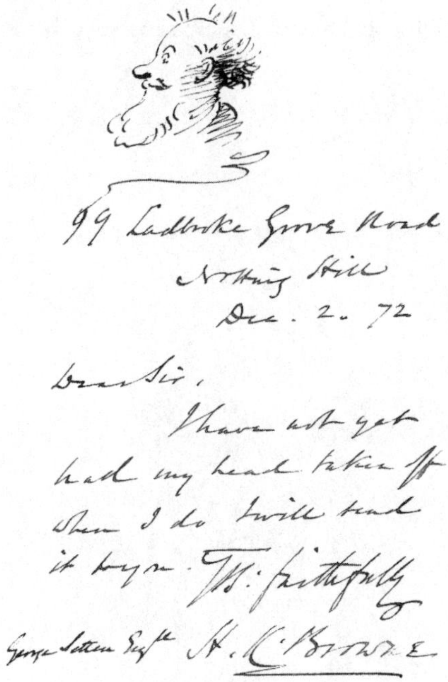

99 Ladbroke Grove Road
Notting Hill
Dec. 2. 72

Dear Sir,

I have not yet had my head taken off. When I do I will send it to you.

Yrs. faithfully,
H.K. Browne

George Setten, Esq.[18]

99 Ladbroke Grove Road
Notting Hill
Dec. 2. 72

Dear Sir,
I have not yet
had my head taken off
When I do I will send
it to you. Yrs: faithfully

George Setten Esq H. K. Browne

Self-portrait in letter, 1872

Even though the Brownes' fourth son, Thomas Hablot, may not have taken art training, he inherited the family talent and became a jeweller. He left England for Australia in 1882, when he was twenty-eight. But it is Gordon Frederick, the Brownes' youngest son, whose prolific career most resembled his father's. Gordon studied art at Heatherly's and in South Kensington, and became in his time almost as famous as Phiz. A frequent contributor to *Punch*, he also illustrated the works of Shakespeare, Scott, Milton, Bunyan, Defoe, Grimm, Swift, and Dumas, among others, but is remembered for his illustrations of boys' books, in particular the work of G.A. Henty.

Gordon's art training certainly shows; his figure drawing is more competent than Phiz's, and he was enormously popular with the public, but the sparkle, the grotesque razzle-dazzle, the wild invention of his father and his brother, Charles Michael, is missing, and as so often happens with the passage of time, originality becomes more valuable than technique.

Word of Charles Dickens's sudden death spread around London like wildfire. He was felled by a stroke on the evening of 9 June 1870. Gravediggers

Gordon Browne, self-caricature

hollowed out his last resting place in Poets' Corner in Westminster Abbey, next to those of Handel and Macaulay, and close to the memorials of Shakespeare, Chaucer and Milton. He was buried early in the morning of the 14th in a private ceremony. (Dickens had expressed the wish to be buried in an unannounced ceremony, preferably in Rochester, but the Dean of Westminster prevailed over the location.) By evening, crowds were gathering at Westminster to pay tribute. The Dean gave permission for the grave to be left open, and thousands of weeping people thronged into the Abbey to throw blossoms onto the coffin.

It is impossible to know whether Phiz was part of the crowd, but it seems more likely that he retired to his studio, turning his mind back to the beginning of the association, remembering the good times, the laughter, and the heady partnership. The only mention of his reaction to Dickens's death appeared in the *Frankfurter Zeitung*. The writer commented, 'Just after the death of Charles Dickens, "Phiz" was considerably affected by the mere mention of the name of that illustrious novelist, which seemed to stir up in his breast feelings of regret at losing such a friend.'[19] The newspaper must have sent a journalist to London to cover the story of Dickens's death, and the enterprising writer found his way to Phiz's door.

During the early 1870s Phiz managed to complete a commission he had begun in 1866. F. W. Cosens, the Dickens collector, had asked him to make replicas of all his illustrations for the Dickens novels. Cosens describes meeting Phiz:

> I remember to have had only two or three interviews with him, and as a stranger, found him shy and nervous. I desired to secure any sketches he might have of the illustrations to Dickens, but understood him to say he had none, as he drew them on the blocks. He evidently did not like the drudgery of reproduction, and named such terms as he thought would deter me; but finding the honorarium was of great importance to him the bargain was struck. The work extended over some years, and the later productions evince haste and inferiority. The work can hardly be called water-colour drawing, as it is simply sketching, slightly heightened by colour-washing.[20]

Ironically, Phiz did not own any of the books by Dickens containing his own illustrations and found himself in the awkward position of having to borrow them from Cosens in order to make the copies. In spite of his illness (which struck just a year after he began work), Phiz completed 405

Certificate self-portrait sketch, *David Copperfield*, 1866

drawings over four years. He wrote a note of authentication with an amusing self-portrait sketch to accompany each volume.

It is easy to imagine that Phiz hears of Dickens's death as he starts work on the 405th drawing. His pencil moves automatically over the page and Dr Manette appears, still miserably hunched on his bench, still reading, in a perfect composition within the arch of his cell. The huge chains still hang down and the walls still look damp to the touch. But Phiz does not copy the upright pitcher at Dr Manette's feet, the pitcher with its promise of plenty. He leaves it out; the well is dry.[21]

The 1870s were an appalling decade for Phiz. His career in book-illustrating was all but dead, but he struggled on, relying on hare-brained schemes and the unswerving belief that things would always somehow work out to his benefit. In 1869, he began a long association with *Judy*, the comic magazine, an association which would endure until his death. Sometimes he created his own letterpress for the illustrations. Edward Dalziel, the chief proprietor of *Judy*, says that he was always willing to exert himself on behalf of the magazine.[22]

Having had no book commissions for four years, Phiz decided in 1876

Final sketch of Dr Manette for F. W. Cosens, 1870

to publish a book on his own account, *All About Kisses*, an amusing trifle in verse about how, where, and whom to kiss. The 100 wood engravings are full of humour but crude, and Phiz may have been unable to afford a good cutter. It is unlikely that he made much money from this project. Money problems were compounded by the death of Octavius on 25 July of the same year. The annual £120 was no longer forthcoming from the next generation.

Phiz lacked funds, but he was certainly not short of friends. Edgar comments that even though his father did not venture much into society, he welcomed visitors to the house, and in this way reconnected with the London art world. Phiz's favourite friend was Fred Barnard, a young illustrator, a rhymester, actor, jokester, and one-man vaudeville show. Barnard had studied art at Heatherly's and with Bonnat in Paris at the same time as Walter. He first visited Phiz as an admirer, but soon became his friend. In spite of the difference in ages, the two men hit it off immediately, mining the same vein of humour, and entering into a series of ill-advised schemes with Barnard always eager to egg Phiz on. One of these schemes was to create a huge, didactic painting, 'The Drunken Helot', as a warning about the perils of drinking (a jab at Cruikshank's 'The Bottle'?). Barnard offered himself up as the model and spent an entire evening lurching around, entertaining the Brownes with demonstrations of various types of drunkenness. Phiz and Barnard chose Sparta as their background, and peopled the scene with women and children gathered beside a fountain, all eyes fixed on the staggering slave. Phiz made an admirable drawing of the scene, intending some day to create a huge oil painting, but somehow never found time to complete it.

Help of a more practical nature came from another good friend, Luke Fildes, the artist who illustrated Dickens's last, unfinished, novel *The Mystery of Edwin Drood*. In 1878, Fildes suggested that Phiz apply for a Government pension, and Phiz set about the task enthusiastically, sending off a draft for Robert Young to edit. Phiz's accompanying note to Young reads: 'Many thanks for the "petition" – it seems the correct thing. If Dizzy [the Prime Minister, Benjamin Disraeli] is benign, I shall henceforth become his steady supporter and a true Conservative (of the pension) as long as I live.'[23] The draft itself reads as follows:

I am sixty-three years old, and have been before the public forty-five years as an artist, constantly illustrating from month to month all sorts of books and authors – Bulwer, Dickens, Lever, Ainsworth, and many others; magazines, papers, periodicals of all sorts, comic and serious. It is just possible I have helped to amuse a few in my time, and in my earlier days I was a bit of a favourite, I think, but the present generation 'knoweth not Joseph'. I have had a large family, nine still living – four girls and one boy still dependent on me. I have had one paralytic attack, and I have been blinded of one eye for five months by acute rheumatism, but I am all right now.[24]

The mention of rheumatism, Phiz's euphemism for his paralytic illness, implies that he suffered the temporary blindness in 1867.

But Dizzy was not benign, and Phiz wrote again to Young saying, 'Things are as bad as they can be; so I suppose, as "it is a long lane that has no turning", my luck will turn sooner or later. Somehow, in spite of the black look of things, I have a sort of conviction that I shall die tolerably "*comfortable*". However, *faith* is a great thing, isn't it, my boy?'[25]

Luke Fildes was determined to extricate Phiz from the financial strait-jacket. When he learned that the petition for a Government pension was unsuccessful, he tried another tack. He knew that the Royal Academy had granted George Cruikshank an annuity, and saw no reason why the Academy should not do the same for Phiz. Together with his friends, the artists William Frith and H.T. Wells,[26] he presented a strong case – and was successful. In 1879, a year in which Phiz had complained, 'My occupation seems gone, extinct. . . . I have not had a single thing to do this year,'[27] he was granted an annuity by the Royal Academy, an annuity awarded to him in acknowledgement of his distinguished services to Art. He showed his gratitude to Fildes in a letter written from Ladbroke Grove on 15 February 1879.

> My dear Sir,
> I have written to Mr Wells to thank him for his aid in getting the annuity from the R.A. – still I feel I must be originally indebted to you for getting it afloat – and as I have sent Mr Wells a slight sketch – just to show that although I can get no work to do from publishers, I am not – (at least in my estimation) quite used up – altho' I may have outlived former friends – I also take the liberty of sending you one as a memorial – which you will gratify me by accepting.
> Yrs. truly, H.K. Browne[28]

Phiz was even more pleased by the recognition of his body of work than by the funds, although they did enable him to move one last time. He sought sea, bracing air, and sunshine away from city smoke, and moved with Susannah, his four daughters, and two maidservants to 8 Clarendon Villas in Hove, then a little town on the outskirts of Brighton. Soon after they moved in, and in spite of the fact that Number 8 was a small, terrace house, Phiz and Susannah had no hesitation in welcoming two of Charles Michael's children from India, four-year-old Josephine and two-year-old Mike. With doting grandparents and aunts, these children would certainly not have lacked affection, and their arrival prompted Phiz's daughters to start a kindergarten.

Eric Gill, the great sculptor and letterer, attended their school and described the Misses Browne as dear kind people. One of his memories of the kindergarten was an early attempt at sculpting. Fiona MacCarthy writes: 'He was handed out some clay, about the size of a plover's egg, with the suggestion that he should make something out of it by squeezing it. This flummoxed him completely since he was given no instructions.'[29] This comment sheds light on the Misses Brownes' educational philosophy.

Phiz was absolutely right when he told Robert Young that he believed that he would die 'tolerably comfortable'. Although the house was crowded, Phiz had a small but regular income, ready access to sea breezes, the affectionate company of women (seven in all), and little children playing at his feet. Without pressure from authors and publishers, he could sketch and paint what he wished, and his remarkable Prospero-like self-portrait came from this final, fertile period. Just before he died, his old friend George Halse successfully persuaded him to provide images for a collection of short stories, *A Salad of Stray Leaves*; and they also collaborated on *The Legend of Sir Juvenis*, a project that Gordon completed after his father's death.[30]

'[In Hove] he seems to have recovered much of his gaiety and his strength,' says Arthur Allchin, 'while his unfailing energy induced him to work daily for many hours, filling portfolios with sketches which he trusted would prove valuable to those he was soon to leave. He even thought of returning to etching, which he had long laid aside'. Allchin then continues gloomily, 'The plates were ordered, but were never used, since when they arrived the hand that should have worked on them was fast stiffening in death.'[31]

On 6 July 1882 Phiz suffered a cerebral haemorrhage. He died on 8 July and on his death certificate, the cause of death is given as 'Progressive Paralysis several years Cerebro & Spinal Effusion 2 days'. He is described as an etcher and painter, his age is given as sixty-six, and the certificate is signed by Susannah, who was present at his death.

Other than a few standard obituaries, the news of Phiz's death barely made a ripple in the press, but *Punch*, rather than publishing a staid account of his life, celebrated his achievement in verse:

'PHIZ'
HABLOT K. BROWNE. ARTIST. BORN, 1815. DIED, JULY, 1882.

The Lamp is out that lighted up the text
   Of DICKENS, LEVER – heroes of the pen.
Pickwick and *Lorrequer* we love, but next
   We place the man who made us see such men.
What should we know of *Martin Chuzzlewit*,
   Stern *Mr Dombey*, or *Uriah Heep*?
Tom Burke of Ours? – Around our hearths they sit,
   Outliving their creators – all asleep!
     No sweeter gift ere fell to man than his
      Who gave us troops of friends – delightful PHIZ!

He is not dead! There in the picture-book
   He lives with men and women that he drew;
We take him with us to the cozy nook

Where old companions we can love anew.
Dear Boyhood's friend! We rode with him to hounds;
    Lived with dear *Peggotty* in after years;
Missed in old Ireland where fun knew no bounds;
    At *Dora's* death we felt poor *David's* tears!
    There is no death for such a man – he is
        The spirit of an unclosed book! immortal PHIZ!

The Extra-Mural Cemetery, where Phiz was laid to rest, is a handsome, seventy-acre Victorian establishment, part of Brighton's Lewes Road Cemeteries. It opened its gates for business in 1851 and at the time of Phiz's death still had the look of a verdant, rolling hillside. Nowadays, it bills itself as one of the most delightful spots in Brighton, and its brochure requests that you listen for the call of woodpeckers and song thrushes, admire the ornamental trees and shrubs, and pay attention to holes that shelter badgers, foxes, and squirrels as you make your way to your destination. Phiz is in good company; the cemetery is also the last resting place of his contemporaries Thomas Hughes, author of *Tom Brown's Schooldays*; Maria Pattle Jackson, sister of Julia Margaret Cameron, and grandmother of Virginia Woolf; Arthur Tidman Gill and his wife, Rose, whose tombstone was carved by their son, Eric Gill; George Harrison, the great cycling pioneer; and Thomas Sayers, the bare-knuckled boxing champion of England.

Phiz was buried at the top of the hill, in a private ceremony attended by three friends, George Halse, Robert Harrison, and Dr Ambler, and four of his five sons, Edgar, Walter, Thomas, and Gordon; Charles would have been in India. Susannah and the four daughters did not attend, and would have read the burial service quietly at home.

The memorial was probably erected by his sons some time after the event; it bears no evidence of straitened circumstances, being a large chunk of Carrara marble, six feet high, two and a half feet wide, and five inches thick. When first installed, it towered over a low stone wall (now missing) with an iron railing, forming a rectangular 'bed'. The lead-letter inscription, leaving enough room for Susannah to be added later, read:

SACRED
TO THE MEMORY
OF
HABLOT KNIGHT BROWNE

WHO DIED JULY 8th 1882
AGED 67[32]
REST FOR THE TOILING HAND
REST FOR THE THOUGHTWORN BROW
REST FOR THE WEARY WAYSORE FEET,
REST FROM ALL LABOUR NOW

Twenty years later, the following inscription was added:
ALSO
SUSANNAH
WIFE OF THE ABOVE WHO DEPARTED THIS LIFE
FEB.10th 1902,
AGED 78
'UNTIL THE DAY DAWN AND THE SHADOWS FLEE AWAY.'[33]

19

The Gallery

Laugh! He will make you laugh. He will dash off pleasantries for you with a few touches of chalk and a slight wash of colour . . . He will take you and show you the happy and beautiful side of childhood. He will amuse you frankly and cheerfully with the mishaps of the hunting-field. But always he seems to return to the old, old morality. . . . He was a professional jester, and wore the cap and bells, but beneath his mirth was a deeper meaning.

Edgar Browne[1]

Shortly after Phiz died, Edgar organised an exhibition of 409 of his father's images. He was aware that Phiz had shown oil paintings at the Royal Academy – 'A Grave Hint' in 1841, and 'Death's Revel' and 'Death's Banquet' in 1871 – and had also exhibited pictures at the Hyde Park Corner Free Exhibition and, in later years, at the Society of British Artists; but he wanted to mount a show devoted to his father's entire range. The public, who knew Phiz almost exclusively as an illustrator, was amazed by

'The Picture Gallery – Sir Andrew Puzzled', Charles Lever, *Roland Cashel*, 1850 the variety, in both quality and quantity, of watercolours and drawings (often in series), oil paintings, and designs for statuettes and candlesticks. The exhibition opened at the Arts Club in Liverpool in January 1883 and was a grand success. Fred Barnard wrote a letter of thanks to Edgar, expressing his deep feelings about Phiz's work:

> . . . One of the greatest lessons I learnt from going carefully through the exhibition was this – that however repulsive and even squalid the subject may be that he chooses, there is always the same charming undercurrent of graceful composition. In everything he touched you can always feel that a keen sense of beauty was at the bottom of it. It comes all the more charmingly from his pencil, for it appears so thrown out in an unconscious and spontaneous manner. This particular sense of beauty of composition, which lies at the root and is the very grammar of all arts, is the rarest gift and the most difficultly learnt task of all, seems to come to him perfectly naturally. It never obtrudes itself, but it is always felt.[2]

The show was later transferred to the Fine Arts Gallery in London in a somewhat smaller version, and one of its visitors was seventeen-year-old Beatrix Potter, who later became the writer and illustrator of *The Tale of Peter Rabbit* and other famous children's books. She records in her journal:

> Saturday, December 15th.
> . . . The most interesting pencil drawings were the originals of *Dombey & Son*, *Bleak House* and *David Copperfield*. These drawings and some others of the same kind were simply marvellous. They were drawn for the most part on scraps of paper, blue very often, scribbled in the pencil. I do not think the engravings, good as they are, do them justice. There is a wonderful difference of expression in the faces, however small. . . .
> There were few drawings, if any, which could be called caricatures, and if there was a keen sense of the ridiculous, there was an equally strong one of beauty.[3]

It is odd how Beatrix Potter responds to Phiz's etchings; most people would agree that he comes brilliantly alive when armed with a stylus. His preliminary sketches, mere aides-memoires for composition, are often carelessly drawn with a blunt pencil – but perhaps they came closer to her own art.

Illustrating was the way for Phiz to earn money, but he never gave up the idea of being a painter. He executed watercolours not just for profit but for pleasure, turning out hundreds of pictures, many of which are graceful and pleasing, particularly the landscapes. The author, John Fowles, has one such picture hanging over his desk. It portrays the countryside around Banstead, and he describes it as 'spacious and very skilled', admitting he was lucky enough to buy it for £2, although the asking price was £5, 'as the dealer didn't have a clue on something signed H.K.B.'[4] Coincidentally, Edgar reproduced this very landscape on page 234 of *Phiz and Dickens*.

Phiz was neither as prolific nor as skilled at painting in oil as he was in watercolour. But even if oil painting does not show him at his best, how liberating it must have felt to uncoil from his perch over a steel plate and fling himself recklessly at an immense subject. With what glee he set about designing those two enormous cartoons, 'A foraging party of Caesar's forces surprized by Britons' (size 18' by 18'), and 'Henry II defied by a Welsh mountaineer', his tongue-in-cheek entries in the contest for decorating the newly rebuilt Houses of Parliament, and displayed in Westminster Hall in 1843. 'He astonished the public almost to amazement', says Charles Gordon Browne. 'Nothing could have been funnier than the expression of the figures in these works'.[5]

Not all of Phiz's oil paintings were immense like the grim 'Death's Revel' (7' 8" by 4'). 'The Country Manager Rehearses a Combat' which Phiz probably painted close to the time he etched the plate of the same subject for *Nicholas Nickleby* is 12" x 10½".[6] In the 1840s, he completed a series of six charming images[7] which average 6" by 5". They appear to illustrate scenes from a book, not by Dickens, but possibly *The Vicar of Wakefield*. These images and 'The Country Manager . . .' reveal how good an oil painter Phiz might have been if he had had more time at his disposal – and the inclination to study technique.

Five years after his death, when income was scarce, Susannah and her daughters decided to cash in on the work he had left to them for exactly such a time. The auction took place at Sotheby, Wilkinson & Hodge's house on the Strand, on 5 December 1887. By this date, Phiz was squarely out of fashion, and the sale did not realise as much money as the family hoped. But its 345 items further revealed the range of Phiz's work: classical poses, hunting scenes, moral admonishment, comic moments, and even designs for an eau de Cologne stand, a clock, an epergne, and a yachting trophy. Most interestingly, four engravings were included (engraving being the technique Phiz had disliked so heartily in the early days at Finden's). It is possible that they were executed for Elhanan Bicknell, since Phiz received a sudden payment of £250 from Bicknell in 1851[8] (but it is also possible that this payment was a legacy from Phiz's sister, Lucinda Bicknell, who died in 1850). The first engraving, 'On the Scheldt', is after Turner, Bicknell's great favourite. The other three engravings are 'Juno Borrowing the Cestus from Venus', after Angelica Kauffmann, and 'The Bottle' and 'The Drunkard's Children', after Cruikshank.

A flurry of grangerising accompanied the publication in 1884 of the first limited edition of 200 copies of David Croal Thomson's *The Life and Labours of Hablôt Knight Browne*. (To 'grangerise' means to add extra material such as drawings, paintings, letters, and maps to an existing book, and in many cases having the volume bound to specification.) An extraordinary such copy, probably compiled by Frederick Cosens judging from the number of letters addressed to him, contains 1,370 extra illustrations, including ninety-two original drawings, bound into twenty red morocco volumes. The frontispiece at first appears to be Prospero, but it is a circular self-portrait of Phiz, painted in oil. It depicts the artist in old age, wearing a skullcap and his usual dark working clothes. The fineness of his features and flowing white beard are set off by a muddy background. His high brow is creased, his face lean, his eyes cast down. The impression – the impact – of the picture is of a man at peace, even as it reveals the years of hard work and the fatigue.

The hand that painted this late oil does not shake. The self-portrait is the work of an illustrator proving at the end of his life that he could have been a fine artist, one whose special skill was the rendering of faces. Phizzes.

★

Tuesday, June 19,

6A, Crescent Place, Margate.

I did some very good shades myself – of myself – unconsciously – yesterday evening. The baths run along one side of the High Street, flush with the pavement – and I found when I had nearly finished my toilet that the gas-burner was so ingeniously placed, that it was impossible for any bather to avoid casting gigantic studies of the nude upon the window blind. – This sort of thing. – [9]

'Phiz takes a bath', sketch in letter

Epilogue and Acknowledgements

Finding Phiz

Phiz has been the best of companions, his art consistently surprising me and his wit a ready source of encouragement. An object of affection world-wide, he called forth extraordinary willingness from those on whom I leaned for help, and I offer them my warmest thanks.

I am Phiz's great-great-granddaughter, descended through a series of eldest sons. As the only child of an only child, I felt bereft of Browne relatives until seven years ago when I began to unravel the mystery of Phiz's genesis. My father never talked about his ancestors, and as he was no longer around when I began rooting for information, I started alone, at the end, with a grave.

I discovered that Phiz was buried in the Extra-Mural Cemetery in Brighton and, with the aid of my school friend Caroline Jose, found his tombstone standing there, pitted and green from overhanging vegetation, with half its lead inscription missing. As I looked, one of the letters dropped off. I took this as a message to begin, literally, with a clean slate, and set

'My Magnificent Order at the Public House', *David Copperfield*

about having the tombstone restored. Stephen Horlock, the cemetery regis-
trar, was delighted with the idea so long as the restoration maintained the
tombstone's essentially Victorian character. He suggested that I abandon
lead lettering (since marble eventually throws off lead on a vertical tombstone). After we reconstructed the wording, Helen Mary Skelton, the great-
niece of Eric Gill, cut letters in the original script on to a slate panel to
be inserted into the marble. At the time of the restoration I had no idea
about the mysteries of Phiz's birthdate, and as the second digit of his age
was missing in the original wording on the tombstone, I was forced to
choose between 66 and 67 for his age at death. There was no consensus
among the experts I now know I was wrong in terms of the original
inscription, but technically correct – by two days – according to Phiz's
death certificate and funeral announcement.

Once the slate was cut, Tom Tilley's team of monumental masons went
to work. The whole effort took more than a year, and I invited those who
had worked on the project to celebrate, along with Edward Preston and
Andrew Carslake from the Dickens Fellowship, and David and Betty
Dickens. The appointed day, 19 February 1998, dawned raw and misty, but
we made our way up the hill to find Phiz's memorial gleaming through
the drizzle. The stone was pure white, its grey slate panel blackened by
rain, and the ground was covered with marble dust – the masons had
finished their work moments before we arrived. David Dickens placed a
bunch of bright tulips beside the stone with a note that read 'From the
Dickens family, with admiration and respect', and I read aloud Phiz's obituary from *Punch*. Then we made our way down the hill to The Bear, an
ancient pub that Phiz may have known, and we all had a jolly time.

A few years before my father died, he announced he would give me 'The
Books', and a large, black, tin trunk was hauled up from the coal cellar. Its
contents included some works illustrated by Phiz, including a first bound
edition of *The Pickwick Papers* inscribed 'To Kate With Hablot's Love – Jan.
1. 1838'; the 1838–1841 Charles Knight pictorial edition of the complete
works of Shakespeare; and a large portfolio of drawings. The books were in
disrepair, but I found a bookbinder to mend them, and in this way I began
to care for Phiz. But with no family history available, I had to enter his
world through Dickens, and it was at the Charles Dickens Museum that I
first stumbled on the trail of lost relations. After a day in the files, I asked
David Parker, the curator, if there was any late-breaking news about Phiz.

'Alas', he said, 'there never is.'

And then he added, 'But there's a man in Scotland who says he's a relative and he owns Phiz's sideboard. I've written to him, but got no reply. You might be luckier'.

I was. I found Gordon Anderson on the island of Mull. He is descended from Phiz's second son, Charles Michael, and the sideboard turned out to be Phiz's desk, an elegant, gleaming piece with, on the inside, a much scratched, pitted, ink-stained, tilt-top working surface. The desk was empty except for Phiz's calling card and some Christmas decorations.

Gordon said that his sister, Margaret MacKenzie, was the family genealogist. I visited her in Vancouver, and she produced Phiz's blanket chest, stuffed with photographs, two paintings by Phiz, and literally hundreds of drawings by Phiz's sons, Charles Michael and Gordon, all of which she made available to me. Then she forwarded me to Peter Browne, who owned – *mirabile dictu* – a handwritten family history.

Peter, a witty journalist, is descended from Phiz's son Gordon, and he lives in Twickenham, near London, not far from the site of The Lodge, Thomas and Ann Moxon's home, and close to the ferry that Phiz drew in *Little Dorrit*. The handwritten history was Rita Browne's word-for-word copy of *Notes to Assist Future Authors of the History of the Huguenot Family of Browne*, compiled by Phiz's nephews Charles Gordon Browne and Algernon Sidney Bicknell in 1905, with additional information added by Rita in 1929. Peter lent it to me, and it became my required reading.

I profited greatly from the kindness of the Dickens Fellowship in London, especially Michael Slater – and Allan Clack who visited and photographed all Phiz's many London residences. Allan also helped hunt down Le Brun and Brunet at the Huguenot Library, but hit the same dead end that earlier researchers did. What he found, however, was the address of Lieutenant Commander Kendall Moxon Browne, who had visited the library in 1969. I knew that the Moxon Brownes were descended from Phiz's brother Octavius, so I shot an arrow in the air, in the form of a letter to the thirty-year-old address in Devon. It hit home. On my next trip to London, I met Kendall's son, Bob. As I walked into his house, he said:

'Before we go any further, I must tell you that my family has always believed Phiz was illegitimate'.

Fuel for the fire of my conjecture! I told Bob I had drawn the same conclusion, and revealed my theory about Kate and Captain Hablot. Bob demurred at first, insisting that Phiz's talent came directly from William Loder Browne, but when I suggested that Phiz did indeed inherit it from William, via Kate, Bob struck his head and said:

'That's it! Oh, yes! Of course!'

Since that moment, Robert Moxon Browne QC and his wife, Kicki, have showered me with kindness – sharing family records, books, pictures, and a place to stay in London – and Bob has examined my ideas while adding his own considered opinions. The ideal sleuth, he discovered Browne loot in the hands of Sue Lowther-Pinkerton, Prue Craig-Waller, and Simon Pardoe, more new cousins. They possessed examples of work by Simon Browne, John Henry Browne, and Kate herself, and my visits to their respective homes made me feel like Howard Carter entering the tomb of Tutankhamen three times over; actually being able to study the images revealed in stunning clarity the imprimatur of Phiz's artistic inheritance.

While on the subject of new-found cousins, I thank yet another – Marcus Bicknell – for his help and for the magnificent celebration at the Garrick Club. He gathered together seven Bicknells, all descended from Phiz's sister Lucinda, for lunch in a private dining room. They included a sprightly nonagenarian, Claud, who invited me to visit him in the Lake District to view the bust of Lucinda and portraits of Elhanan Bicknell, an invitation I accepted with alacrity. My debt of gratitude to all my new-found cousins – Gordon, Margaret, Peter, Bob, Sue, Pru, Simon, Marcus, and (the now late) Claud – is enormous. I thank them for their encouragement and for so unselfishly sharing their inherited material.

I was at a loss when trying to hunt down the elusive Captain Hablot until I approached Napoleon on the Internet. The electronic path led to Terry Senior, an expert on Napoleonic generals and colonels in particular, but willing to take on an exceptional captain. He procured Nicolas Hablot's *états de service* from Vincennes, and in a stroke of brilliance downloaded the page containing the name 'Hablot' in the telephone book for the department of Meuse. I wrote to all sixteen Hablots, asking about Nicolas. The response was immediate and fascinating: three emails from teenagers wanting a pen pal; a film about the church in Dugny-sur-Meuse where Nicolas was baptised; and, best of all, a letter from Pascal Hablot, the family historian, with enclosures: the registrations of baptism, marriage, and burial for Nicolas Hablot, and the newspaper cutting about the discovery of his tombstone. It was clearly time to go to France. My maternal cousin, Petra Molloy, another indefatigable sleuth who has travelled with me for glimpses of Phiz in Greta Bridge, Norwich, Cambridge and Nottingham, joined me in search of Captain Hablot in St Omer, Waterloo, Dugny-sur-Meuse and Carignan. Pascal hoped to join us in Dugny but his duties as police chief of Rouen prevented this; in his place, Denis

Bonfils, a writer, and Bruno Frémont, the local doctor and historian, showed us around. With their help, I was able to picture Nicolas's village life before he joined Napoleon's army.

Gérard Hablot, Pascal's brother, appeared the next day to drive us to Carignan, where Nicolas lived after his marriage. A marathon runner, Gérard lives life at full tilt, and we swooped north in teeming rain and found our way to the town hall, which we left with two useful items: the Lavorels' address, where pigs had snouted up Nicolas's tombstone and the location of Anne Thérèse Hablot's grave in the local cemetery. The rain continued to lash down as we approached the Lavorels' neat little house. No one was home, so we tapped on the neighbour's door. A diminutive old man appeared, and set off through the rain to show us the exact location of the tombstone's discovery at a moment when the Lavorels were digging a foundation for their pig pen.

Searching for other family members, I realised I could fulfil a lifelong ambition to visit Australia and New Zealand while hunting down information about Phiz's brothers Gordon, Octavius, and Decimus, and his son, Thomas Hablot. My husband Jim and I set off, and in Sydney my godchild, Belinda Bolding, helped us find records for Thomas Hablot and his descendants; in Melbourne, Jim and I rented bicycles and rode out to St Kilda to search, in vain, for 'Charnwood', the mansion Octavius built. Elisabeth Neales of the Melbourne Dickens Fellowship later explained that 'Charnwood' was torn down when the area was redeveloped, but she brought photographs of it and information about Octavius's life in Melbourne, as well as a print of the beautiful portrait of him by Georgiana McCrae.

In New Zealand, the Auckland Public Library put me in touch with Barbara Ruck at the Auckland Research Centre and Janet Riddle, of the Mercury Bay Museum at Whitianga. Many thanks to them for enlightening us about life in New Zealand in the early 1800s.

The subject of Phiz's illustrations for Charles Lever is vast and the path virtually untrodden. My friend, Margie Deverell, met me in Dublin, and we made a pilgrimage to Templeogue House where Phiz visited Lever during the years 1842–1845. In Coleraine, Marjorie Geary of the Irish Records Office introduced me to the works of Lever experts Tony Bareham and Stephen Haddelsey. A year later I visited Portstewart and trawled with the generous and knowledgeable Tony Bareham through his massive Lever collection. I met Stephen Haddelsey in Nottingham Castle museum, where I had gone to see Phiz's drawing, 'An Italian Peasant Girl'. He and I conversed for hours about the impact of Phiz's images on Lever's work. I thank Stephen and Tony for sharing their knowledge of the under-appreciated (in this era) but captivating Charles Lever.

It has been my privilege to meet the group of authors who wrote about Phiz in a sudden flurry of interest in the 1960s and 1970s: Michael Steig, John Harvey, Jane Rabb Cohen, Simon Houfe, and John Buchanan-Brown. They have all been unstintingly encouraging and enlightening. I visited Michael Steig in Vancouver, and he produced various items from his collection of Phiz-illustrated books for me to examine. When he decided to sell his collection he contacted me, and I bought the lot. I thank him profoundly each time I need to consult a specific image and find it on my bookshelf.

One disappointment has been my inability to locate any of Phiz's large-scale oil paintings and see for myself whether they are truly as awful as Thomson intimates. Where are 'Sintram and Death descending into the Dark Valley' and the eight-foot-long 'Les Trois Vifs et les Trois Morts'? Where is 'Tam O'Shanter,' once owned by the Forbes collection but sold at Sotheby's in 1995? And where are the cartoons for the House of Commons?

I have been luckier with smaller oil paintings, several of which I have seen in private collections. Perhaps the most extraordinary oil painting of all is the Prospero-like self-portrait, and I must thank my friend Martin Nason for putting me on its trail, and for all his other kindness.

Many dealers have helped with wisdom and goods: Paul Goldman; Brian Lake and Janet Nassau of Jarndyce; William Drummond; Peter Allen (of Robert Temple) and his online archive; Ed Nudelman; Phillip Pirages; James Cummins; and the ever-seductive Alibris.com.

The Victoria and Albert Museum, the British Library, the British Museum Department of Prints and Drawings, the London Metropolitan Archives, the Norwich Record office, the *Punch* Archives, and the Charles Dickens Museum are Phiz gold mines. I have also profited from examining collections of his work in the United States at the Free Library in Philadelphia (special thanks to William Lang, Karen Lightner, and Joel Sartorius); the Library of Congress; the New York Public Library; the Princeton University Library; the Beinecke Library at Yale; the Boston Public Library; the Pierpont Morgan Library; the Huntington Library; and the Houghton Library at Harvard. These last two each provided me with a month's fellowship, sublime stretches of time in which to look and look again. There are no greater allies than well-tuned library people, and I owe special gratitude to Jacqueline Dugas, Alan Jutzi, and Christopher Addé at the Huntington, and Roger Stoddard, Susan Halpert, Elizabeth Falsey, Thomas Ford, and Joseph Zajac at the Houghton. I am also grateful to the Gelman Library at George Washington University.

My principal readers have been Robert Pattern, Michael Slater, Bob Moxon Browne, Diana Phillips, and Jim Lester. Bob Patten is the author of *George Cruikshank: Life, Times, and Art*, an exemplary biography. He pushed me into deep water and cheered when I swam. Michael Slater shared his vast knowledge and offered this sound advice: 'Keep Dickens at bay.' The last three have kindly read many drafts, an affliction they endured with good humour and bite. Diana, in particular, infused the work with her deep knowledge of the art, behaviour, and literature of the nineteenth century.

I thank them all profoundly.

I would also like to thank Cedric Dickens for all the fun; Scip Barnhart and Chris Mona, my printmaking teachers; Brian Walker, comic strip artist and Phiz aficionado; Stephen Massil at the Huguenot Library; Carol Digel, Pat Vinci, Herb Moskovitz, and the late, truly great, Martha Rosso of the Philadelphia Dickens Fellowship; Nancy Moore and John Luccarelli of the Pittsburgh Dickens Fellowship; Tony Williams, Thelma Grove, and everyone at the Dickens Fellowship Headquarters in London; Andrew Xavier and Florian Schweizer, curator and assistant curator at the Charles Dickens Museum; the Friends of Christchurch, Spitalfields; the Friends of West Norwood Cemetery; the Friends of the Dickens Project in Santa Cruz; Anita O'Brien of the Cartoon Art Trust; Jack Strang of *Huguenot Heritage*; and Mary Burdett; Carolyn Campbell; Andrew Carslake; Jonathan Chaves; Robert Colby; Bill and Jennifer Cordeaux; R.E.G. Davies; Sarah deLima; Miriam Dow; John Fowles; Lady Dorothy Gilbertson; Paul Graham; Sarah and Christopher Gregory; Marie-Agnès Hablot; Joan and Peter Hockaday; Patricia Jenkyns; John Jordan; Pat and Paul Kaplan; Toby, Alison, and Jane Lester; Niall McGarry; Maire McQueeney; Helena Michie; Sally Montgomery; Andrew Mooney; Rosemary Pruniaux; Jeremy Rex-Parkes; Joanna Rottke; Evan Summer; Alan Watts and Jim Wheaton.

Special thanks to the team at Chatto & Windus, especially Jenny Uglow, my editor, for being so incredibly adept, and Gillian Kemp for her copy-editing. And warmest gratitude to Jim Lester for his photographs and for sharing his wife with another man for seven years. And now I come round again to Phiz, who presented the challenge, provided me with a family, and led me into such a rollicking adventure.

Appendix I

Works Illustrated by Phiz

*Wood engravings † Browne and others
Works are published in London unless otherwise indicated.

1836

Charles Dickens (as Timothy Sparks), *Sunday Under Three Heads**
Charles Dickens, *The Strange Gentleman* (frontispiece)
Henry Winkles, *Cathedral Churches of England and Wales*, Vol. I†

1837

Edward Caswall (as 'Quiz'), *Sketches of Young Ladies*
Charles Dickens, *Posthumous Papers of the Pickwick Club*
John Woods, *History of London*†

1838

Edward Caswall, *Morals from the Churchyard**
Charles Dickens (as 'Boz'), *Sketches of Young Gentlemen*
Richard Falconer, *Voyages* (two plates)
James Grant, *Sketches in London*
Stephen Oliver (Music by Daniel Blake), *The Old English Squire* (a song)
R.S. Surtees, *Jorrocks' Jaunts and Jollities*
Henry Winkles, *Cathedral Churches of England and Wales*, Vol. II†

1839

W.A. Chatto (as 'Joseph Fume'), *A Paper of Tobacco**
Charles Dickens, *Nicholas Nickleby*
Charles Lever, *Harry Lorrequer*. Dublin
J.P. Robertson, *Solomon Seesaw*
Douglas Jerrold (as 'Captain Barrabas Whitefeather'), *The Handbook of Swindling*

1840

(Anon.) *The Legend of Cloth Fair*

Capt. R.N. Chamier, *The Spitfire: A Nautical Romance*

Charles Dickens (as 'Boz'), *Sketches of Young Couples*

Henry Fielding, *Life of Mr. Jonathan Wild*

Theodore Hook, *Precepts and Practice*

G.W.M. Reynolds, *Robert Macaire in England*

1841

(Anon.) *Legendary Tales of the Highlands*

Charles Dickens, *Master Humphrey's Clock* (including *The Old Curiosity Shop* and *Barnaby Rudge*)* †

Charles Dickens (ed.) *The Pic-Nic Papers* †

Theodore Hook, *The College Scout*

Theodore Hook, *Peter Priggins*

Charles Lever, *Charles O'Malley*. Dublin

W.J. Neale, *Paul Periwinkle*

'Cavendish Pelham' (ed.), *The Chronicles of Crime* (some of these plates reappear in 1871 in L. Benson's *Book of Remarkable Trials* *)

Frances Trollope, *Charles Chesterfield*

1842

Cornelius Mathews, *The Career of Puffer Hopkins*. New York

W.H. Maxwell, *Rambling Recollections of a Soldier of Fortune**

G.T. Miller, *Godfrey Malvern*

Sir Walter Scott, *Waverly Novels* (Abbotsford Edition) Vol I *†

1843

(Anon.) *Samuel Sowerby*. Includes twenty plates from *The Commissioner*

William Carleton, *Traits and Stories of the Irish Peasantry*†

G.P.R. James, *The Commissioner*. Dublin. Contains twenty-eight plates, twenty of which appear in *Samuel Sowerby*

Mark Lemon, *A Shilling's Worth of Nonsense**

Charles Lever, *Our Mess*. Vol. I *Jack Hinton;* Vols. II & III *Tom Burke of 'Ours'*. Dublin

A.R. Smith, *The Wassail Bowl*

1844

W.H. Ainsworth, *Revelations of London* (completed as *Auriol* in 1865)

Charles Dickens, *Martin Chuzzlewit*

George Raymond, *Memoirs of Robert William Elliston, Comedian,* Vol. II†

1845

(Anon.) *Fiddle Faddle's Sentimental Tour*
William Carleton, *Valentine McClutchy.* Dublin
Charles Lever, *Nuts and Nutcrackers* (Etchings and wood engravings)
Charles Lever, *The O'Donoghue.* Dublin
Charles Lever, *St. Patrick's Eve* (Etchings and wood engravings)
Charles Lever (as Tillbury Tramp), *Tales of the Trains**
G.H. Rodwell, *Memoirs of an Umbrella**

1846

William Carleton, *Tales and Stories of the Irish Peasantry.* Dublin
Daniel Defoe, *Robinson Crusoe**
'Democritus,' *Medical and Christian Dissection of Teetotalism*
G.P.R. James, *The Commissioner.* Dublin
Charles Rowcroft, *Fanny the Little Milliner*†
Sir Walter Scott, *Waverly Novels* (Abbotsford Edition) Vol. X*†

1847

W.H. Ainsworth, *Old St Paul's*†
(Anon.) *The Long Lost Found*
Charles Lever, *The Knight of Gwynne*
John Smith, *Irish Diamonds; or, a Theory of Irish Wit and Blunders**
R.S. Surtees, *Hawbuck Grange*
*The Illustrated Musical Almanac for 1847** †

1848

H.K. Browne, *Dombey and Son, the Four Portraits*
H.K. Browne, *Dombey and Son, Full-length Portraits*
H.K. Browne, *Four plates to illustrate the cheap edition of* The Old Curiosity
   Shop
George Lillie Craik, *The Romance of the Peerage, or Curiosities of Family History*
Charles Dickens, *Dombey and Son*
W.B. Jerrold, *The Disgrace to the Family*
Augustus and Horace Mayhew, *The Image of his Father*
John Milton, *L'Allegro and II Penseroso** †
Angus B. Reach, *Christmas Cheer in Three Courses,* containing *The Romance
   of a Mince-Pie** which appeared as a single volume later in the year

1849

W.H. Ainsworth, *Crichton*
H.K. Browne, *Four Plates to illustrate the cheap edition of* Barnaby Rudge
James Hannay, *Hearts are Trumps**
G.P.R. James, *The Fight of the Fiddlers**
Charles Lever (as 'Con Cregan'), *The Confessions of Con Cregan*
Albert Smith, *The Pottleton Legacy*
'Sparkle', *Scraps & Sketches for an Idle Half-Hour*

1849–1854

Edward Bulwer-Lytton, octavo series, frontispieces for *Eugene Aram; Godolphin; Last of the Barons; Last Days of Pompeii; Night and Morning; Rienzi; Pelham; Paul Clifford; What Will He Do With It?; A Strange Story**

1850

Lord Byron, *The Poetical Works of Lord Byron*†
J.A. Couts, *A Practical Guide for the Tailor's Cutting Room: Being a Treatise on Measuring and Cutting Clothing in all Styles, and for Every Period of Life from Childhood to Old Age.* Lithographs
Charles Dickens, *David Copperfield*
Charles Lever, *Roland Cashel*
Samuel Lover, *Metrical Tales**†
John Smith, *Sketches of Cantabs*

1851

H.K. Browne, *Home Pictures*
W.G. Fearnside, (ed.) *Holmes Great Metropolis*
S. Le Fanu, *The Fortunes of Colonel Torlogh O'Brien*
S. Le Fanu, *Ghost Stories and Tales of Mystery*
John Poole, *The Comic Miscellany**†

1852

Ann Hawkshaw, *Aunt Effie's Rhymes for Little Children**
H.K. Browne, *The Five Senses*
Charles Lever, *The Daltons*
Julia Maitland, *The Doll and Her Friends; or Memoirs of the Lady Serafina**
Harriet Myrtle, *A Day of Pleasure*
F.E. Smedley, *Lewis Arundel*

1853

William Carleton, *Traits and Stories of the Irish Peasantry* †
Charles Dickens, *Bleak House*
F.E. Smedley, *The Fortunes of the House of Colville*

1854

John Absolon and H.K. Browne, et al. *The Favourite Picture-book: A Gallery of Amusement and Instruction of the Young*†
Mrs Bray, *A Peep at the Pixies**
Lord Byron, *Poetical Works**†
Lady Pamela Campbell, *The Cabin by the Wayside**
'Christian Le Ros', *Christmas Day and How it was Spent**
Charles Lever, *The Dodd Family Abroad*
Horace Mayhew, *Letters left at a Pastry-cook's**
Harriet Myrtle, *The Water Lily**
F.E. Smedley, *Harry Coverdale's Courtship*

1855

(Anon.) *A Dozen Pairs of Wedding Gloves**
Mary and Elizabeth Kirby, *The Discontented Children**
R.E. Egerton–Warburton, *Three Hunting Songs*

1856

Maria Edgeworth, *The Parents' Assistant; or Stories for Children**
Mary and Elizabeth Kirby, *The Talking Bird; or, The Little Girl Who Knew What was Going to Happen**
Charles Lever, *The Martins of Cro'Martin*

1857

W.H. Ainsworth, *The Spendthrift**
H.K. Browne, *Merry Pictures**†
Charles Dickens, *Little Dorrit*
Henry Fielding, *Amelia**
Henry Fielding, *Joseph Andrews**
Henry Fielding, *Tom Jones**
Theodore Hook, *Precepts and Practice*
George Raymond, *Life and Enterprises of Robert William Elliston*
Tobias Smollett, *Humphrey Clinker**
Tobias Smollett, *Peregrine Pickle**
Tobias Smollett, *Roderick Random**

1858

W.H. Ainsworth, *Mervyn Clitheroe*
(Anon.) *Aunt Mavor's Third Book of Nursery Rhymes**
(Anon.) *Christmas Cheer**
Margaret Gatty, *Legendary Tales**
Robert Hardwick, *London at Dinner or Where to Dine**
Mrs Kirby, *The Discontented Children and How they were Cured**
Augustus Mayhew, *Paved with Gold*
Walter Thornbury, *The Buccaneers**
E. Townsend (ed.) *Acting Proverbs; or, Drawing room theatricals* (Cover design)

1859

R. Brough, *Ulf the Minstrel** (illustrations reissued in 1870 in *The Little Red Man*)
Charles Dickens, *A Tale of Two Cities*
Charles Lever, *Davenport Dunn*
Harriet Beecher Stowe, *The Minister's Wooing*

1860

(Anon.) *Twigs for Nests*
W.H. Ainsworth, *Ovingdean Grange**
E.L. Blanchard, *Dinner and Diners at Home and Abroad: With Piquant Plates and Choice Cuts, Comical, Anatomical and Gastronomical: Forming a Comprehensive Dining Directory for all Palates and all Pockets*
Halwin Caldwell, *The Art of Doing Our Best**† (Published as *Determined to Succeed* in the U.S.)
Thomas Moore, *Lalla Rookh**†
Robert Paltock, *The Adventures of Peter Wilkins**
J.R. Ware, *The Fortunes of the House of Pennyl**
Grace and Philip Wharton, *Wits and Beaux of Society**

1861

(Anon.) *Confessions of a Page**
(Anon.) *Grimm's Goblins**
(Anon.) *New Mysteries of London**
George Halse, *Agatha* (wood engravings and etchings)
Charles Lever, *One of Them*
H. Cholmondeley Pennell, *Puck on Pegasus**†
Jonathan Swift, *Gulliver's Travels**
You Know Who, *Our Choir in 1860–61*

1862

H.K. Browne, *Hunting Bits*
H.K. Browne, *The Times Such as They Are** (a broadside)
M. Bentham-Edwards, *Snowflakes**
Charles Lever, *Barrington*

1864

George Halse (as 'Rattlebrain'), *Sir Guy de Guy**
Mark Lemon, *Tom Moody's Tales**
C.H. Ross, *The Strange Adventures of Two Single Gentlemen**
Anthony Trollope, *Can You Forgive Her?*†

1865

The Attractive Picture Book: A New Book from the Old Corner†
W.H. Ainsworth, *Auriol* (published as *Revelations of London* in 1844)
Charles Lever, *Luttrell of Arran*
John Mills, *Stable Secrets: or Puffy Doddles, His Sayings and Sympathies**
R.S. Surtees, *Mr Facey Romford's Hounds*†

1866

(Anon.) *The Young Ragamuffin**
Thomas Hood, *Penny Readings**
Lindon Meadows, *Dame Perkins and Her Grey Mare* (graphotype)

1867

Six young widows and a spinster lady of a certain age. *Ghost Wives: A Christmas Story**†

1868

H.K. Browne, *London's Great Outing* (graphotype)
H.K. Browne, *Racing and Chasing* (graphotype)

1869

H.K. Browne, *The Derby Carnival* (graphotype)
H.K. Browne, *The Derby Day. The Road and the Course. A Series of Eight Illustrations* (graphotype)
H.K. Browne, *Sketches of the Seaside and the Country* (graphotype)

1871

Capt. L. Bevan (ed.) *Book of Remarkable Trials* (wood engravings of some designs from *The Chronicles of Crime*, 1841)*

Charles Dickens, *Posthumous Papers of the Pickwick Club* (Household Edition). Fifty-seven new designs.*
Martin Legrand, *The Cambridge Freshman**
Rev. P.B. Power, *The Oiled Feather**

1875

H.K. Browne (as 'Damocles'), *All About Kisses**
Wilkie Collins, *Antonina*. (Frontispiece for new edition, engraved by Robert Young)
Dulken (ed.) *Fairy Tales**
Charles Lever, *Novels* (Harry Lorrequer Edition) Vols XXII–XXXI* (including four woodcuts in each of the following: *The Fortunes of Glencore, Tony Butler, Sir Jasper Carew, Maurice Tiernay, Horace Templeton, Sir Brook Fossbrooke, A Day's Ride*)
Edmund B. Tuttle, *Border Tales around the Campfire, in the Rocky Mountains**

1879

W.H. Ainsworth, *The Star Chamber**
Jonathan Swift, *Gulliver's Travels**

1882

George Halse, *A Salad of Stray Leaves**

No date

John Absolon, *Tales and Rhymes*
(Anon.) *Ruth, the Murdered Child**† (early 1880s)
(Anon.) *The Battle and the Breeze**† (early 1860s)
(E.H. Burrage?) *Rags and Riches: A Story of Three Poor Boys**
Robert Emmett, *Follow my Leader; or Lionel Wilful's Schooldays**
Handy Andy, A Tale of Irish Life (Cover attributed to Phiz by Sadleir)
Peter Parley's Annual: Phelim O'Flynn*†
Albert Smith and Angus B. Reach (eds.) *The Man in the Moon*

Posthumous

1883

*New Mysteries of London**
H.K. Browne, *Phiz's Baby Sweethearts**
H.K. Browne, *Phiz's Funny Alphabet**
H.K. Browne, *Phiz's Funny Stories**
H.K. Browne, *Phiz's Merry Hours**

(All four reprinted from *A Toy Book by 'Phiz'*)
William Shakespeare, *Works* (Phelps edition)[1]

1885

By the Author of 'Ralph Rattleton', *Charley and Tim at Scarum School**

1890

(Anon.) *The Frog would a'wooing go***†

Magazines

New Sporting Magazine, 1839–1843
London Magazine, 1840
Punch, 1842–1844; 1861–1869
Great Gun, 1844
Illustrated London News, 1844–1861
Ainsworth's Magazine, 1844
Illuminated Magazine, 1843–1845
Sharpe's London Magazine, 1845–1847
Union Magazine, 1846
Man in the Moon, 1847
Life, 1850
Illustrated London Magazine, 1853–1855
Illustrated Times, 1855–1856
Once a Week, 1859–1865
Autograph Mirror, 1865–1866
Judy, 1869–1882

Occasional contributions to: *New Monthly Magazine*; *Tinsley's Magazine*; *London Society*; *St James's Magazine*; *Illustrated Gazette*; *Sporting Times*; *The Welcome Guest*.

A complete list of works illustrated by Phiz is a tantalising dream. Consider this a work in progress which you are invited to make contributions.

Appendix 2

Charles Lever Works Illustrated by Phiz
FP fontispiece; TP tailpiece; engs engravings

Harry Lorrequer, 1839	21 steels inc. F & TP
Charles O'Malley, Vol. I, 1841	22 steels inc. F & TP
Charles O'Malley, Vol. II, 1841	22 steels inc. F & TP
Jack Hinton, 1843	26 steels plus 9 wood engs
Tom Burke of 'Ours', Vol. I, 1844	24 steels inc. FP
Tom Burke of 'Ours', Vol. II, 1844	20 steels inc. FP
The O'Donohue, 1845	26 steels inc. FP
St Patrick's Eve, 1845	4 steels, inc. FP. 12 wood engs, inc. TP
Tales of the Trains, 1845	14 wood engs
The Knight of Gwynne, 1847	40 steels inc. FP & TP
Confessions of Con Cregan, Vol. I, 1849	14 steels, 21 wood engs inc. F & TP 2 questionable ch. tailpieces. G.H. Thomas takes over woods at Ch. 14
Confessions of Con Cregan, Vol. II, 1869	15 steels, inc. FP & TP G.H. Thomas woods
Roland Cashel, 1850	40 steels inc. FP & TP
The Daltons, 1850–2	48 steels inc. FP & TP
The Dodd Family Abroad, 1852–4	40 steels inc. FP & TP
The Martins of Cro'Martin, 1856	40 steels inc. FP & TP
Nuts and Nutcrackers (1845), Third edition, 1857	6 steels inc. FP and 52 wood engs
Davenport Dunn, 1859	44 steels inc. F & TP

One of Them, 1861	30 steels inc. FP & TP
Barrington, 1863	26 steels inc. FP & TP
Luttrell of Arran, 1863	32 steels inc. FP & TP

Novels (Harry Lorrequer Edition) Vols XXII – XXXI (1878), includes four new wood engravings in each of the following books which had originally appeared without illustrations: *The Fortunes of Glencore, Tony Butler, Sir Jasper Carew, Maurice Tiernay, Horace Templeton, Sir Brook Fossbrooke, A Day's Ride.*

Notes

Full title of each book is given on first mention, with short title thereafter.

Abbreviations
P Let. *The Letters of Charles Dickens* (Pilgrim Edition) (eds) Madeleine House, Graham Storey, Kathleen Tillotson. 12 volumes, Oxford: Clarendon Press, 1965–2002.
ALS Autographed manuscript

Prologue

1. F.G. Kitton, *Dickens and His Illustrators*. London: George Redway, 1899, p. 63.
2. Edgar Browne, *Phiz and Dickens*. London: James Nisbet, 1913, pp. 7–8.

Chapter 1

1. *Punch*. Obituary. 22 July 1882.
2. Charles Gordon Browne and Algernon Sidney Bicknell's *Notes to Assist the Future Authors of the History of the Huguenot Family of Browne*. Handwritten manuscript, 1903. (Henceforth referred to as *Notes*.) A copy was made by Rita Gwendoline Browne in 1929. The text is identical apart from a few additions, using information she gathered between 1903 and 1929. These handwritten books are in the hands of, respectively, Robert Moxon Browne, QC, and Peter Browne.
3. Letter to Eliza Moxon, 28 Oct. 1839. In *Notes*, p. 15.
4. Ibid.
5. Charles St Denys Moxon, *History of the Browne Family*, 1877. (Henceforth C. Moxon.) Unpublished. Unpaginated. (Moxons and Brownes had a habit of intermarrying. Charles St Denys Moxon was the eldest son of Thomas Moxon of Leyton and Bessie Browne.)
6. *Notes*, p. 15.
7. *Publications of the Huguenot Society*, Vol. XXXIX. Register of the French Church of St Jean, Spitalfields.
8. The entries in the burial registry read: 'Burial. 1747. Oct. 30th. Eleanor

233

Brown. Brick Lane. W [i.e. woman].' 'Burial. 1747/48. Jan. 8th. Michael Brown. Brick Lane. M [i.e. man]'

9. *Notes*, p. 21. Present whereabouts of ring unknown.

10. Simon's sister, Elizabeth, a silk weaver, stayed in London, became a rigid Calvinist, and remained in Spitalfields throughout her long life. She married another Huguenot, Henry Sluce (Sélous). Later, when he spent too long lingering at death's door, she encouraged him in ringing tones: 'Sélous, old man, get on with your dying.' (Quoted in handwritten notes sent to Rita Browne by Alfred Moxon.)

11. Marriage register, St Stephen's.

12. Norfolk Record Office, Gildengate House, Norwich.

13. Algernon Sidney Bicknell, *Five Pedigrees*. London: Sherwood, n.d., p. 35.

14. *Notes*, p. 29.

15. Simon and Ann are buried in a vault in St Stephen's, Norwich, which lies under the pavement of the south aisle. Their handsome memorial slab, which they share with her mother and brother, is still in pristine condition.

16. C. Moxon.

17. Ibid.

18. *Notes*, p. 67.

19. The marriage licence, quoted in *Notes*, p. 67, reads:

William Browne of the Parish of Saint Andrew, Holborn, in the County of Middlesex, Bachelor, and Katherine Hunter of the same Parish, a minor, were married in this Church by licence, by & with the consent of Thomas Hunter the natural & lawful father of the said minor, on the seventh day of July in the year one thousand seven hundred and ninety two, by me Robert Cooper, Curate.
This marriage was solemnized between us {William Browne
{Katherine Hunter
in the presence of us {Sarah Hunter
{T. Hunter

20. David Croal Thomson, *Life and Labours of Hablôt Knight Browne*. London: Chapman and Hall, 1884, p. 18.

21. Letter to his daughter, Lucinda, 31 Aug. 1795. In *Notes*, p. 66.

22. 'Mrs Moxon & my Aunt' refer to John Henry's sister, Ann Moxon, and her mother-in-law.

23. Letter to William Loder Browne, 6 May 1797. In *Notes*, p. 32.

Chapter 2

1. See Arthur Allchin, 'An Illustrator of Dickens: Hablot Knight Browne.' *Century Magazine*, 1893, pp. 386–394.
2. French Army records, Vincennes.
3. Interestingly, French still has a firm hold on Simon's descendants. My children, his three-times-great-grandchildren, both have degrees in French, and my eight-year-old granddaughter speaks French with a perfect accent.
4. *Notes*, p. 79.
5. Ibid.
6. William Thackeray, *Vanity Fair*, Ch. 32.
7. Scott Bowden, *Armies at Waterloo*. Arlington, TX: Empire Games Press, 1983, p. 82.
8. *The Times*, 22 June 1815.
9. Ibid.
10. E. Browne, p. 1.

Chapter 3

1. Alec Guinness, *A Positively Final Appearance*. Harmondsworth: Penguin, 1999, p. 101.
2. Cedric Dickens, *The Miracle of Pickwick*. London: Dickens Publishing for the Dickens House, 2001, p. 45.
3. *Notes*, p. 101.

Chapter 4

1. Bound album of juvenilia titled 'Original Sketches by Phiz (H.K. Browne) from the collection of Mrs Purnell of Bath at whose house H.K. Browne used to stay.' Watermark 1827. Now in my collection.
2. Date given in Rita Browne's copy of *Notes*.
3. In *Notes* he is referred to as William Le Breton, but William L. Breton is the name he signed on his paintings and which appears on his death certificate and tombstone.
4. Charles V. Hagner, *Early History of the Falls of Schuylkill, Manayunk*. Philadelphia: Claxton, Remsen, and Haffelinger, 1869, p. 89.
5. Martin Snyder, 'William L. Breton, Philadelphia Artist.' *Pennsylvania Magazine of History and Biography*, 1961, pp. 178–209. Snyder admires Breton's unusual ability to create a primitive atmosphere and describes his work as carrying 'a sense of detachment from everyday affairs, of countrified simplicity; the ancient character of the structure is conveyed by more than its lines alone.' Joseph Jackson, in his *Encyclopedia of*

Philadelphia, Vol. II, p. 327, records that Breton was 'the son of a London publisher' (another of William's lies!), and comments, '[Breton] was not a great artist, but a most useful and sympathetic one to have appeared at the time he did.'

6. John F. Watson, *Annals of Philadelphia, and Pennsylvania, in the Olden-Time*. Philadelphia, 1830. The manuscript can be seen in The Historical Society of Pennsylvania.

7. C. Moxon, n.p.

8. *Notes*, p. 3.

9. *Notes*, p. 83.

10. Ibid., pp. 85–87.

11. Ibid., pp. 113–115.

12. Ibid., p. 99.

Chapter 5

1   *The Westminster Review*, XXXIV (June 1840), pp. 6–7.

2   E. Browne, pp. 57–58.

3   Ibid., p. 55.

4   Ibid., p. 62.

5   Thomson, p. 20.

6   Frederic Kitton, *Phiz: A Memoir*, London: W. Satchell, 1882, p. 8.

7   Allchin, p. 2.

8   E. Browne, p. 4.

9   Kitton, *Phiz*, p. 8.

10 George Cruikshank, 'John Gilpin's Ride,' *The Diverting History of John Gilpin*, etching, 1828 (Princeton University Library). The image is one of six vignettes sewn into a twenty-page, 5¼" x 4⅛", booklet.

11 'John Gilpin's Race' was a popular favourite with children. The artist, George Augustus Sala (1828–1896), who must have been very small at the time, recalls seeing in a shop window in Wardour Street 'a certain print by a young man named HABLOT BROWNE, representing the involuntary flight of John Gilpin, scattering the pigs and poultry in his never-to-be-forgotten ride.' (Kitton, *Phiz*, p. 8.) Sala's comment is revealing because it reflects the embellishments of childhood. There is a complete shortage of poultry in Browne's print, and Sala certainly cannot mistake the lone dog in the lower right-hand corner of the picture for a chick. It is, of course, possible that Browne made more than one plate, and that the etching of John Gilpin was an early demonstration of his ability to duplicate plates even as he added differences and improvements. But it is more likely that little

Sala saw what he wanted to see: pigs and chicks. Incidentally, Cowper's poem mentions dogs and a donkey, while Cruikshank's woodcut contains one dog, several chickens, but no pigs.

12 The entry for H.K. Browne in George Cruikshank's address book has, in place of an address, the words 'The Phiz'. This seems to award Phiz a measure of respect, while the lack of an address reminds us that he was a moving target, changing his residence as his mood or finances dictated.

13 Furnival's Inn was torn down in 1898 to make room for the giant offices of the Prudential Insurance Company.

14 Diary entry for Saturday, 6 January 1838. P Let., 1:630

15 *Notes*, p. 141.

16 Alexander Gilchrist, *Life of William Etty, R.A.* London: Bogue, 1855.

17 Joseph Grego, *Pictorial Pickwickiana; Charles Dickens and his Illustrators*, London: Chapman and Hall, 1899, p50

Chapter 6

1. G.K. Chesterton, *Charles Dickens: A Critical Study*. NY: Dodd Mead, 1913.

2. Private collection.

3. Robert Hanna has made careful comparisons between Elizabeth Dickens's handwriting and that for the play. He continues to examine the handwriting of others in Dickens's circle, trying to establish the identity of the transcriber.

4. Kitton, *Dickens*, p. 62.

5. Charles Dickens (as Timothy Sparks), *Sunday Under Three Heads*. London: Chapman and Hall, 1836, p. 31.

6. Walter Dexter and J.W.T. Ley, *The Origin of Pickwick*. London: Chapman and Hall, 1936, p. 60. The history of the disasters that occurred before Phiz was hired is painstakingly described by Dexter and Ley, and also by Joseph Grego in *Pictorial Pickwickiana*.

7. See Dexter, p. 54.

8. Ibid., p. 51.

9. Ibid., p. 124.

10. Buss's statement in Dexter, p. 133.

11. E. Browne, p. 102.

12. In Kitton, *Dickens*, p. 62.

13. Grego, p. 133.

14. Thomson, p. 91.

15. E. Browne, p. 241.

16. Ibid., pp. 235–236.

17. Thackeray (1811–1863) originally intended to become an artist, and often illustrated his own works. He was not the last young man to apply for the job. On 23 August, nineteen-year-old John Leech (the future illustrator of Dickens's Christmas books) submitted a design he made from the story of Tom Smart and the chair. Leech left the picture for Dickens to examine, and shortly received the following letter:

Sir,

I have to acknowledge the receipt of your design from the last Pickwick, which I think extremely well conceived and executed.

I can only repeat, however, what I at first said when I had the pleasure of seeing you – namely that the plates for the Pickwick Papers are in the hands of a gentleman of very great ability, with whose designs I am exceedingly well satisfied, and from whom I feel it neither my wish, nor my interest, to part. . . . (CD to John Leech, PLet.,? Aug., 1836, 1:168).

18. Kitton, *Dickens*, p. 62.

19. Thomson, p. 92.

20. Ibid., p. 88.

21. In Thomson, p. 235.

22. CD to HKB, PLet., Jan., 1837, 1:222.

23. CD to HKB, PLet., mid-Mar., 1837, 1:242.

24. CD to HKB, PLet., mid-Aug., 1836, 1:163.

25. CD to Chapman and Hall, PLet., 19 Oct., 1836, 1:184.

26. CD to Harley, PLet., 19 Dec., 1836, 1:214.

27. Albert Johanssen, *Phiz. Illustrations from the Novels of Charles Dickens*. Chicago: University of Chicago Press, 1956.

28. Buss's statement in Dexter, p. 135.

29. CD to Bentley, PLet., 28 Jan., 1837, 1:230.

30. See John Harvey, *Victorian Novelists and their Illustrators*. London: Sidgwick & Jackson, 1970, p. 188.

31. Thomson, p. 29. Harvey appears to have solved the problem of Croal Thomson's arbitrary figure: 'The accounts of Bradbury and Evans in the Forster Collection state that, for *Dombey*, Browne was given £25.4s.0d. for "Etching No. 1 in duplicate" and £6 for "Biting in Plates". This totals £31.4s.0d., and Thomson may have derived his

opulent figure of fifteen guineas by dividing in half this payment for etching "in duplicate", making £15.12s.0d. But for "No. 1" which has the date 30 Sept. 1846, and clearly refers to the monthly part, and not the plate, *two* designs were etched in duplicate. Browne's payment is really for four etchings, and as the payment for biting in was passed on, presumably, to his lifelong assistant, Robert Young, it would appear that Browne received, per etching, a quarter of £25.4s.0d., or six guineas.' Harvey, pp. 187–188.

32. See Kitton, *Dickens*, p. 65.

Chapter 7

1. Thomson, p. 35.
2. Herring fry, then in season. The whitebait dinner was a yearly banquet for cabinet ministers, held in memory of the massive engineering effort from 1705 to 1720 to save the lowlands on the Essex bank of the Thames.
3. E. Browne, p. 43.
4. Private collection.
5. 'Young, beautiful, and good, God in His Mercy Numbered her with his Angels At the early age of Seventeen.' Epitaph composed by Dickens on Mary Hogarth's tombstone in Kensal Green Cemetery.
6. CD to John Forster, PLet., 2 July, 1837, 1:281.
7. Ibid.
8. Lady De Lancey, *A Week at Waterloo in June 1815*. London: John Murray, 1906.
9. CD to Basil Hall, PLet., 16 Mar., 1841, 2:236.
10. Thomas Noon Talfourd, *Vacation Rambles and Thoughts*. Quoted in *The Illuminated Magazine*, Vol. IV, p. 231.
11. In Michael Slater, *Douglas Jerrold, 1803–1857*. London: Duckworth, 2002, p. 130.

Chapter 8

1. E. Browne, p. 239.
2. Charles Dickens, Preface to cheap edition of *Nicholas Nickleby*. 1848.
3. Frederic Kitton, *The Dickens Country*. London: Adam and Charles Black, 1905, p. 125.
4. *Nicholas Nickleby*, p. 88 (Penguin).
5. CD to Catherine Dickens, PLet., 1 Feb., 1838, 1:365–366.
6. Kitton, *Dickens Country*, p. 126.
7. *Nicholas Nickleby*, p. 140.

8. Ibid., p. 90.

9. Charles Dickens, 1839 preface to *Nicholas Nickleby*.

10. E. Browne, pp. 11–12.

11. Illustrations to *Nicholas Nickleby*, Huntington Library, HM 39999.

12. CD to Mrs Hall, PLet., 29 Dec., 1838, 1:481.

13. *Nicholas Nickleby*, p. 223.

14. Ibid., p. 120.

15. A visit to Bowes is a must for the lover of Phiz and Dickens. All the buildings – St Giles's church, Dotheboys Hall, the castle ruins, and the Ancient Unicorn – are still standing, and it is possible to locate the graves of William Shaw and George Ashton Taylor. A good plan is to walk around the village and then, as Phiz and Dickens did, repair to the Ancient Unicorn for refreshment. If you're lucky, the innkeeper's wife will take you through to the dining room and show you the corner where the two young men sat to warm themselves. You may also, like her, be lucky enough to see figures in Victorian dress reflected in a long mirror at the other end of the room.

16. See Kitton, *Dickens*, p. 115.

17. In *The Dickensian*, Vol. 37, No. 257, 1 Dec. 1940, p. 28.

18. CD to J.P. Harley, PLet., ?24 Oct., 1838, 1:444.

19. CD's diary, PLet., 29 Oct. – 7 Nov., 1838, 1:634–636.

20. CD to Catherine Dickens, PLet., 1 Nov., 1838, 1:447.

21. Ibid., 1:448.

22. See Edgar Johnson, *Charles Dickens*. New York: Simon and Schuster, 1952, p. 225.

24. CD's cheque-book counterfoils, PLet., 30 Nov., 1838, 1:645.

Chapter 9

1. PLet., 1:549 FN1.

2. Michael Steig, *Dickens and Phiz*. Bloomington: Indiana University Press, 1978, p. 5.

3. Charles Dickens, *Sketches of Young Couples*, Conclusion.

4. Edgar F. Howden, ed., *The Letters and Private Papers of William Makepeace Thackeray*. (Supplement to Gordon N. Ray), 2 vols, New York: Garland, 1994, Vol I, p. 126. Richard Tattersall (1785–1859) was proprietor of the famous turf establishment bearing his name in Grosvenor Place. Robert Smith Surtees's *Jorrocks' Jaunts and Jollities: or the Hunting, Racing, Driving, Sailing, Eating, Eccentric and Extravagant Exploits of the Renowned Sporting citizen, Mr. John Jorrocks of St. Botolph Lane and Great Coram*

Street with illustrations by Phiz, had been published in book form in 1838 and 1839, and was about to reappear in 1843. Thackeray himself was still living at 13 Great Coram Street.

5. *The London and Westminster Review*, xxxii, 1839, p. 304.

6. Quoted in and translated by Jonathan Mayne, ed., *The Painter of Modern Life and Other Essays*. London: Phaidon, 1964, p. 178.

7. See Michael Diamond's fascinating article, 'Charles Dickens as Villain and Hero in Reynolds's Newspaper.' *The Dickensian*, Summer 2002, Vol. 98, p. 127.

8. James Grant, *Sketches in London*. London: Orr, 1838. Preface.

9. See Kitton, *Dickens*, p. 79.

10. For more details of the publishing history, see Robert Patten, *Charles Dickens and His Publishers*. Santa Cruz: Dickens Project, p. 117. Reprint of Oxford: Oxford University Press, 1978.

11. CD to George Cattermole. PLet., ?21 Jan., 1849, 2:12.

12. Patten, p. 58.

13. Clear and detailed explanations of the various printing techniques – etching, wood engraving, lithography – used by Phiz can be found in Bamber Gascoigne, *How to Identify Prints*. London: Thames and Hudson, 1986.

14. E. Browne, p. 256.

15. Jane Rabb Cohen, *Dickens and His Principal Illustrators*. Columbus: Ohio State University, 1980, p. 75.

16. Steig, p. 56.

17. Ibid., p. 53.

18. Email to VBL, 29 Mar., 2002.

19. Email to VBL, 21 April, 2003.

20. CD to Cattermole, PLet., 7 Aug., 1840, 2:110.

21. CD to Cattermole, PLet., 13 Aug., 1840, 2:115.

22. CD to Samuel Williams, PLet., 31 Mar., 1840, 2:48.

23. Harvey, p. 117.

24. CD to J.P. Harley, PLet., 16 Oct., 1840, 2:137.

25. *The Old Curiosity Shop*, end of Ch. 67.

26. Ibid., end of Ch. 71.

27. CD to Cattermole, PLet., 14 Jan., 1841, 2:183.

28. In Kitton, *Dickens*, p. 115.

29. CD to Basil Hall, PLet., 15 Jan., 1841, 2:184.

30. CD to Cruikshank, PLet., ?3 Oct., 1839, 1:589.

31. Cruikshank to CD., PLet., 1:589 FN. 4.

32. The best estimate for their totals for the entire miscellany is 157 for

Phiz and thirty-nine for Cattermole. It is impossible to be precise because some of the illustrations are unsigned, and experts still argue about which artist did a couple of them.

33. Cohen, p. 77.
34. John Ruskin, *The Works of John Ruskin*, Vol. 22, *Ariadne Florentina*. London: George Allen, 1906, p. 467.
35. CD to Cattermole, PLet., 28 Jan., 1841, 2:197.
36. CD to Cattermole, PLet., 30 Jan., 1841, 2:198.
37. CD to Forster, PLet., 9 Feb., 1841, 2:207.
38. CD to Maclise, PLet., 10 Feb., 1841, 2:208.
39. CD to Basil Hall. PLet., 16 Mar., 1841, 2:234.
40. In Kitton, *Dickens*, p. 83.
41. Phiz to CD, PLet., 27 Mar., 1841, 2:244 FNI (Manuscript in Huntington Library.)
42. Editors of Punch, *A Shilling's Worth of Nonsense*. London: Orr, 1843.
43. CD to Leech, PLet., 5 Nov., 1842, 2:359.
44. Frederick Evans, quoted in E. Browne, p. 22.
45. CD to Leech, PLet.,7 Nov., 1842, 2:361.
46. British Museum, Dept. of Prints and Drawings.
47. Harvey, p. 134.
48. CD to Phiz, PLet., ?June, 1844, 3:140.

Chapter 10

1. CD to Walter Landor, PLet., 11 Feb., 1840, 2:23.
2. A. W. Venner to Jessie Browne, 5 Sept., 1917. Quoted in *Notes*, p. 330.
3. There is no Burn Street in Stepney. Burn was probably a mistranscription of Burr.
4. Thomson, p. 38.
5. *Notes*, p. 147.
6. Thomson, p. 24.
7. *Notes*, p. 147.
8. CD uses this genderless phrase twice on the third page of *OCS*.
9. Thomson, p. 26.
10. Alfred Moxon notebook.
11. E. Browne, p. 26.
12. Charles Dickens Museum collection, No. B129.
13. In Thomson, p. 25.
14. It has been suggested to me that what I take to be the 'y' in Wordyworth is actually an 's'. I have examined Phiz's letters very carefully, and the only example I have yet found of a long 's' is when the letter is

doubled, as in 'blessings'. His 's' on other occasions does not trespass below the line.

15. E. Browne, p. 32.
16. Ibid., p. 27.
17. Ibid., p. 30.
18. Ibid., p. 29.
19. Ibid., pp. 34–35.
20. Ibid., p. 240.
21. Ibid., p. 243.
22. Ibid., p. 46.
23. Ibid., p. 41.
24. Ibid., p. 43.
25. W.J. Fitzpatrick, *The Life of Charles Lever*, Vol. II. London: Chapman and Hall, 1879, p. 51.
26. CD to W.H. Wills, PLet., 4 Sept., 1860, 9:303.

Chapter 11

1. Thomas Moore, quoted in W.J. Fitzpatrick, *The Life of Charles Lever*, Rev. ed., London: Ward, Lock, 1884, p. 369. For the life of me, I cannot find the original line in Moore.
2. *Jack Hinton*, Ch. 10.
3. A.J. Symington, *Samuel Lover, A Biographical Sketch*. London: Blackie & Son, 1880, p. iii.
4. In Edmund Downey, *Charles Lever, His Life in His Letters 2 vols.* Blackwood, 1906, Vol I, p. 151.
5. E. Browne, p. 173.
6. W.J. Fitzpatrick, *The Life of Charles Lever*, 2 Vols. London: Chapman and Hall, 1879, Vol I, p.267.
7. In Downey, Vol I, p. 289.
8. Fitzpatrick, Rev. ed., p. 209.
9. Ibid, p. 23.
10. Ibid., p. 13.
11. Interview with Tony Bareham, 25 May 2003. (*Charles Lever: New Evaluations* was published by Colin Smythe in 1991.)
12. Downey, Vol I, p. 57.
13. John Dryden, *Epistle* 'To my honoured kinsman John Driden', 1700.
14. Fitzpatrick, Rev. ed., p. 98.
15. Ibid., p. 85.
16. Downey, Vol I, p. 107.

17. Fitzpatrick, Note, p. 183.
18. Downey, Vol II, p. 338.
19. *Harry Lorrequer*, Ch. 55.
20. Downey explains: 'This was an epithet applied to the "Repealers" who followed O'Connell's leadership.'
21. Downey, Vol I, p. 109.
22. Lionel Stevenson, *Dr Quicksilver*. London: Chapman and Hall, 1939, p. 104.
23. Downey, Vol I, pp. 184–88.
24. Stephen Haddelsey, *Charles Lever: The Lost Victorian*. Gerrards Cross: Colin Smythe, 2000, p. 25.
25. Downey, Vol II, p. 401.
26. Ibid., p. 347.
27. Ibid., p. 358.
28. Downey, Vol I, p. 367.
29. Ibid., p. 340.
30. Fitzpatrick, Rev. ed., p. 221.
31. Ibid., p. 93.
32. Perhaps Phiz was making a reference to the great French artist whom he may have wrongly considered to be one of his ancestors.
33. *St Patrick's Eve*, Ch. 1.
34. Fitzpatrick, Rev. ed., p. 259.
35. Dickens had just staged an extravagant production of Ben Jonson's *Every Man in his Humour*.
36. In E. Browne, p. 184.
37. In Fitzpatrick, Rev. ed., p. 215.
38. *Con Cregan*, Ch. 24.
39. *The Martins of Cro' Martin*, Ch. 29.
40. George Stubbs (1724–1806). Anatomist and outstanding painter of horses and other animals.
41. Fitzpatrick, Rev. ed., p. 353.

Chapter 12

1. Author's collection. The man with gamp and flat hat is probably a self-portrait. The torn letter from Dickens to Phiz, on which Phiz has doodled, was in a scrapbook put together by Mike, one of Phiz's grandchildren.
2. ALS, Princeton, AM 19311.
3. Cohen, p. 90.

4. Edgar Allan Poe, 'A Chapter on Autography' (Part III), *Graham's Magazine*, Jan. 1842, p. 44.

5. Cornelius Mathews, *The Career of Puffer Hopkins*. New York: Appleton, 1842, Preface.

6. CD to Forster, PLet., 30 Aug., 1846, 4:613.

7. CD to Thomas Mitton, PLet., 30 Aug., 1846, 4:615.

8. CD to Forster, PLet., ?6 Sept., 1846, 4:620.

9. CD to Forster, PLet., 26–29 Oct., 1846, 4:649.

10. In Cohen, p. 90.

11. Forster collection, Victoria and Albert Museum Library, 48.6.514.

12. See John Forster, *The Life of Charles Dickens*, London: Cecil Palmer, 1872-74 p. 478.

13. CD to Forster, PLet., 4 Nov., 1846, 4:653.

14. CD to Forster, PLet., ?Nov.–Dec., 1846, 4:671.

15. PLet., ?Nov–Dec., 1846, FN4 4:671.

16. *Punch*, 28 Aug., 1847, p. 75.

17. CD to Forster, PLet., ?12 Dec., 1846, 4:679.

18. *Dombey and Son*, Ch. 11.

19. CD to Catherine Dickens, PLet., 19 Dec., 1846, 4:681.

20. One of Mrs Gamp's words.

21. CD to Phiz, PLet., 15 Mar., 1847, 5:35.

22. Q.D. Leavis, 'The Dickens Illustrations: Their Function.' In *Dickens the Novelist* by F.R. and Q.D. Leavis. New York: Pantheon, 1970, p. 355.

23. *Dombey and Son*, Ch. 55.

24. The confusing word 'aquatint' simply means an imitation of a watercolour wash, but the technique itself is vastly more complex, and best described by Bamber Gascoigne: 'An aquatint achieves gradations of tone through a very fine network, etched to various depths by the action of acid. The network, entirely random in its patterning, encloses tiny islands of white. It is these islands which are the essential characteristic of the medium, for they are caused by the separate globules of the aquatint ground which have adhered to the plate. These globules prevent the acid from attacking the copper immediately below them, only allowing it to operate in the gaps between them.' The globules themselves were created by spreading and heating resin on the plate.

25. Philip Collins, '*Dombey and Son* – Then and Now.' *Dickensian*, 63, 1967.

26. CD to Phiz, PLet., 13 June, 1848, 5:335.

27. Robert Patten, 'Frank Stone'. Entry in *Oxford Reader's Companion to Dickens*, ed. Paul Schlicke. Oxford: OUP, 1999, p. 540.

28. PLet., FN5, 5:284.

29. Thomson, p. 177.
30. Gordon N. Ray, ed., *The Letters and Private Papers of William Makepeace Thackeray.* Cambridge, Mass: Harvard University Press, 1945, p. 326.
31. Ibid., p. 327.
32. S.M. Ellis, *William Harrison Ainsworth and his Friends.* London: John Lane, 1911, p. 75.
33. Ibid., p. 262.
34. Sales description by Charles Sessler, Bookseller, 1314 Walnut Street, Philadelphia, located in the Couts album in the Huntington Library.
35. CD to Phiz, PLet., 4 May, 1849, 5:531–2.
36. Forster, p.528
37. PLet., 5 May, 1849, 5:532. FN1.
38. Kittan, *Phiz*, p.12.
39. CD to Miss Browne, PLet., 27 July, 1849, 5:581.
40. CD to Forster, PLet., 21 Sept., 1849, 5:610.
41. Cohen, p. 101.
42. This image forms the centrepiece of a fascinating article by Robert Patten, 'Serial Illustration and Storytelling in *David Copperfield.*' In *The Victorian Illustrated Book*, ed. Richard Maxwell. Charlottesville: University Press of Virginia, 2002, pp. 91–128.
43. In Johnson, p. 674.
44. E. Browne, p. 48.
45. CD to Forster, PLet., 21 Oct., 1850, 6:195.
46. Phiz was referring to the Parnassus Plays, satires produced at St John's College, Cambridge, at the end of the sixteenth century. In Part I, Philomusus and Studioso travel to Parnassus by way of Trivium. On their way home they are reduced to being shepherds. Part II skewers the academic life.
47. Fitzpatrick, p. 330.
48. Thomson, p. 211.
49. *Diogenes*, No. 36 (3 September 1853), p. 151.
50. Refers to the real Simon Pure, a character in Susannah Centlivre's *A Bold Stroke for a Wife* (1710), Act. V, sc. 1.
51. Undated letter from Phiz to CD in the Mabel Bradbury Album at the *Punch* Library and Archive, Basil Street, London.
52. Harvey, p. 153.
53. Cohen, p. 109.
54. CD to Phiz, PLet., 29 June, 1853, 7:107.

55. CD to Phiz, PLet., 6 July, 1853, 7:111.
56. See Harvey, p. 160.
57. Cohen, p. 114.
58. Brian Rosenberg, *Little Dorrit's Shadows*. Columbia, MO: University of Missouri Press, 1996. Even Queenie Leavis points out that the illustrations for novels after *Bleak House* were unnecessary but for the habit of having illustrations. See *Dickens the Novelist*, p. 361.
59. Steig, p. 158.
60. Paul Schlicke, *Oxford Reader's Companion to Dickens*. Oxford: OUP, 1999, p. 339.
61. CD to W.H. Wills, PLet., 19 Oct., 1855, 7:722.
62. CD to Phiz, PLet., 8 Nov., 1856, 8:219.
63. CD to Phiz, PLet., 6 Dec., 1856, 8:232.
64. CD to Phiz, PLet., 10 Feb., 1857, 8:280.
65. Steig, p. 171.

Chapter 13

1. CD to Forster, PLet., 6 July, 1859, 9:
2. CD to Angela Burdett Coutts, PLet., 5 Sept., 1867, 8:432.
3. CD to John Forster, PLet, 15 Mar., 1858, 8:531.
4. CD to Wills, PLet, 3 April, 1858, 8:541.
5. CD to Angela Burdett Coutts, PLet., 9 May, 1858, 8:558
6. CD to Edmund Yates, PLet., 8 June 1858, 8:558
7. Email, 16 Jan., 2003.
8. Michael Steig, *Dickens and Phiz*, Bloomington: Indiana University Press, 1978, p. 312.
9. CD to Edward Chapman, PLet., 16 Oct., 1859, 9:136.
10. Dickens actually wrapped it up after the eighth number.
11. In PLet., N1 9:87.
12. E. Browne, p. 223.
13. Quoted in PLet., 9:87 FN1.
14. Augustus Mayhew, *Paved with Gold*. London: Chapman and Hall, 1858, p. 146.
15. Ibid., p. 9.
16. In Thomson, p. 177.
17. W. Harrison Ainsworth, *Mervyn Clitheroe*. London: Routledge, 1858, pp. 255–256.
18. H. B. Stowe, *Sunny Memories of Foreign Lands*. London: Routledge, 1855, p. 153.

19. Richard B. Sewall, *Life of Emily Dickinson*. New York: Farrar, Straus and Giroux, 1974, p. 57.
20. Written c. 1859, when Dickinson was twenty-eight years old.
21. See Philip Collins's interesting article, 'Bruce Castle: a School Dickens Admired', in *The Dickensian*, 1955, Vol. 51, pp. 174–181.
22. See letter to Forster, PLet, 30 Nov., 1846, 4:652.
23. Lucy Crump, ed., *Letters of George Birkbeck Hill*, London: Edward Arnold, 1906, p. 7.
24. Phiz's copies of Charles Knight's pictorial edition of the works of Shakespeare, published in a series of volumes between the years 1838 and 1841, are in my possession. I believe that Phiz, quite flush during those years, made a lifelong investment in these beautifully bound books as they appeared, one by one.
25. E. Browne, p. 112. Distemper is a mixture of powdered colour, glue or gum, and water.
26. E. Browne, p. 256.
27. The original sketches are in the Huntington Library.

Chapter 14

1. Richard Cobden (1804–1865) and John Bright (1811–1889) were statesmen and reformers known for their brilliant oratory. Perhaps it was their very prolixity, rather than their principles, that irritated Phiz.
2. E. Browne, p. 236.
3. Ibid., p. 238.
4. *Notes*, p. 145.
5. Ibid.
6. Thomson, pp. 29–30.
7. E. Browne, p. 237
8. In E. Browne, p. 237.
9. Thomson, p. 238.
10. Ibid., p. 217.
11. N. John Hall, *Trollope and His Illustrators*. New York: St Martin's, 1980, p. 91.
12. A. Trollope to George Smith, 12 August 1864. N. John Hall, ed., *The Letters of Anthony Trollope*. Stanford: Stanford University Press, 1983, p. 282.
13. See Downey, Vol. 2. pp. 37–38.
14. This composite of Lutyens's character comes from Mary Lutyens and Jane Ridley's descriptions of him.

Chapter 15

1. Dickens used Phiz as late as 1858 for the frontispieces of the Library Edition's *Oliver Twist* and *Sketches by Boz*, both of which were originally illustrated by George Cruikshank. Dickens may have intended this as a slap in the face for Cruikshank, who insisted he was the originator of *Oliver Twist*.

2. In Kitton, *Dickens and His Illustrators*, p. 113. Trollope also disparaged Dickens, using the word 'puppets', when he declared:

   'I do acknowledge that Mrs. Gamp, Micawber, Pecksniff, and others have become household words in every house, as though they were human beings; but to my judgement they are not human beings, nor are any of the characters human which Dickens has portrayed. It has been the peculiarity and the marvel of this man's power, that he has invested his puppets with a charm that has enabled him to dispense with human nature. . . . Nor is the pathos of Dickens human. It is stagey and melodramatic.'

   Anthony Trollope, *An Autobiography*, ed. Frederrick Page, Oxford Universtiy Press, 1950 , pp. 248-49. N. D. Is it any wonder, if this is Trollope's opinion of Dickens, that he resented having 'a Dickens look' for his writing?

3. CGB's circumspect use of the word 'away' may imply that Kate returned to France to teach.

4. One of whom was Algernon Sidney Bicknell, co-author of *Notes to Assist . . .*

5. Richard Stewart Dobbs, *Reminiscences of Christian Life in India*, Dublin: George Herbert, 1881, p.119.

6. Kate's red granite memorial bears the following words at the head: 'Sacred to the memory of Katherine Anne Browne, Eldest Daughter of the late W.L. Browne, Esq. Died Sep. 4th, 1862. Blessed are the Dead that Die in the Lord.' Later the names of her sister, Emma Grant, and Emma's daughter, Margaret, were added to the long slab. Coincidentally, my father was cremated at West Norwood cemetery. When I first saw Kate's tombstone and realised there was space for yet another name, I asked for and received permission to add my father's, Hablot Robert Edgar, to the slab. In this way, the names Kate and Hablot are united in her last resting place. I had the letterer add the words '*Je t'aime*' to the foot of the stone.

7. Service record for Captain Nicolas Hablot, French army records, Vincennes.
8. Marriage certificate.
9. 'Here lies Nicolas Hablot, late grenadier officer in the Old Guard, died 8 February 1836.'

Chapter 16

1. Robert McCrum, *My Year Off: Recovering Life After a Stroke*. New York: W.W. Norton, 1998, p. 19.
2. Buchanan-Brown, p. 28; Steig, p. 314; Kitton, *Phiz*, p. 15; Spielmann, p. 451; Cohen, p. 122; Allchin, p. 293; C.G. Browne, p. 147; Thomson, p. 31.
3. Thomson, p. 31.
4. E. Browne, p. 313.
5. Ibid., p. 314.
6. Thomson, p. 31.
7. Balmorals are stout boots which lace up the front. Phiz was picking Walter's Balmorals up from the cobbler and sending them to him by train.
8. In Kitton, *Phiz*, p. 18.
9. In Thomson, pp. 38–39.

Chapter 17

1. E. Browne, p. 238.
2. Ibid., p. 239.
3. Leap with forelegs together.
4. Phiz, *The Derby Carnival*. London: H. Vickers, 1869.

Chapter 18

1. This must refer to Robert Young.
2. Guinness, p. 101.
3. This Hablot would, in turn, name his only son, my father, Hablot Robert Edgar, also nicknamed Phiz.
4. Rudyard Kipling, *Departmental Ditties*.
5. *Notes*, p. 159.
6. Edward Stirling's production at the Adelphi. CD saw it on 21 Nov. 1838 and wrote to Forster, 'The tableaux from Browne's sketches exceedingly good.' PLet. ?23 Nov., 1838, 1:459.
7. C.G. Browne, p. 159.
8. M.H. Spielmann, *The History of 'Punch.'* London: Cassell, 1895, p. 539.
9. Phiz's fourth son.

10. In Kitton, *Phiz: A Memoir*. p. 19.
11. Ibid.
12. Letter in Victoria and Albert Museum library.
13. Kitton, *Phiz*, p. 21.
14. A prudish character in Thomas Morton's *Speed the Plough*.
15. Quoted in Thomson, p. 35.
16. E. Browne, p.17. Park, a good friend, is a mysterious figure. He failed to attain fame in the sculpting world and even Edgar could find no record of his work.
17. Letter in twenty-volume extra-illustrated *Life and Labours of Hablôt Knight Browne*, reproduced by kind permission of Phillip Pirages.
18. Beinecke Library Rare Books and Manuscripts, Yale University, H 1274.
19. In Kitton, *Dickens*, p. 113.
20. Letter from F.W. Cosens to Kitton. In Kitton, *Dickens*, p. 118.
21. This drawing can be seen in the Houghton Library, Harvard University.
22. Thomson, p. 219.
23. In Thomson, p. 33.
24. Ibid., p. 32.
25. Ibid., p. 33.
26. W.P. Frith (1819–1909), subject painter, famous for 'Derby Day'; and H.T. Wells (1828–1903), portrait painter.
27. In Thomson, p. 32.
28. In the Victoria and Albert Museum Library.
29. Fiona MacCarthy, *Eric Gill*. London: Faber, 1989, p. 14.
30. Phiz's sketches and a copy of the completed book can be seen at the British Library.
31. Allchin, p. 393.
32. It now reads 'Aged 66'. See explanation in Epilogue.
33. *Song of Solomon* 2:17.

Chapter 19

1. Address to the Liverpool Arts Club, January 1883.
2. Letter from Fred Barnard to Edgar Browne in author's collection.
3. Beatrix Potter, *The Journal of Beatrix Potter from 1881–1897*. London: Warne, 1966, p. 57.
4. Letter from John Fowles to author, 11 Nov., 1996.
5. *Notes*, p. 143.
6. Private collection. To the best of my knowledge this painting is unique in being a Phiz oil painting of a Dickens subject.

7. Private collection.
8. See letter of thanks from Phiz to Bicknell, 13 June 1851. Charles Dickens Museum, B109.
9. Letter from Phiz to his son, Walter. In Kitton, *Phiz,* p. 13.

Appendix 1

1. This is Phelps's edition in two volumes, and includes on its title page the words 'embellished with beautiful steel engravings by "Phiz".' This runs counter to Thomson's claim that they are wood engravings after Browne's designs.

Index

Numbers in italics refer to illustrations